UNITED NATIONS CONFERENCE ON TRADE AND DEVELOPMENT

UNCTAD

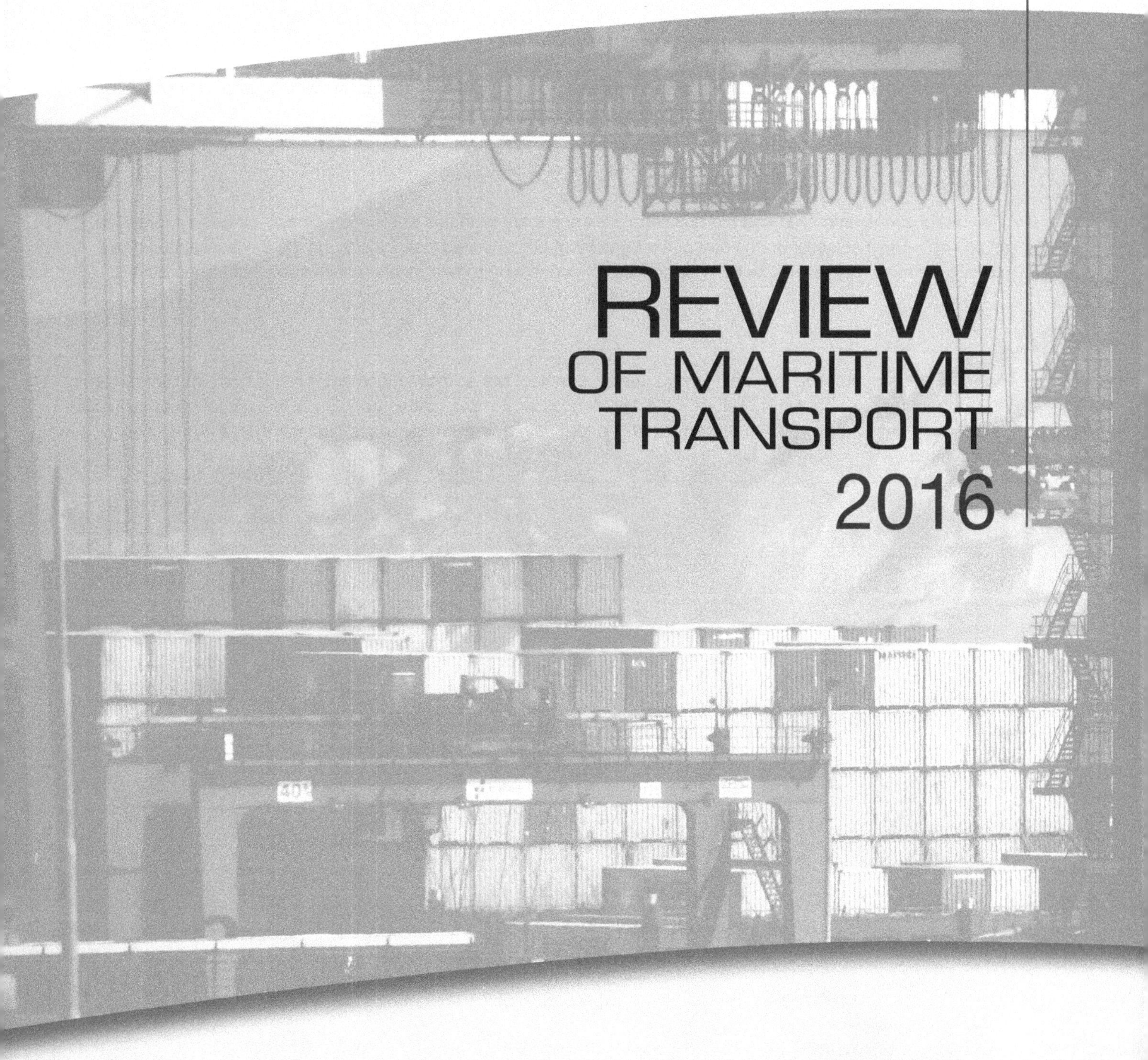

REVIEW OF MARITIME TRANSPORT 2016

UNITED NATIONS
New York and Geneva, 2016

NOTE

The *Review of Maritime Transport* is a recurrent publication prepared by the UNCTAD secretariat since 1968 with the aim of fostering the transparency of maritime markets and analysing relevant developments. Any factual or editorial corrections that may prove necessary, based on comments made by Governments, will be reflected in a corrigendum to be issued subsequently.

*

* *

Symbols of United Nations documents are composed of capital letters combined with figures. Use of such a symbol indicates a reference to a United Nations document.

*

* *

The designations employed and the presentation of the material in this publication do not imply the expression of any opinion whatsoever on the part of the Secretariat of the United Nations concerning the legal status of any country, territory, city or area, or of its authorities, or concerning the delimitation of its frontiers or boundaries.

*

* *

Material in this publication may be freely quoted or reprinted, but acknowledgement is requested, with reference to the document symbol (UNCTAD/RMT/2016). A copy of the publication containing the quotation or reprint should be sent to the UNCTAD secretariat at the following address: Palais des Nations, CH1211 Geneva 10, Switzerland.

UNCTAD/RMT/2016

UNITED NATIONS PUBLICATION

Sales no. E.16.II.D.7

ISBN 978-92-1-112904-5

eISBN: 978-92-1-058462-3

ISSN 0566-7682

ACKNOWLEDGEMENTS

Preparation of the UNCTAD *Review of Maritime Transport 2016* was coordinated by Jan Hoffmann with administrative support and formatting by Wendy Juan, under the overall guidance of Shamika N. Sirimanne. Contributors were Regina Asariotis, Hassiba Benamara, Jan Hoffmann, Anila Premti, Vincent Valentine and Frida Youssef.

The publication was edited by Deniz Barki and Lucy Deleze-Black. The cover was designed by Sophie Combette. The desktop publishing was carried out by Nathalie Loriot.

The considered comments and valuable input provided by the following reviewers are gratefully acknowledged: Samantha Barnwell, Alex Charvalias, Trevor Crowe, Jörg Erdtmann, Mahin Faghfouri, Dalibor Gogic, Ki-Soon Hwang, Rouben Indjikian, Ulrich Malchow, Hafiz Mirza, José María Rubiato, Ma Shuo, Dong-Wook Song, André Stochniol, Antonella Teodoro, Miluše Tichavska, Wang Wei and Clarksons Research. Thanks are also due to Vladislav Shuvalov for reviewing the publication in full.

TABLE OF CONTENTS

LIST OF TABLES, FIGURES AND BOXES

Table

Figures

Boxes

ABBREVIATIONS

AEO	authorized economic operator
AIS	Automatic Identification System
BWM Convention	Ballast Water Management Convention (full title, International Convention for the Control and Management of Ships' Ballast Water and Sediments)
CMA CGM	Compagnie maritime d'affrètement – Compagnie générale maritime
CO_2	carbon dioxide
ConTex	Container Ship Time Charter Assessment Index
dwt	dead-weight tons
GDP	gross domestic product
HNS Convention	International Convention on Liability and Compensation for Damage in Connection with the Carriage of Hazardous and Noxious Substances by Sea
ILO	International Labour Organization
IMO	International Maritime Organization
ISO	International Organization for Standardization
LSCI	Liner Shipping Connectivity Index
MARPOL	International Convention for the Prevention of Pollution from Ships
MEPC	Marine Environment Protection Committee
NO_x	nitrogen oxides
ppm	parts per million
SOLAS	International Convention for the Safety of Life at Sea
SO_x	sulphur oxides
TEU	20-foot equivalent unit
UN/LOCODE	United Nations Code for Trade and Transport Locations
VGM	verified gross mass

EXPLANATORY NOTES

The *Review of Maritime Transport 2016* covers data and events from January 2015 until June 2016. Where possible, every effort has been made to reflect more recent developments.

The terms "countries" and "economies" refer to countries, territories or areas.

All references to dollars ($) are to United States dollars, unless otherwise stated.

The terms "ton" and "mile" refer to metric ton (1,000 kg) and nautical mile, respectively, unless otherwise specified.

In tables and figures:

- Because of rounding, totals of percentages presented may not add up to 100
- The following symbols are used:

  .. not available

  — (em-dash) amount is nil.

Since 2014, the *Review of Maritime Transport* does not include printed statistical annexes. Instead, UNCTAD has expanded the coverage of statistical data online via the following links:

Overview: http://stats.unctad.org/maritime

Seaborne trade: http://stats.unctad.org/seabornetrade

Merchant fleet by flag of registration: http://stats.unctad.org/fleet

Merchant fleet by country of ownership: http://stats.unctad.org/fleetownership

National maritime country profiles: http://unctadstat.unctad.org/CountryProfile/en-GB/index.html

Ship building by country in which built: http://stats.unctad.org/shipbuilding

Ship scrapping by country of demolition: http://stats.unctad.org/shipscrapping

Liner Shipping Connectivity Index: http://stats.unctad.org/lsci

Liner Shipping Bilateral Connectivity Index: http://stats.unctad.org/lsbci

Containerized port traffic: http://stats.unctad.org/teu.

Vessel groupings used in the Review of Maritime Transport

Grouping	Constituent ship types
Oil tankers	Oil tankers
Bulk carriers	Bulk carriers, combination carriers
General cargo ships	Multi-purpose and project vessels, roll-on/roll-off cargo, general cargo
Container ships	Fully cellular container ships
Other ships	Liquefied petroleum gas carriers, liquefied natural gas carriers, parcel (chemical) tankers, specialized tankers, reefers, offshore supply, tugs, dredgers, cruise, ferries, other non-cargo
Total all ships	Includes all vessel types mentioned above

Approximate vessel size groups referred to in the *Review of Maritime Transport*, according to generally used shipping terminology

Crude oil tankers

Very large crude carrier	200,000 dwt* plus
Suezmax crude tanker	120,000–200,000 dwt
Aframax crude tanker	80,000–119,999 dwt
Panamax crude tanker	60,000–79,999 dwt

Dry bulk and ore carriers

Capesize bulk carrier	100,000 dwt plus
Panamax bulk carrier	65,000–99,999 dwt
Handymax bulk carrier	40,000–64,999 dwt
Handysize bulk carrier	10,000–39,999 dwt

Container ships

"Neo-Panamax" container ship	Ships now able to transit the expanded locks of the Panama Canal, with up to a maximum 49 m beam and 366 m in length overall
Panamax container ship	Container ships above 3,000 20-foot equivalent units with a beam below 33.2 m, i.e. the largest size of vessels able to transit the old locks of the Panama Canal

Source: Clarkson Research Services.
* Dwt, dead-weight tons.
Note: Unless otherwise specified, the ships covered in the Review of Maritime Transport include all propelled seagoing merchant vessels of 100 gross tons and above, excluding inland waterway vessels, fishing vessels, military vessels, yachts and offshore fixed and mobile platforms and barges (with the exception of floating production storage and offloading units and drillships).

EXECUTIVE SUMMARY

The present edition of the *Review of Maritime Transport* takes the view that the long-term growth prospects for seaborne trade and maritime businesses are positive. There are ample opportunities for developing countries to generate income and employment and help promote foreign trade.

Seaborne trade

In 2015, world gross domestic product expanded by 2.5 per cent, the same rate as in 2014. Diverging individual country performances unfolded against the background of lower oil and commodity price levels, weak global demand and a slowdown in China. In tandem, global merchandise trade by volume weakened, increasing by only 1.4 per cent, down from 2.3 per cent in 2014.

In addition in 2015, estimated world seaborne trade volumes surpassed 10 billion tons – the first time in the records of UNCTAD. Shipments expanded by 2.1 per cent, a pace notably slower than the historical average. The tanker trade segment recorded its best performance since 2008, while growth in the dry cargo sector, including bulk commodities and containerized trade in commodities, fell short of expectations.

UNCTAD expects world gross domestic product to further decelerate to 2.3 per cent in 2016, while, according to estimates by the World Trade Organization, merchandise trade volumes are expected to remain steady and grow at the same rate as in 2015. Growth in world seaborne trade shipments is expected to pick up marginally in 2016, with the estimated pace remaining relatively slow on a historical basis.

While a slowdown in China is bad news for shipping, other countries have the potential to drive further growth. South–South trade is gaining momentum, and planned initiatives such as the One Belt, One Road Initiative and the Partnership for Quality Infrastructure, as well as the expanded Panama Canal and Suez Canal, all have the potential to affect seaborne trade, reshape world shipping networks and generate business opportunities. In parallel, trends such as the fourth industrial revolution, big data and electronic commerce are unfolding, and entail both challenges and opportunities for countries and maritime transport.

Maritime businesses

The world fleet grew by 3.5 per cent in the 12 months to 1 January 2016 (in terms of dead-weight tons (dwt)). This is the lowest growth rate since 2003, yet still higher than the 2.1 per cent growth in demand, leading to a continued situation of global overcapacity.

The position of countries within global container shipping networks is reflected in the UNCTAD liner shipping connectivity index. In May 2016, the best-connected countries were Morocco, Egypt and South Africa in Africa; China and the Republic of Korea in Eastern Asia; Panama and Colombia in Latin America and the Caribbean; Sri Lanka and India in South Asia; and Singapore and Malaysia in South-East Asia.

Different countries participate in different sectors of the shipping business, seizing opportunities to generate income and employment. As at January 2016, the top five shipowning economies (in terms of dwt) were Greece, Japan, China, Germany and Singapore, while the top five economies by flag of registration were Panama, Liberia, the Marshall Islands, Hong Kong (China) and Singapore. The largest shipbuilding countries are China, Japan and the Republic of Korea, accounting for 91.4 per cent of gross tonnage constructed in 2015. Most demolitions take place in Asia; four countries – Bangladesh, India, Pakistan and China – accounted for 95 per cent of ship scrapping gross tonnage in 2015. The largest suppliers of seafarers are China, Indonesia and the Philippines. As countries specialize in different maritime subsectors, a process of concentration of the industry occurs. As each maritime business locates in a smaller number of countries, most countries host a decreasing number of maritime businesses, albeit with growing market shares in the subsectors.

Policymakers are advised to identify and invest in maritime sectors in which their countries may have a comparative advantage. Supporting the maritime sector is no longer a policy choice. Rather, the challenge is to identify and support selected maritime businesses. Policymakers need to carefully assess the competitive environment for each maritime subsector they wish to develop, and to consider the value added of a sector for the State economy, including possible synergies and spillover effects into other sectors – maritime and beyond. Policymakers should also take into account the fact that the port and shipping business is a key enabler of a country's foreign trade. Apart from possibly generating income and employment in the maritime sector, it is generally even more important to ensure that a country's traders have access to fast, reliable and cost-effective port and shipping services, no matter who is the provider.

Freight rates and maritime transport costs

In 2015, most shipping segments, except for tankers, suffered historic low levels of freight rates and weak earnings, triggered by weak demand and oversupply of new tonnage. The tanker market remained strong, mainly because of the continuing and exceptional fall in oil prices.

In the container segment, freight rates declined steadily, reaching record low prices as the market continued to struggle with weakening demand and the presence of ever-larger container vessels that had entered the market throughout the year. In an effort to deal with low freight rate levels and reduce losses, carriers continued to consider measures to improve efficiency and optimize operations, as in previous years. Key measures included cascading, idling, slow steaming, and wider consolidation and integration, as well as the restructuring of new alliances.

The same was true of the dry bulk freight market, which was affected by the substantial slowdown in seaborne dry bulk trade and the influx of excess tonnage. Rates fluctuated around or below vessels' operating costs across all segments. As in container shipping, measures were taken to mitigate losses and alliances were reinforced, as illustrated by the formation in February 2015 of the largest alliance of dry bulk carriers, Capesize Chartering.

Market conditions in the tanker market, however, were favourable. The crude oil and oil product tanker markets enjoyed strong freight rates throughout 2015, mainly triggered by a surge in seaborne oil trade and supported by a low supply of crude tanker fleet capacity.

Ports

The report describes the work of UNCTAD in helping developing countries improve port performance, with a view towards lowering transport costs and achieving better integration into global trade. It explores new datasets in port statistics and presents an overview of what these reveal about the port industry in 2015.

The overall port industry, including the container sector, experienced significant declines in growth, with growth rates for the largest ports only just remaining positive. The 20 leading ports by volume experienced an 85 per cent decline in growth, from 6.3 per cent in 2014 to 0.9 per cent in 2015. Of the seven largest ports to have recorded declines in throughput, Singapore was the only one not located in China. Nonetheless, with 14 of the top 20 ports located in China, some ports posted impressive growth, and one (Suzhou) even grew by double digits. The top 20 container ports, which usually account for about half of the world's container port throughput and provide a straightforward overview of the industry in any year, showed a 95 per cent decline in growth, from 5.6 per cent in 2014 to 0.5 per cent in 2015.

Legal issues and regulatory developments

During the period under review, important developments included the adoption of the 2030 Agenda for Sustainable Development in September 2015 and the Paris Agreement under the United Nations Framework Convention on Climate Change in December 2015. Their implementation, along with that of the Addis Ababa Action Agenda, adopted in July 2015, which provides a global framework for financing development post-2015, is expected to bring increased opportunities for developing countries.

Among regulatory initiatives, it is worth noting the entry into force on 1 July 2016 of the International Convention for the Safety of Life at Sea amendments related to the mandatory verification of the gross mass of containers, which will contribute to improving the stability and safety of ships and avoiding maritime accidents. At the International Maritime Organization, discussions continued on the reduction of greenhouse gas emissions from international shipping and on technical cooperation and transfer of technology particularly to developing countries. Also, progress was made in other areas clearly related to sustainable development. These included work on technical matters related to the imminent entry into force and implementation of the International Convention for the Control and Management of Ships' Ballast Water and Sediments (2004) and on developing an international legally binding instrument under the United Nations Convention on the Law of the Sea on the conservation and sustainable use of marine biological diversity of areas beyond national jurisdiction.

Continued enhancements were made to regulatory measures in the field of maritime and supply chain security and their implementation. Areas of progress included the implementation of authorized economic operator programmes and an increasing number of bilateral mutual recognition agreements that will, in due course, form the basis for the recognition of authorized economic operators at a multilateral level. As regards suppression of maritime piracy and armed robbery, in 2015, only a modest increase of 4.1 per cent was observed in the number of incidents reported to the International Maritime Organization, compared with 2014. The number of crew members taken hostage or kidnapped and those assaulted, and the number of ships hijacked, decreased significantly compared with 2014. In this respect, a circular on combating unsafe practices associated with mixed migration by sea and interim guidelines on maritime cyber risk management were approved at the International Maritime Organization. In the context of International Labour Organization conventions, progress was also made on the issue of recognition of seafarers' identity documents and on improving their living and working conditions.

1

DEVELOPMENTS IN INTERNATIONAL SEABORNE TRADE

In 2015, world gross domestic product (GDP) expanded by 2.5 per cent, the same rate as in 2014. Diverging individual country performances unfolded against the background of lower oil and commodity price levels, weak global demand and a slowdown in China. In tandem, global merchandise trade by volume weakened, increasing by only 1.4 per cent, down from 2.3 per cent in 2014.

In addition in 2015 – for the first time in the records of UNCTAD – world seaborne trade volumes were estimated to have surpassed 10 billion tons. Shipments expanded by 2.1 per cent, a pace notably slower than the historical average. The tanker trade segment recorded its best performance since 2008, while growth in the dry cargo sector, including bulk commodities and containerized trade, fell short of expectations.

UNCTAD expects world GDP to further decelerate to 2.3 per cent in 2016, while, according to estimates by the World Trade Organization, merchandise trade volumes are expected to remain steady and grow at the same rate as in 2015. Growth in world seaborne trade shipments is expected to pick up marginally in 2016, with the estimated pace remaining relatively slow on a historical basis.

While a slowdown in China is bad news for shipping, other countries have the potential to drive further growth. South–South trade is gaining momentum, and planned initiatives such as the One Belt, One Road Initiative and the Partnership for Quality Infrastructure, as well as the expanded Panama Canal and Suez Canal, all have the potential to affect seaborne trade, reshape world shipping networks and generate business opportunities. In parallel, trends such as the fourth industrial revolution, big data and electronic commerce (e-commerce) are unfolding and entail both challenges and opportunities for countries and maritime transport.

This chapter covers developments in January 2015–July 2016. Section A reviews the overall performance of the global economy and world merchandise trade; section B, developments in world seaborne trade, including by market segment; and section C, relevant trends and developments that may increase growth, reinvigorate trade and boost maritime transport activities and seaborne trade volumes, and that entail both challenges and opportunities These need to be further monitored and taken into account when devising maritime transport policies and making growth projections and investment decisions in transport. Section D concludes with an outlook.

A. WORLD ECONOMIC SITUATION AND PROSPECTS

Although a number of factors are increasingly redefining seaborne trade patterns, maritime trade flows continue to be largely determined by developments in the macroeconomic landscape. Seaborne trade volumes have generally moved in tandem with economic growth, industrial activity and merchandise trade, albeit at varied speeds (figure 1.1).

1. World economic growth

Falling short of expectations and below the pre-financial crisis levels, growth in world GDP expanded by 2.5 per cent in 2015, the same rate as in 2014 (table 1.1). Diverging individual country performances unfolded against the background of lower oil and commodity price levels, weak global demand and a slowdown in China. China's transition from an investment and export led-growth model has had an impact on global manufacturing activity, aggregate demand, investment and commodity prices. An additional factor dampening global growth was the reduced positive effect of lower oil prices, partly offset by the negative impact on investment in the oil sector and the import demand of oil-exporting countries.

Developing country growth decelerated from 4.4 per cent in 2014 to 3.9 per cent in 2015, although still accounting for 70 per cent of global expansion (International Monetary Fund, 2016). China's economy has slowed over the past few years, although it is still growing at a relatively high rate; GDP growth decelerated from 7.2 per cent in 2014 to 6.9 per cent in 2015. China may be said to be growing at two speeds, with its manufacturing sector facing overcapacity and limited growth, while its consumer-driven services sector is growing at a rapid pace (The Economist Intelligence Unit, 2016a). India is now growing faster than China, as its GDP growth, supported by factors such as infrastructure investment, accelerated to 7.2 per cent in 2015. Apart from developments in China and continuing weak demand conditions, other

Figure 1.1. Organization for Economic Cooperation and Development industrial production index and indices for world gross domestic product, seaborne trade and merchandise trade, 1975–2015

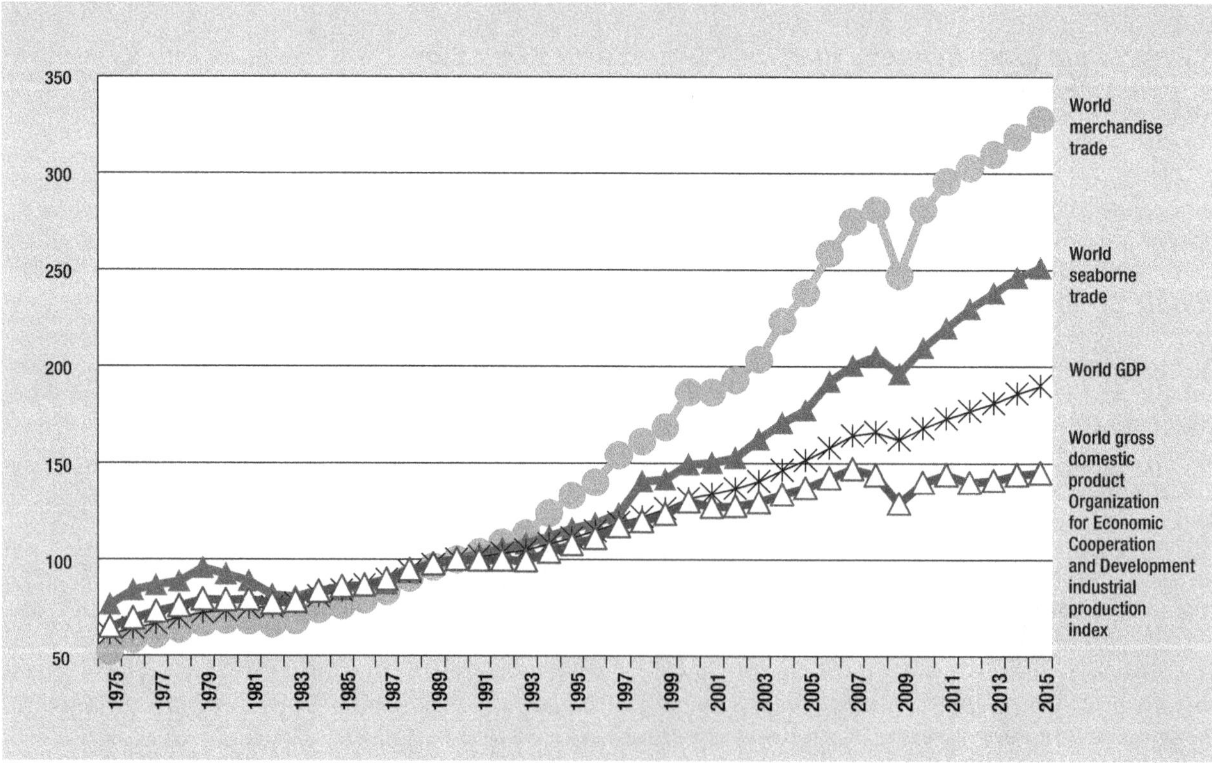

Source: UNCTAD secretariat calculations, based on Organization for Economic Cooperation and Development, 2016; UNCTAD, *Review of Maritime Transport*, various issues; UNCTAD, 2016a; World Trade Organization, 2014; and World Trade Organization, 2016.

Note: 1990=100. Indices calculated based on GDP and merchandise trade in dollars and seaborne trade in metric tons.

trends have also affected many developing countries, namely, the recession in Brazil, the low commodity and energy price environment, and geopolitical tensions and domestic conflicts in a number of countries.

Some estimates suggest that a sustained 1 percentage point decline in Brazil, China, India, the Russian Federation and South Africa could reduce growth in other emerging and developing economies by around 0.8 percentage points and global growth by 0.4 percentage points (World Bank, 2016). This is illustrated by GDP growth in Latin America, which has recorded its worst performance since 1999, expanding at merely 0.2 per cent in 2015. Similarly, GDP growth in Africa decelerated from 3.7 per cent in 2014 to 2.9 per cent in 2015. Growth in the least developed countries remained relatively firm, albeit slowing from 5.5 per cent in 2014 to 3.6 per cent in 2015. This rate remains below the Sustainable Development Goals' target of at least 7 per cent GDP growth and may potentially undermine progress in achieving the 2030 Agenda for Sustainable Development and the Goals.

GDP in countries with economies in transition declined by 2.8 per cent, owing to the recessions in the Russian Federation and Ukraine, as well as low commodity prices, net capital outflows, falling real wages, conflicts and unilateral coercive measures. While still fragile, the recovery in developed economies continued in 2015, with GDP expanding by 2.0 per cent, up from 1.7 per cent in 2014. In the United States of America, GDP expanded by 2.6 per cent, while growth in the European Union improved to 2.0 per cent, supported in particular by higher domestic consumption and investment levels and by falling energy prices. GDP growth in Japan remained subdued, at 0.5 per cent, reflecting the country's continued struggle against economic stagnation.

2. World merchandise trade

Global merchandise trade by volume (that is, trade in value terms, adjusted to account for inflation and exchange rate movements) increased by 1.4 per cent in 2015, down from 2.3 per cent in 2014 (table 1.2). Trade in volumes held up relatively well, compared with trade in value, which recorded a decline of 13 per cent, due to fluctuations in commodity prices and exchange rates (World Trade Organization, 2016). Together, the slow recovery in Europe, weaker global investment and the slowdown in large developing economies have depressed global trade. Overall, the

Table 1.1 World economic growth by selected country grouping, 2013–2016 (Percentage change)

	2013	2014	2015	2016 (forecast)
World	2.2	2.5	2.5	2.3
Developed economies	1.1	1.7	2.0	1.6
European Union (28 countries)	0.3	1.4	2.0	1.8
Germany	0.3	1.6	1.7	1.7
France	0.7	0.2	1.2	1.5
Italy	-1.8	-0.3	0.8	0.8
United Kingdom of Great Britain and Northern Ireland	2.2	2.9	2.3	1.8
Japan	1.4	0.0	0.5	0.7
United States	1.7	2.4	2.6	1.6
Developing economies	4.6	4.4	3.9	3.8
Africa	2.0	3.7	2.9	2.0
South Africa	2.2	1.5	1.3	0.3
Asia	5.5	5.5	5.1	5.1
China	7.7	7.3	6.9	6.7
India	6.3	7.0	7.2	7.6
Western Asia	3.4	3.0	2.9	2.1
Developing America	2.7	1.1	0.2	-0.2
Brazil	3.0	0.1	-3.8	-3.2
Least developed countries	4.9	5.5	3.6	3.8
Transition economies	2.0	0.9	-2.8	0.0
Russian Federation	1.3	0.7	-3.7	-0.3

Source: UNCTAD, 2016a.
Note: Calculations for country aggregates based on GDP in constant 2005 dollars.

impact of Asia, which had contributed more than any other region to the recovery of world merchandise trade after the financial crisis, appears to be easing. The contribution to global import growth from Eastern Asia dropped significantly, from an average of 27 per cent in the previous decade to 8.4 per cent in 2015 (United Nations Department of Economic and Social Affairs, 2016). In comparison, Europe contributed 59 per cent to global import growth, in contrast to the negative contribution in 2012 and 2013. With regard to global export growth, Europe contributed 44 per cent and Asia, 35 per cent (World Trade Organization, 2016). Other regions had limited contributions.

Developing country trade was particularly weak in 2015, with export and import volumes, respectively, expanding at the marginal rate of 0.4 per cent, a significant drop from growth in previous years. The contraction of both exports and imports in Eastern Asia had negative impacts on the trade of other developing economies, in particular manufacturing export-dependent economies in developing Asia. China accounted for about 20 per cent of the slowdown in import growth of developing economies and countries with economies in transition in 2014–2015 (United Nations Department of Economic and Social Affairs, 2016). Export growth in the oil-exporting regions of Africa and Western Asia and countries with economies in transition remained positive. With regard to imports, demand in commodity and oil export-dependent countries and regions such as Africa, Latin America and Western Asia and countries with economies in transition either weakened or declined due to erosion in their terms of trade and purchasing power. In contrast, India experienced a surge in its import demand (10.1 per cent).

For the second consecutive year, developed economies were more active in driving global trade, with exports rising slightly (2.2 per cent) while imports grew at a faster pace, by 3.3 per cent. United States exports declined marginally (-0.2 per cent) while in Japan, modest growth, a weaker currency and a slowdown in key trading partners in Eastern Asia dampened both exports and imports. Import demand in the United States and Europe held up relatively well (4.8 per cent and 3.6 per cent, respectively), owing to a stronger dollar and relatively solid economic growth in the Unites States and, arguably, due to recovery in intra-European Union trade.

A trend with potentially long-term implications for seaborne trade and shipping is the apparent weakening of the trade–GDP growth ratio. In recent years, world merchandise trade has been expanding at a relatively slower pace, either matching or below world GDP growth levels, while in earlier years, on average, international trade grew significantly faster than world GDP. The trade–GDP growth ratio was estimated at 0.62 in 2015, down from 0.94 in 2014 and

Table 1.2 Growth in merchandise trade volume by selected country grouping, 2013–2015 (Percentage change)

Exports				Imports		
2013	2014	2015		2013	2014	2015
3.3	2.3	1.4	**World**	2.7	2.4	1.6
2.2	1.9	2.2	**Developed economies**	0.0	2.8	3.3
1.8	1.7	3.2	**European Union**	-0.9	3.3	3.6
-1.5	0.6	-1.0	**Japan**	0.3	0.6	-2.8
2.8	4.4	-0.2	**United States**	1.0	4.3	4.8
4.6	3.1	0.4	**Developing economies**	6.3	2.5	0.4
-0.7	0.0	2.1	**Africa**	6.5	5.7	1.5
1.9	3.3	2.9	**Developing America**	3.6	0.2	-1.8
5.6	3.3	-0.1	**Developing Asia**	6.8	2.6	0.7
6.7	4.9	-0.5	**Eastern Asia**	8.9	2.8	-1.6
7.7	6.8	-0.9	**China**	9.9	3.9	-2.2
4.1	5.2	-0.2	**South Asia**	-0.4	4.6	7.2
8.5	3.5	-2.1	**India**	-0.3	3.2	10.1
4.7	3.5	-0.3	**South-East Asia**	4.3	1.7	2.8
3.8	-2.3	2.0	**Western Asia**	7.4	1.8	2.0
2.3	0.5	0.9	**Transition economies**	-0.5	-7.6	-19.4

Source: UNCTAD secretariat calculations, based on UNCTADstat and national sources.
Note: Trade volumes derived from international merchandise trade values deflated by UNCTAD unit value indices.

1.4 in 2013. While international trade is still influenced by the Great Recession (2009), the question is whether the continued slowdown in merchandise trade results mainly from cyclical factors (weaker GDP growth and macroeconomic cycles) or a break in the long-term trade–GDP relationship, indicating that structural factors are at play, such as the potential start of a de-globalization pattern (box 1.1).

In sum, global recovery continues but at a slower pace, with momentum created by China and other developing economies in Asia increasingly easing. Developments in the economy of China and related spillover effects on other large developing countries impact all countries, both developed and developing. Other factors – namely, lower commodity and oil price levels, eroding terms of trade in many commodity and oil-exporting countries, weaker global demand and investment, geopolitical tensions and political unrest – contribute to heightening uncertainty, increasing downside risks and challenging the outlook for merchandise and seaborne trade. A trend that was reinforced in 2015 and that has a bearing on the long-term outlook for seaborne trade and shipping is the evolving trade–GDP relationship.

B. WORLD SEABORNE TRADE

Maritime transport is the backbone of globalization and lies at the heart of cross-border transport networks that support supply chains and enable international trade. An economic sector in its own right that generates employment, income and revenue, transport – including maritime transport – is cross-cutting and permeates other sectors and activities. Maritime transport enables industrial development by supporting manufacturing growth; bringing together consumers and intermediate and capital goods industries; and promoting regional economic and trade integration.

The importance of transport has been recognized in the Sustainable Development Goals, which have integrated infrastructure and transport as an important consideration. While none of the Goals is exclusively dedicated to transport or maritime transport in particular, transport is considered a critical factor for the effective realization of eight Goals and 11 targets, both directly and indirectly. For instance, as part of the implementation process, the United Nations Inter-agency Expert Group on Sustainable Development

Box 1.1 Global trade slowdown and the trade–gross domestic product relationship

Long-term trade–GDP elasticity was estimated at 1.3 in 1970–1985, 2.2 in 1986–2000, 1.3 in the 2000s and 0.7 in 2008–2013. The estimates suggest that the contribution of cyclical factors to trade slowdown is more pronounced during crises and recession periods. However, reduced elasticities outside periods of crises point to other potential factors.

An oft-cited potential structural factor in the observed reduced elasticity is the recent limited growth in vertical specialization and the global fragmentation of production, reflecting a maturation of value chains (in China and the United States). While the decline in trade elasticities of primary goods and investment goods relates in particular to cyclical factors, lower trade elasticity for intermediate goods mainly reflects structural causes, such as a shift in production and trade patterns in global value chains. Overall decline in the vertical specialization process is evident when considering trade in intermediate goods, especially in Eastern Asia. China's share of intermediate imports as a proportion of its exports of manufacturing goods, which measures the reliance of the manufacturing sector on imported inputs, has declined constantly over the last decade, from almost 60 per cent in 2002 to less than 40 per cent in 2014. Another measure, the share of China's intermediate goods in its total imports, fell from 33 per cent in 2001 to about 18 per cent in 2014. Although still substantially high, vertical specialization in other countries in Eastern Asia has also declined in recent years. These trends are also indicative of a potential re-shoring or near-shoring process (that is, moving manufacturing activity home or closer to home) and of the consolidation of production processes into geographical clusters of production that, together, result in relatively lower levels of trade per unit of output.

Other potential explanatory factors are changes in the composition of global demand, with slow recovery in investment goods that are more trade intensive than government and consumer spending, as well as a shift in the composition of consumer demand away from tradeable (manufactured) goods to services. Globally, the share of capital goods in total imports dropped from 35 per cent in 2000 to 30 per cent in 2014. In the same period, consumer goods, which tend to have lower import content relative to investment goods, maintained their share of about 30 per cent.

Another view is that the decline in the global wage share and related negative impact on domestic demand growth may have also contributed to slower trade growth. The global wage share continued to decline due to continued efforts to raise competitiveness, such as by delocalizing production to low-cost sites. Greater access to global markets has often been associated with a deterioration in national wage income compared with the global level.

While boosting global aggregate demand remains key to stimulating global trade growth, various non-cyclical factors suggest that even if trade recovers gradually, trade elasticities may not return to the high levels of the late 1990s and early 2000s.

Sources: Constantinescu et al., 2015; European Central Bank, 2015; UNCTAD, 2015a; UNCTAD, 2015b; UNCTAD, 2016a; United Nations Department of Economic and Social Affairs, 2016.

Goal Indicators (see http://unstats.un.org/sdgs/iaeg-sdgs) has proposed that freight volumes by mode of transport, including maritime transport, be used to measure progress towards target 9.1 (develop quality, reliable, sustainable and resilient infrastructure, including regional and transborder infrastructure, to support economic development and human well-being, with a focus on affordable and equitable access for all). To put things in perspective, in 2015, world seaborne trade volumes are estimated to have accounted for over 80 per cent of total world merchandise trade. In value terms, some observers have estimated the share of maritime trade at 55 per cent (figure for 2013 from Lloyd's List Intelligence) and others at over two thirds of total merchandise trade (IHS Markit, 2016). Linking the performance of freight volumes, including maritime freight, to target 9.1 highlights the importance of further monitoring, assessing and analysing developments affecting international seaborne trade (UNCTAD, 2016b).

1. Overall seaborne trade

In 2015 – for the first time in UNCTAD records – world seaborne trade volumes[1] were estimated to have exceeded 10 billion tons. However, shipments expanded by 2.1 per cent, a pace notably slower than the historical average and below rates recorded over the last decade, when volumes were lifted by strong import demand from China. Individual performances varied by country and across market segments, with tanker trade performing relatively better than any other sector. A key influence on seaborne trade in 2015 was China. Over the last decade, China has contributed the largest shares of import volume growth, particularly in imports of dry bulk commodities, which fell in 2015, for the first time since the Great Recession. Given the rising contribution of the services sector to the GDP of China, along with the contribution of industry and construction, the implications for seaborne trade patterns and volumes are significant.

In 2015, dry cargo shipments accounted for 70.7 per cent of total seaborne trade volumes, while the remaining share was made up of tanker trade, including crude oil, petroleum products and gas (tables 1.3 and 1.4 (a) and (b) and figure 1.2). Also in 2015, volumes increased by 1.6 per cent, down from 4.1 per cent in 2014. Growth in world seaborne trade by ton–miles – providing a more accurate measure of demand for ship-carrying capacity, as it takes into account distances travelled – also decelerated; world seaborne trade totalled an estimated 53.6 billion ton–miles, up from an estimated 52.7 billion ton–miles in 2014 (figure 1.3). While there are reports of some increases in ship-operating speeds in the tanker sector, overall, the shipping industry seems committed to slow steaming as a way of managing excess capacity and, in view of the design of eco-ships, optimizing for lower speeds.

Table 1.3 Developments in international seaborne trade, selected years (Millions of tons loaded)

	Oil and gas	Main bulk commodities (iron ore, coal, grain, bauxite and alumina and phosphate rock)	Dry cargo other than main bulk commodities	Total (all cargo)
1970	1 440	448	717	2 605
1980	1 871	608	1 225	3 704
1990	1 755	988	1 265	4 008
2000	2 163	1 295	2 526	5 984
2005	2 422	1 709	2 978	7 109
2006	2 698	1 814	3 188	7 700
2007	2 747	1 953	3 334	8 034
2008	2 742	2 065	3 422	8 229
2009	2 642	2 085	3 131	7 858
2010	2 772	2 335	3 302	8 409
2011	2 794	2 486	3 505	8 785
2012	2 841	2 742	3 614	9 197
2013	2 829	2 923	3 762	9 514
2014	2 825	2 985	4 033	9 843
2015	2 947	2 951	4 150	10 047

Source: UNCTAD secretariat calculations, based on data from reporting countries, as published on relevant government and port industry websites, and from specialist sources, as well as Clarksons Research (2006–2015), *Dry Bulk Trade Outlook*.

Note: Data for 2006–2015 have been revised and updated to reflect improved reporting, including more recent figures and better information regarding breakdown by cargo type. Figures for 2015 are estimates based on preliminary data or on the last year for which data were available.

Figure 1.2 International seaborne trade, selected years (Millions of tons loaded)

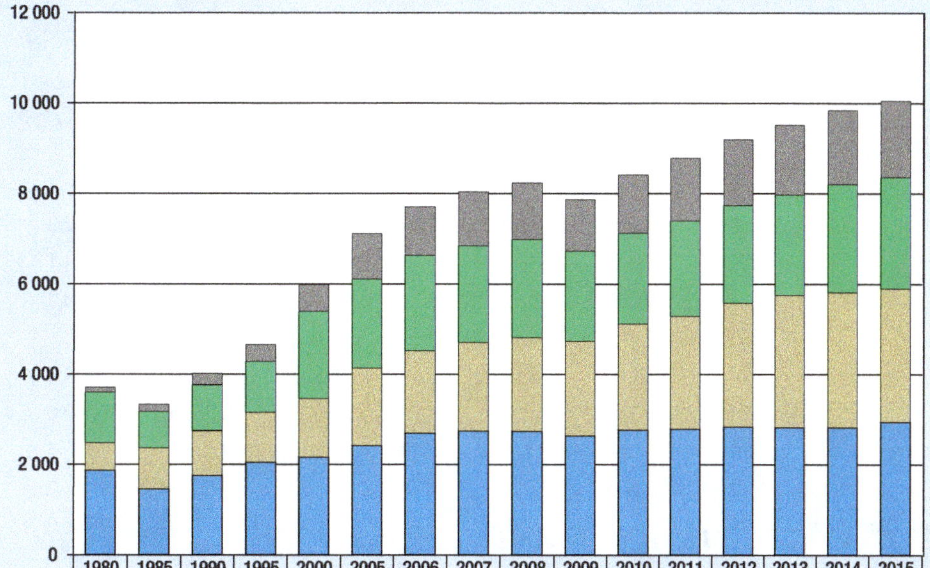

	1980	1985	1990	1995	2000	2005	2006	2007	2008	2009	2010	2011	2012	2013	2014	2015
Containers	102	152	234	371	598	1 001	1 076	1 193	1 249	1 127	1 280	1 393	1 464	1 544	1640	1687
Dry cargo other than main bulk commodities	1 123	819	1 031	1 125	1 928	1 975	2 112	2 141	2 173	2 004	2 022	2 112	2 150	2 218	2393	2463
Main bulk commodities	608	900	988	1 105	1 295	1 711	1 814	1 953	2 065	2 085	2 335	2 486	2 742	2 923	2985	2951
Oil and gas	1 871	1 459	1 755	2 050	2 163	2 422	2 698	2 747	2 742	2 642	2 772	2 794	2 841	2 829	2 825	2 947

Source: UNCTAD, Review of Maritime Transport, various issues.

Figure 1.3 World seaborne trade by cargo type, 2000–2016 (Estimated billions of ton-miles)

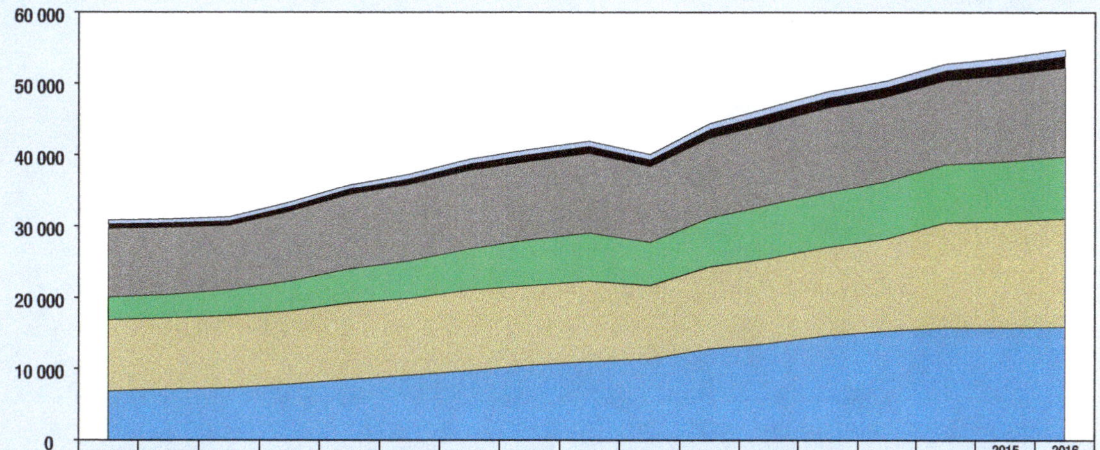

	2000	2001	2002	2003	2004	2005	2006	2007	2008	2009	2010	2011	2012	2013	2014	2015 (estimate)	2016 (forecast)
Chemicals	552	562	593	606	625	651	689	724	736	765	824	864	889	908	914	953	998
Gas	576	591	611	662	719	736	833	913	956	958	1 147	1 344	1 346	1 347	1 392	1 467	1 561
Oil	9 631	9 352	8 971	9 698	10 393	10 729	11 036	11 011	11 200	10 621	11 237	11 417	11 890	11 779	11 717	12 059	12 410
Containers	3 170	3 271	3 601	4 216	4 785	5 269	5 757	6 422	6 734	6 030	6 833	7 469	7 673	8 076	8 237	8 428	8 757
Other (minor bulk commodities and other dry cargo)	9 998	10 023	10 167	10 275	10 729	10 782	11 330	11 186	11 272	10 325	11 504	11 927	12 375	12 952	14 707	14 892	15 156
Main bulk commodities	6 896	7 158	7 331	7 852	8 527	9 107	9 745	10 503	11 028	11 400	12 824	13 596	14 691	15 312	15 768	15 790	15 918

Source: UNCTAD secretariat calculations, based on Clarksons Research, 2016a.

Table 1.4 (a) World seaborne trade by type of cargo and country grouping, 2006–2015 (Millions of tons)

Region or country	Year	Goods loaded				Goods unloaded			
		Total	Crude	Petroleum products and gas	Dry cargo	Total	Crude	Petroleum products and gas	Dry cargo
World	2006	7 700.3	1 783.4	914.8	5 002.1	7 878.3	1 931.2	893.7	5 053.4
	2007	8 034.1	1 813.4	933.5	5 287.1	8 140.2	1 995.7	903.8	5 240.8
	2008	8 229.5	1 785.2	957.0	5 487.2	8 286.3	1 942.3	934.9	5 409.2
	2009	7 858.0	1 710.5	931.1	5 216.4	7 832.0	1 874.1	921.3	5 036.6
	2010	8 408.9	1 787.7	983.8	5 637.5	8 443.8	1 933.2	979.2	5 531.4
	2011	8 784.3	1 759.5	1 034.2	5 990.5	8 797.7	1 896.5	1 037.7	5 863.5
	2012	9 196.7	1 785.7	1 055.0	6 356.0	9 188.5	1 929.5	1 055.1	6 203.8
	2013	9 513.6	1 737.9	1 090.8	6 684.8	9 500.1	1 882.0	1 095.2	6 523.0
	2014	9 843.4	1 706.9	1 118.3	7 018.2	9 836.1	1 850.4	1 127.1	6 858.6
	2015	10 047.5	1 771.0	1 175.9	7 100.6	10 033.4	1 916.2	1 185.2	6 932.0
Developed economies	2006	2 460.5	132.9	336.4	1 991.3	4 164.7	1 282.0	535.5	2 347.2
	2007	2 608.9	135.1	363.0	2 110.8	3 990.5	1 246.0	524.0	2 220.5
	2008	2 715.4	129.0	405.3	2 181.1	4 007.9	1 251.1	523.8	2 233.0
	2009	2 554.3	115.0	383.8	2 055.5	3 374.4	1 125.3	529.9	1 719.2
	2010	2 865.4	135.9	422.3	2 307.3	3 604.5	1 165.4	522.6	1 916.5
	2011	2 982.5	117.5	451.9	2 413.1	3 632.3	1 085.6	581.3	1 965.4
	2012	3 122.9	125.2	459.7	2 538.0	3 700.2	1 092.6	556.5	2 051.1
	2013	3 188.3	114.4	470.5	2 603.4	3 679.4	1 006.7	556.6	2 116.0
	2014	3 343.7	121.8	463.4	2 758.5	3 690.1	964.4	518.9	2 206.8
	2015	3 423.4	135.6	467.2	2 820.6	3 733.7	994.3	530.9	2 208.5
Transition economies	2006	410.3	123.1	41.3	245.9	70.6	5.6	3.1	61.9
	2007	407.9	124.4	39.9	243.7	76.8	7.3	3.5	66.0
	2008	431.5	138.2	36.7	256.6	89.3	6.3	3.8	79.2
	2009	505.3	142.1	44.4	318.8	93.3	3.5	4.6	85.3
	2010	515.7	150.2	45.9	319.7	122.1	3.5	4.6	114.0
	2011	505.0	132.6	42.0	330.5	156.7	4.2	4.4	148.1
	2012	544.2	135.6	40.3	368.3	148.1	3.8	4.0	140.3
	2013	551.9	145.1	32.1	374.8	77.4	1.1	10.6	65.7
	2014	592.7	152.1	36.8	403.8	68.7	0.2	4.2	64.3
	2015	632.3	164.4	43.1	424.7	58.6	0.3	4.3	54.0
Developing economies	2006	4 829.5	1 527.5	537.1	2 765.0	3 642.9	643.6	355.1	2 644.3
	2007	5 017.2	1 553.9	530.7	2 932.6	4 073.0	742.4	376.3	2 954.3
	2008	5 082.6	1 518.0	515.1	3 049.6	4 189.1	684.9	407.2	3 097.0
	2009	4 798.4	1 453.5	502.9	2 842.0	4 364.2	745.3	386.9	3 232.1
	2010	5 027.8	1 501.6	515.6	3 010.5	4 717.3	764.4	452.0	3 500.9
	2011	5 296.8	1 509.4	540.4	3 247.0	5 008.8	806.7	452.1	3 750.0
	2012	5 529.6	1 524.9	555.0	3 449.7	5 340.1	833.1	494.7	4 012.4
	2013	5 773.4	1 478.5	588.2	3 706.7	5 743.4	874.2	527.9	4 341.3
	2014	5 907.1	1 432.9	618.2	3 855.9	6 077.3	885.7	604.1	4 587.5
	2015	5 991.8	1 470.9	665.6	3 855.3	6 241.0	921.6	649.9	4 669.5

Table 1.4 (a) World seaborne trade by type of cargo and country grouping, 2006–2015 (Millions of tons) *(continued)*

Region or country	Year	Goods loaded				Goods unloaded			
		Total	Crude	Petroleum products and gas	Dry cargo	Total	Crude	Petroleum products and gas	Dry cargo
Africa	2006	721.9	353.8	86.0	282.2	349.8	41.3	39.4	269.1
	2007	732.0	362.5	81.8	287.6	380.0	45.7	44.5	289.8
	2008	766.7	379.2	83.3	304.2	376.6	45.0	43.5	288.1
	2009	708.0	354.0	83.0	271.0	386.8	44.6	39.7	302.5
	2010	754.0	351.1	92.0	310.9	416.9	42.7	40.5	333.7
	2011	723.7	338.0	68.5	317.2	378.2	37.8	46.3	294.1
	2012	757.8	364.2	70.2	323.4	393.6	32.8	51.0	309.8
	2013	815.3	327.5	82.4	405.3	432.2	36.6	65.3	330.3
	2014	757.4	299.3	74.3	383.7	469.6	37.2	71.0	361.5
	2015	756.1	294.7	58.6	402.8	483.6	39.4	70.1	374.2
Americas	2006	1 030.7	251.3	93.9	685.5	373.4	49.6	60.1	263.7
	2007	1 067.1	252.3	90.7	724.2	415.9	76.0	64.0	275.9
	2008	1 108.2	234.6	93.0	780.6	436.8	74.2	69.9	292.7
	2009	1 029.8	225.7	74.0	730.1	371.9	64.4	73.6	234.0
	2010	1 172.6	241.6	85.1	846.0	448.7	69.9	74.7	304.2
	2011	1 239.2	253.8	83.5	901.9	508.3	71.1	73.9	363.4
	2012	1 282.6	253.3	85.9	943.4	546.7	74.6	83.6	388.5
	2013	1 263.7	240.0	69.8	953.9	569.4	69.4	89.4	410.7
	2014	1 292.2	232.6	76.4	983.1	571.7	65.1	99.8	406.8
	2015	1 327.6	223.5	83.8	1 020.3	593.6	65.8	101.1	426.7
Asia	2006	3 073.1	921.2	357.0	1 794.8	2 906.8	552.7	248.8	2 105.3
	2007	3 214.6	938.2	358.1	1 918.3	3 263.6	620.7	260.8	2 382.1
	2008	3 203.6	902.7	338.6	1 962.2	3 361.9	565.6	286.8	2 509.5
	2009	3 054.3	872.3	345.8	1 836.3	3 592.4	636.3	269.9	2 686.2
	2010	3 094.6	907.5	338.3	1 848.8	3 838.2	651.8	333.1	2 853.4
	2011	3 326.7	916.0	388.2	2 022.6	4 108.8	697.8	328.0	3 082.9
	2012	3 480.9	905.8	398.1	2 177.0	4 386.9	725.7	355.5	3 305.7
	2013	3 686.9	909.4	435.2	2 342.4	4 728.7	767.4	369.2	3 592.1
	2014	3 849.4	899.4	466.5	2 483.6	5 023.1	782.5	429.2	3 811.4
	2015	3 899.9	951.0	522.3	2 426.7	5 151.3	815.6	474.6	3 861.1
Oceania	2006	3.8	1.2	0.1	2.5	12.9	0.0	6.7	6.2
	2007	3.5	0.9	0.1	2.5	13.5	0.0	7.0	6.5
	2008	4.2	1.5	0.1	2.6	13.8	0.0	7.1	6.7
	2009	6.3	1.5	0.2	4.6	13.1	0.0	3.6	9.5
	2010	6.5	1.5	0.2	4.8	13.4	0.0	3.7	9.7
	2011	7.1	1.6	0.2	5.3	13.5	0.0	3.9	9.6
	2012	8.3	1.6	0.8	5.9	13.0	0.0	4.6	8.4
	2013	7.5	1.6	0.8	5.1	13.1	0.8	4.1	8.2
	2014	8.1	1.6	0.9	5.5	12.9	0.9	4.1	7.9
	2015	8.2	1.7	0.9	5.5	12.5	0.9	4.1	7.5

Source: UNCTAD secretariat calculations, based on data from reporting countries, as published on relevant government and port industry websites, and from specialist sources.

Note: Data for 2006–2015 have been revised and updated to reflect improved reporting, including more recent figures and better information regarding breakdown by cargo type. Figures for 2015 are estimates based on preliminary data or on the last year for which data were available.

Table 1.4 (b) World seaborne trade by type of cargo and country grouping, 2006–2015 (Percentage share)

Region or country	Year	Goods loaded				Goods unloaded			
		Total	Crude	Petroleum products and gas	Dry cargo	Total	Crude	Petroleum products and gas	Dry cargo
World	2006	100.0	23.2	11.9	65.0	100.0	24.5	11.3	64.1
	2007	100.0	22.6	11.6	65.8	100.0	24.5	11.1	64.4
	2008	100.0	21.7	11.6	66.7	100.0	23.4	11.3	65.3
	2009	100.0	21.8	11.8	66.4	100.0	23.9	11.8	64.3
	2010	100.0	21.3	11.7	67.0	100.0	22.9	11.6	65.5
	2011	100.0	20.0	11.8	68.2	100.0	21.6	11.8	66.6
	2012	100.0	19.4	11.5	69.1	100.0	21.0	11.5	67.5
	2013	100.0	18.3	11.5	70.3	100.0	19.8	11.5	68.7
	2014	100.0	17.3	11.4	71.3	100.0	18.8	11.5	69.7
	2015	100.0	17.6	11.7	70.7	100.0	19.1	11.8	69.1
Developed economies	2006	32.0	7.4	36.8	39.8	52.9	66.4	59.9	46.4
	2007	32.5	7.5	38.9	39.9	49.0	62.4	58.0	42.4
	2008	33.0	7.2	42.3	39.7	48.4	64.4	56.0	41.3
	2009	32.5	6.7	41.2	39.4	43.1	60.0	57.5	34.1
	2010	34.1	7.6	42.9	40.9	42.7	60.3	53.4	34.6
	2011	34.0	6.7	43.7	40.3	41.3	57.2	56.0	33.5
	2012	34.0	7.0	43.6	39.9	40.3	56.6	52.7	33.1
	2013	33.5	6.6	43.1	38.9	38.7	53.5	50.8	32.4
	2014	34.0	7.1	41.4	39.3	37.5	52.1	46.0	32.2
	2015	34.1	7.7	39.7	39.7	37.2	51.9	44.8	31.9
Transition economies	2006	5.3	6.9	4.5	4.9	0.9	0.3	0.3	1.2
	2007	5.1	6.9	4.3	4.6	0.9	0.4	0.4	1.3
	2008	5.2	7.7	3.8	4.7	1.1	0.3	0.4	1.5
	2009	6.4	8.3	4.8	6.1	1.2	0.2	0.5	1.7
	2010	6.1	8.4	4.7	5.7	1.4	0.2	0.5	2.1
	2011	5.7	7.5	4.1	5.5	1.8	0.2	0.4	2.5
	2012	5.9	7.6	3.8	5.8	1.6	0.2	0.4	2.3
	2013	5.8	8.3	2.9	5.6	0.8	0.1	1.0	1.0
	2014	6.0	8.9	3.3	5.8	0.7	0.0	0.4	0.9
	2015	6.3	9.3	3.7	6.0	0.6	0.0	0.4	0.8
Developing economies	2006	62.7	85.6	58.7	55.3	46.2	33.3	39.7	52.3
	2007	62.4	85.7	56.9	55.5	50.0	37.2	41.6	56.4
	2008	61.8	85.0	53.8	55.6	50.6	35.3	43.6	57.3
	2009	61.1	85.0	54.0	54.5	55.7	39.8	42.0	64.2
	2010	59.8	84.0	52.4	53.4	55.9	39.5	46.2	63.3
	2011	60.3	85.8	52.2	54.2	56.9	42.5	43.6	64.0
	2012	60.1	85.4	52.6	54.3	58.1	43.2	46.9	64.7
	2013	60.7	85.1	53.9	55.4	60.5	46.4	48.2	66.6
	2014	60.0	83.9	55.3	54.9	61.8	47.9	53.6	66.9
	2015	59.6	83.1	56.6	54.3	62.2	48.1	54.8	67.4

Table 1.4 (b) World seaborne trade by type of cargo and country grouping, 2006–2015 (Percentage share) *(continued)*

Region or country	Year	Goods loaded				Goods unloaded			
		Total	Crude	Petroleum products and gas	Dry cargo	Total	Crude	Petroleum products and gas	Dry cargo
Africa	2006	9.4	19.8	9.4	5.6	4.4	2.1	4.4	5.3
	2007	9.1	20.0	8.8	5.4	4.7	2.3	4.9	5.5
	2008	9.3	21.2	8.7	5.5	4.5	2.3	4.7	5.3
	2009	9.0	20.7	8.9	5.2	4.9	2.4	4.3	6.0
	2010	9.0	19.6	9.4	5.5	4.9	2.2	4.1	6.0
	2011	8.2	19.2	6.6	5.3	4.3	2.0	4.5	5.0
	2012	8.2	20.4	6.6	5.1	4.3	1.7	4.8	5.0
	2013	8.6	18.8	7.6	6.1	4.5	1.9	6.0	5.1
	2014	7.7	17.5	6.6	5.5	4.8	2.0	6.3	5.3
	2015	7.5	16.6	5.0	5.7	4.8	2.1	5.9	5.4
Americas	2006	13.4	14.1	10.3	13.7	4.7	2.6	6.7	5.2
	2007	13.3	13.9	9.7	13.7	5.1	3.8	7.1	5.3
	2008	13.5	13.1	9.7	14.2	5.3	3.8	7.5	5.4
	2009	13.1	13.2	7.9	14.0	4.7	3.4	8.0	4.6
	2010	13.9	13.5	8.7	15.0	5.3	3.6	7.6	5.5
	2011	14.1	14.4	8.1	15.1	5.8	3.7	7.1	6.2
	2012	13.9	14.2	8.1	14.8	5.9	3.9	7.9	6.3
	2013	13.3	13.8	6.4	14.3	6.0	3.7	8.2	6.3
	2014	13.1	13.6	6.8	14.0	5.8	3.5	8.9	5.9
	2015	13.2	12.6	7.1	14.4	5.9	3.4	8.5	6.2
Asia	2006	39.9	51.7	39.0	35.9	36.9	28.6	27.8	41.7
	2007	40.0	51.7	38.4	36.3	40.1	31.1	28.9	45.5
	2008	38.9	50.6	35.4	35.8	40.6	29.1	30.7	46.4
	2009	38.9	51.0	37.1	35.2	45.9	34.0	29.3	53.3
	2010	36.8	50.8	34.4	32.8	45.5	33.7	34.0	51.6
	2011	37.9	52.1	37.5	33.8	46.7	36.8	31.6	52.6
	2012	37.8	50.7	37.7	34.3	47.7	37.6	33.7	53.3
	2013	38.8	52.3	39.9	35.0	49.8	40.8	33.7	55.1
	2014	39.1	52.7	41.7	35.4	51.1	42.3	38.1	55.6
	2015	38.8	53.7	44.4	34.2	51.3	42.6	40.0	55.7
Oceania	2006	0.0	0.1	0.01	0.0	0.2	—	0.7	0.1
	2007	0.0	0.1	0.01	0.0	0.2	—	0.8	0.1
	2008	0.1	0.1	0.01	0.0	0.2	—	0.8	0.1
	2009	0.1	0.1	0.02	0.1	0.2	—	0.4	0.2
	2010	0.1	0.1	0.0	0.1	0.2	—	0.4	0.2
	2011	0.1	0.1	0.0	0.1	0.2	—	0.4	0.2
	2012	0.1	0.1	0.1	0.1	0.1	—	0.4	0.1
	2013	0.1	0.1	0.1	0.1	0.1	—	0.4	0.1
	2014	0.1	0.1	0.1	0.1	0.1	—	0.4	0.1
	2015	0.1	0.1	0.1	0.1	0.1	—	0.3	0.1

Source: UNCTAD secretariat calculations, based on data from reporting countries, as published on relevant government and port industry websites, and from specialist sources.

Note: Data for 2006–2015 have been revised and updated to reflect improved reporting, including more recent figures and better information regarding breakdown by cargo type. Figures for 2015 are estimates based on preliminary data or on the last year for which data were available.

In 2015, dry cargo shipments increased by 1.2 per cent, a much slower pace than the 5 per cent growth in 2014. Trade in dry bulk commodities totalled 4.8 billion tons, with volumes declining by a marginal 0.2 per cent, the first decline since 2009. Growth was constrained by a fall in shipments of the five major dry bulk commodities (-1.3 per cent), in particular coal (-6.9 per cent), which contracted for the first time in about three decades. The slowdown in construction and infrastructure investment by China and the decline in steel output have affected iron ore trade, which accounted for 13.6 per cent of total seaborne trade in 2015. Heavily concentrated in China, iron ore trade expanded by 1.9 per cent in 2015, a significant slowdown from the double-digit rate of 12.5 per cent in 2014.

Minor bulk commodities (agribulks, metals and minerals and manufactures), many of which are also linked to steel production, are estimated to have increased by 1.5 per cent, supported, in particular, by growing exports of steel products from China. Accounting for over one third of all dry cargo, volumes of other dry cargo (general cargo, break bulk and containerized cargo) are estimated to have increased at the slower pace of 2.6 per cent, with a total of 2.53 billion tons in 2015. Reflecting sluggish intra-Asian trade and a drop in volumes in Eastern Asia–Europe trade, growth in containerized trade, which accounted for about two thirds of other dry cargo, is estimated to have decelerated significantly, from 6.1 per cent in 2014 to 2.9 per cent in 2015. Total containerized trade volumes are estimated at 1.69 billion tons, equivalent to 175 million twenty-foot equivalent units (TEUs).

In contrast, and supported in particular by an ample supply of oil cargo and lower oil prices, the tanker sector experienced one of its best performances since 2008. Crude oil shipments are estimated to have increased by 3.8 per cent in 2015, following two consecutive annual contractions in 2013 and 2014. According to UNCTAD, petroleum products and gas trade together expanded by 5.2 per cent in 2015, up from 2.6 per cent in 2014. A breakdown of this total, based on estimates by Clarksons Research, indicates that in 2015, trade in petroleum products increased faster than trade in gas.

Developing countries continued to contribute larger shares to the total volumes of international seaborne trade. Their contribution with regard to global goods loaded is estimated at 60 per cent, and their import demand as measured by the volume of goods unloaded increased, reaching 62 per cent (figures

Figure 1.4 (a) World seaborne trade by country grouping, 2015 (Percentage share of world tonnage)

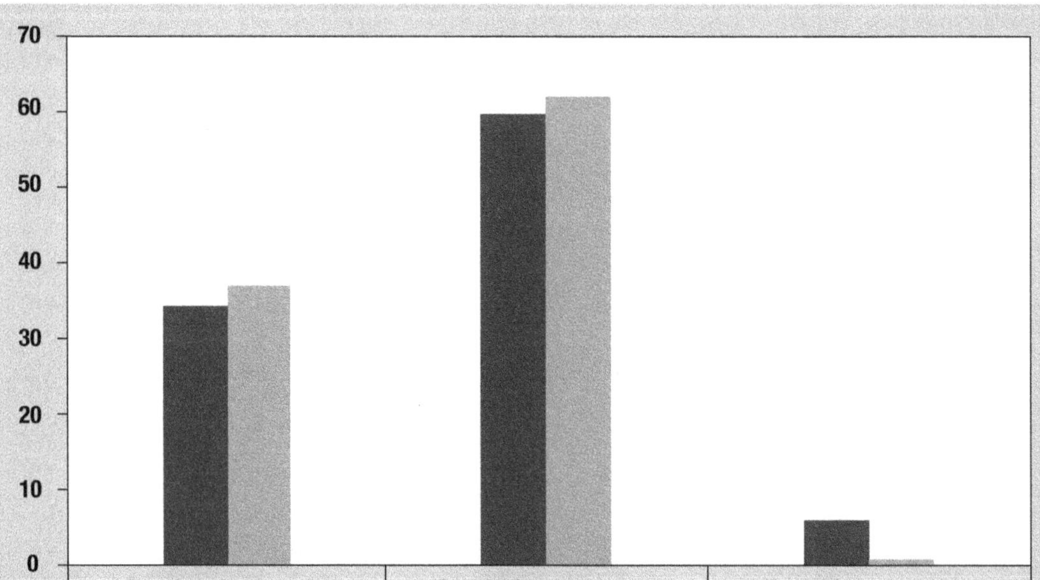

	Developed economies	Developing economies	Transition economies
Loaded	34	60	6
Unloaded	37	62	1

Source: UNCTAD secretariat calculations, based on data from reporting countries, as published on relevant government and port industry websites, and from specialist sources.

Note: Estimated figures are based on preliminary data or on the last year for which data were available.

Figure 1.4 (b) Developing country participation in world seaborne trade, selected years (Percentage share of world tonnage)

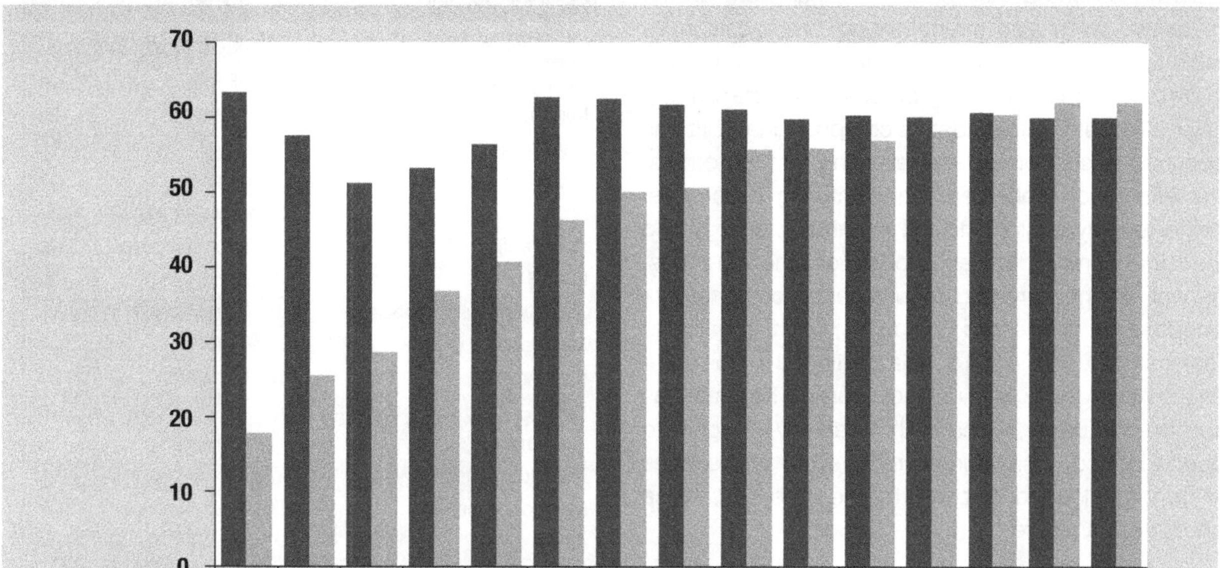

	1970	1980	1990	2000	2005	2006	2007	2008	2009	2010	2011	2012	2013	2014	2015
Loaded	63	58	51	53	56	63	62	62	61	60	60	60	61	60	60
Unloaded	18	26	29	37	41	46	50	51	56	56	57	58	60	62	62

Source: UNCTAD, *Review of Maritime Transport*, various issues.

Figure 1.4 (c) World seaborne trade by region, 2015 (Percentage share of world tonnage)

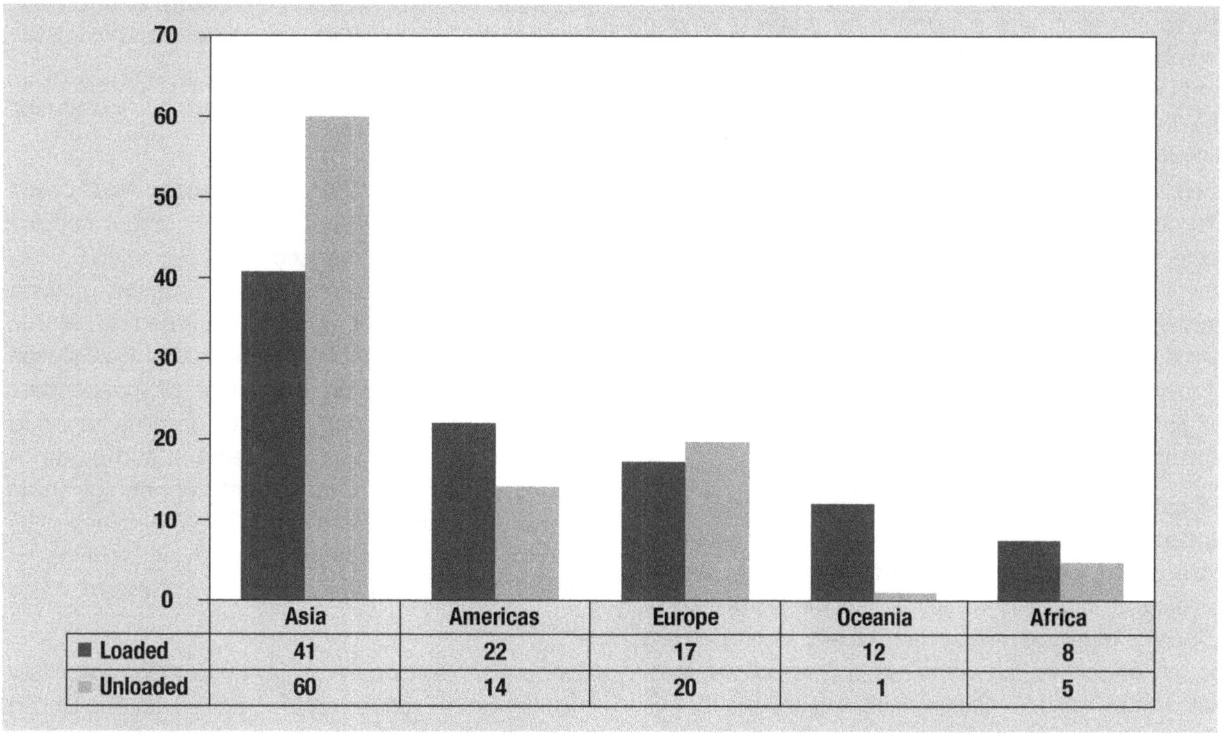

	Asia	Americas	Europe	Oceania	Africa
Loaded	41	22	17	12	8
Unloaded	60	14	20	1	5

Source: UNCTAD secretariat calculations, based on data from reporting countries, as published on relevant government and port industry websites, and from specialist sources.

Note: Estimated figures based on preliminary data or on the last year for which data were available.

1.4 (a) and (b)). Developing countries remained key world importers and exporters in 2015 and have consolidated their position as suppliers of raw materials, while also strengthening their position as large sources of consumer demand and main players in globalized manufacturing processes (figure 1.4 (b)). Over the past four decades, a compositional shift has occurred in seaborne trade reflecting, among others, the effects of globalized manufacturing processes, longer supply chains and the expanding energy and industrial commodity needs of developing countries, as well as their growing requirements for consumer goods and processed products. With regard to regional influence, in 2015, Asia continued to dominate as the main loading and unloading area. The Americas surpassed Europe, Africa and Oceania with regard to goods loaded, while Europe received larger volumes of goods unloaded, followed by the Americas, Africa and Oceania (figure 1.4 (c)).

2. Seaborne trade by cargo type

(a) Tanker trade

(i) Crude oil

In 2015, oil remained the leading fuel, accounting for one third of global energy consumption. Global oil consumption was supported by demand among members of the Organization for Economic Cooperation and Development, in particular the United States and the European Union, and also partly sustained by China and India, where oil consumption expanded by 6.3 per cent and 8.1 per cent, respectively (British Petroleum, 2016). Global oil production expanded at a faster pace, resulting in continued downward pressure on oil prices. Underpinned by these developments, global crude oil trade reversed the 2014 trend and expanded by 3.8 per cent in 2015, with total volumes reaching an estimated 1.77 billion tons. An overview of global consumers and producers of oil and gas is presented in table 1.5.

Global seaborne oil trade expanded faster than underlying oil demand, suggesting that end-user oil demand was not the only factor at play. Ample oil supply, low oil price levels, additions to refinery capacity, improved refinery margins and stock-building activity all contributed to the rise in crude oil volumes, which in turn led to infrastructure bottlenecks, delays and greater demand for oil storage. Lower oil prices and improved refinery margins supported imports into Europe, as well as shipments within the region and

Table 1.5 Major producers and consumers of oil and natural gas, 2015 (Percentage of world market share)

World oil production		*World oil consumption*	
Western Asia	32	Asia–Pacific	34
North America	19	North America	23
Transition economies	15	Europe	13
Developing America	11	Western Asia	11
Africa	10	Developing America	9
Asia–Pacific	9	Transition economies	6
Europe	4	Africa	4
Oil refinery capacities		***Oil refinery throughput***	
Asia–Pacific	33	Asia–Pacific	34
North America	21	North America	22
Europe	15	Europe	16
Western Asia	10	Western Asia	10
Transition economies	9	Transition economies	8
Developing America	8	Developing America	7
Africa	4	Africa	3
World natural gas production		***World natural gas consumption***	
North America	26	North America	25
Transition economies	22	Asia–Pacific	20
Western Asia	17	Transition economies	16
Asia–Pacific	15	Western Asia	14
Europe	7	Europe	13
Developing America	7	Developing America	8
Africa	6	Africa	4

Source: UNCTAD secretariat calculations, based on British Petroleum, 2016.

Note: Oil includes crude oil, shale oil, oil sands and natural gas liquids, but excludes liquid fuels from other sources such as biomass and coal derivatives.

from both Western Africa and Western Asia. Crude oil imports into China accounted for about half the growth, as volumes increased by an estimated 9.3 per cent (Clarksons Research, 2016d). Together, growing refinery throughput in China, the need to fill the country's strategic petroleum reserve and liberalization of the market, allowing a number of independent refineries to either import crude oil or refine imported volumes, boosted China's oil demand and crude oil imports. India – the third largest importer of crude oil after the United States and China – increased its imports, while increasingly diversifying sources of supply, including Latin America and Western Africa (Tusiani, 2016).

Two major developments in 2015 had potentially important ramifications on crude oil trade. The United States lifted a 40-year ban on crude oil exports, and export shipments are reported to have since been made. In the short term, continued lower oil price levels and limited adequate export facilities are holding back oil export growth. However, exports from the United States are expected to redraw the future energy map as the country's shale oil production increases (Miller, 2016). In addition, some sanctions on the Islamic Republic of Iran have been lifted, allowing for the return of its crude oil to the market, which is expected to add more pressure on oil supply and weigh down price levels, although the pace at which its exports will fully recover remains uncertain, given continued obstacles arising from some outstanding issues, including financial, legal and insurance-related issues (Danish Ship Finance, 2016).

(ii) Refined petroleum products

Trade in petroleum products and gas increased by 5.1 per cent in 2015, reaching a total volume of 1.17 billion tons. UNCTAD data do not allow for a breakdown of such trades. However, estimates, for example by Clarksons Research, indicate that trade increased in petroleum products by 6.2 per cent, to above 1 billion tons, and in gas by 3.5 per cent, to 328 million tons. Import demand in Asia, as well as strong demand in Australia resulting from the closure of some refineries in 2014 and 2015, helped support trade. Import growth was also fuelled by strong import demand in India, driven largely by the removal of diesel subsidies in late 2014. Imports in Europe also increased on the back of lower oil price levels, which supported growth in refinery throughputs and intra-European trade. In parallel, and in addition to end-user demand, lower oil price levels triggered greater trading activity and generated arbitrage opportunities, further supporting trade in petroleum products. With regard to cargo types, strong demand for gas and transportation fuels, as well as storage activity with regard to diesel, supported demand for petroleum products. With regard to supply, increased refinery throughput resulting from the availability of domestic crude oil boosted export volumes from the United States, while growing refinery capacity in Western Asia, in particular in Saudi Arabia, supported export volumes from the region.

(iii) Gas

Global natural gas trade carried by sea in liquefied form, which accounted for nearly one third of world natural gas trade in 2015, expanded by 1.6 per cent, down from 2.5 per cent in 2014. Total volumes reached 338.3 billion cubic metres (British Petroleum, 2016). Export growth was driven by growing shipments from Australia, Indonesia, Malaysia, Papua New Guinea and Qatar, among others. Rising import demand in Europe and Western Asia helped partly offset volume declines in some key liquid natural gas importing countries such as Japan. The largest importer, Japan reduced its imports, possibly owing to a mild winter, reduced coal prices and the restart of two nuclear reactors in 2015 (World Nuclear Association, 2016). The Republic of Korea, the second largest importer, also reduced its imports by 15 per cent (British Petroleum, 2016). Imports into China fell by 3.3 per cent due to the economic slowdown, a mild winter and expansion of the country's domestic gas production. In addition, although starting from a low base, liquefied natural gas imports to the United States increased by over 50 per cent, while exports increased eightfold (British Petroleum, 2016). In 2015, the high cost of onshore import facilities resulted in the use of alternative and new solutions, including the use of regasification equipment on board ships, liquid natural gas regasification carriers as mobile import terminals and floating storage and regasification units (Clarksons Research, 2016e). In July 2015, 19 countries were reported to be exporting liquid natural gas, and 16 countries are reported to have started importing liquid natural gas over the past 10 years (Clarksons Research, 2015a). Trade in liquefied petroleum gas, which competes with naphtha for use as a feedstock in the petrochemical sector, is estimated to have expanded by 8.3 per cent in 2015, owing to continued export growth in the United States and rising demand in the petrochemical and household sectors in Asia, notably in China and India.

(b) Dry cargo trade: Major and minor dry bulk commodities and other dry cargo

In 2015, global dry bulk shipments contracted by 0.2 per cent, and their volume was estimated at 4.8 billion tons. In contrast to the average annual growth of 7 per cent in recent years, dry bulk trade contracted due to the 1.3 per cent decline in trade in the five major dry bulk commodities (iron ore, coal, grain, bauxite and alumina and phosphate rock). In 2015, shipments of the five major bulk commodities totalled 2.95 billion tons. In less than 15 years, China's import volumes increased nearly sevenfold, from 319 million tons in 2000 to 2.1 billion tons in 2015. The concentrated growth, both in China and in two key commodities – iron ore and coal – heightened the vulnerability of shipping and seaborne trade to fluctuations affecting demand and to developments in China's economy. This became evident in 2015, when China's steel output, which accounted for nearly half of global output, declined (by 2.3 per cent) for the first time since 1981 (World Steel Association, 2016). Reduced steel production in China compressed the country's demand for imports of iron ore, as well as other related commodities and metals. An overview of global players in the dry bulk sector is presented in table 1.6.

Table 1.6 Major dry bulk commodities and steel: Main producers, users, exporters and importers, 2015 (Percentage of world market shares)

Steel producers		*Steel users*	
China	50	China	46
Japan	6	United States	7
India	6	India	5
United States	5	Japan	4
Russian Federation	4	Republic of Korea	4
Republic of Korea	4	Russian Federation	3
Germany	3	Germany	3
Brazil	2	Turkey	2
Turkey	2	Mexico	1
Ukraine	1	Brazil	1
Other	17	Other	24
Iron ore exporters		***Iron ore importers***	
Australia	54	China	70
Brazil	27	Japan	10
South Africa	5	Europe	8
Canada	3	Republic of Korea	5
Ukraine	1	Other	7
Sweden	1		
Other	9		
Coal exporters		***Coal importers***	
Australia	33	India	19
Indonesia	32	Japan	16
Russian Federation	9	Europe	15
Colombia	7	China	14
South Africa	7	Republic of Korea	11
United States	5	Taiwan Province of China	5
Canada	2	Malaysia	2
Other	5	Thailand	2
		Other	16
Grain exporters		***Grain importers***	
United States	22	Asia	33
Russian Federation	19	Africa	22
European Union	14	Developing America	19
Ukraine	11	Western Asia	16
Argentina	9	Europe	7
Canada	8	Transition economies	3
Other	17		

Source: UNCTAD secretariat calculations, based on Clarksons Research, 2016f; International Grains Council, 2016; and World Steel Association, 2016.

(i) Iron ore

Following strong expansion (12.6 per cent) in 2014, world seaborne iron ore trade is estimated to have grown by 1.9 per cent in 2015, the slowest pace since 1999. Seaborne iron ore shipments totalled 1.36 billion tons, with import volumes into China – accounting for over two thirds of world iron ore imports – increasing by 2.8 per cent, a slower pace than the 15 per cent expansion in 2014. The slowdown was partly due to reduced steel production and to reliance on existing stocks. With regard to supply, in 2015, major iron ore exporters, namely, Australia and Brazil – accounting for over 80 per cent of the global iron ore market – continued production and increased their global shipments.

(ii) Coal

In 2015, for the first time in about three decades, world seaborne coal (steam and coking) shipments fell, by 6.9 per cent, and total volumes fell to 1.13 billion tons, with a division of 78 and 22 per cent, respectively, between steam and coking coal. Steam coal exports are estimated to have dropped by 7.5 per cent to 881 million tons, while coking coal shipments are estimated to have dropped by 5.3 per cent to 248 million tons, owing mainly to contraction in China's coal imports (-31.4 per cent), in particular steam coal. This contraction was caused by the slowdown in China's economic growth, restrictions on low-quality coal imports and air pollution control measures introduced in China. After overtaking China as the world's leading steam coal importer in mid-2015, India saw its steam coal imports decline by 3.2 per cent due to reduced power demand and growing domestic output. Meanwhile, India's coking coal imports increased by 8.9 per cent, stimulated by infrastructure development and manufacturing activity. In Europe, the Large Combustion Plant Directive of the European Union, which aims to reduce carbon emissions, constrained the region's coal imports, resulting in steam and coking coal imports falling by 9.6 per cent and 6.2 per cent, respectively. In Japan, falling steel output was a drag on coking coal imports, with volumes falling by 4.5 per cent in 2015. With regard to exports, in 2015, Australian shipments to China fell by 35 per cent, as China began to make greater use of domestic coal, renewables and uranium (Catlin, 2015). Other exporters, including Indonesia and South Africa, and in North America, remain vulnerable to developments in China's economy, as well as the potential for India to increase domestic production, which may offset its coal import requirements. Vulnerabilities also arise, for example, in connection with logistical disruptions in Indonesia, as well as from intense competition among producers (Catlin, 2015).

(iii) Grain

In 2015, global trade in grains (wheat, coarse grain and soybeans) increased by an estimated 4.9 per cent, reaching 453 million tons. Wheat and coarse grains, accounting for 71.5 per cent of the total, expanded by 2.9 per cent, while soybean shipments increased by 10.3 per cent. The slowdown from the double-digit growth rates in 2014 reflects high grain stockpiles and weaker import demand in some of the largest grain-importing countries, especially in North Africa and Western Asia. The Islamic Republic of Iran scaled back its imports and was reported to have introduced taxes to limit imports and promote domestic production. Improved domestic harvests, including in China and Egypt, and moves to increase reliance on local harvests, such as in Algeria, contributed to limited shipping volumes.

(iv) Bauxite and alumina, and phosphate rock

In 2015, global bauxite and alumina trade volumes expanded by 18.1 per cent, in contrast to the negative performance in 2014 (-24.5 per cent). China's ability to secure sources of bauxite other than from Indonesia, and its growing alumina production capacity, contributed to the growth. Following Indonesia's ban on the export of bauxite in January 2014, stocks of bauxite lessened, while bauxite production in China increased, together with imports from countries other than Indonesia. In 2015, China imported 20 million tons of bauxite from Australia, 28 per cent more than in 2014, and bauxite production in Malaysia increased to 21.20 million tons, from 3.26 million tons in 2014, and nearly all bauxite was exported to China in both years (United States Department of the Interior and United States Geological Survey, 2016). With regard to phosphate rock (used as fertiliser or industrial input), following an estimated growth of 1.0 per cent in 2015, global shipments are estimated at 29.8 million tons. Some projects are planned for 2019, including in Algeria, Australia, Brazil, China, Egypt, Jordan, Kazakhstan, Peru, the Russian Federation and Tunisia. Offshore mining projects are planned in Namibia for after 2019. Current projects in Africa are not expected to begin production until after 2020 (United States Department of the Interior and United States Geological Survey, 2016).

(v) Minor bulk commodities

In 2015, trade in minor bulk commodities increased at an estimated 0.4 per cent, with total volumes reaching 1.74 billion tons. Manufactures (steel products and forest products) accounted for 43.0 per cent of the total, followed by metals and minerals (37.1 per cent) and agribulks (19.9 per cent). While shipments of manufactures and agribulks increased, by 1.9 per cent and 2.9 per cent, respectively, shipments of metals and minerals declined, by 2.4 per cent. Growth in manufactures reflected the increase in steel production in China and exports to China, and the weakened domestic demand for steel. Protectionist measures in some importing countries such as India and in the European Union may have affected exports of steel products from China. Exports of metals and minerals fell as nickel ore volumes dropped (-21.4 per cent), and the effect of the export ban imposed on nickel ore from Indonesia in January 2014 continued to be felt. With regard to imports, demand from China weakened with the reduction in stainless steel consumption and the introduction of pollution control measures.

(vi) Containerized trade

In 2015, total containerized trade across the mainlane East–West, secondary East–West, intraregional, South–South and North–South routes recorded a significant slowdown, with volumes increasing by 2.4 per cent to reach 175 million TEUs (figures 1.5 and 1.6). Three main factors combined to limit containerized trade growth, namely, the decline in volumes on the headhaul of the Eastern Asia–Europe trade route; the limited growth of North–South trade, owing to the impact of low commodity prices on the terms of trade and purchasing power of commodity-exporting countries; and the pressure on intra-Asian trade resulting from the slowdown in China (table 1.7).

Figure 1.5 Global containerized trade by route, 2015 (Percentage share in twenty-foot equivalent units)

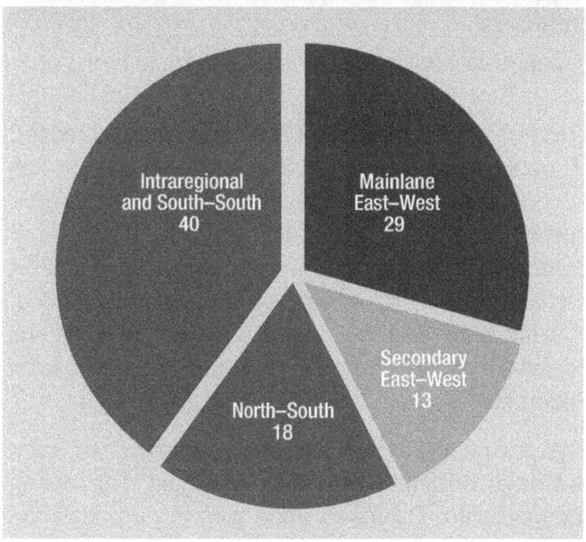

Source: UNCTAD secretariat calculations, based on Clarksons Research, 2016b.

Figure 1.6 Global containerized trade, 1996–2016 (Millions of twenty-foot equivalent units and percentage annual change)

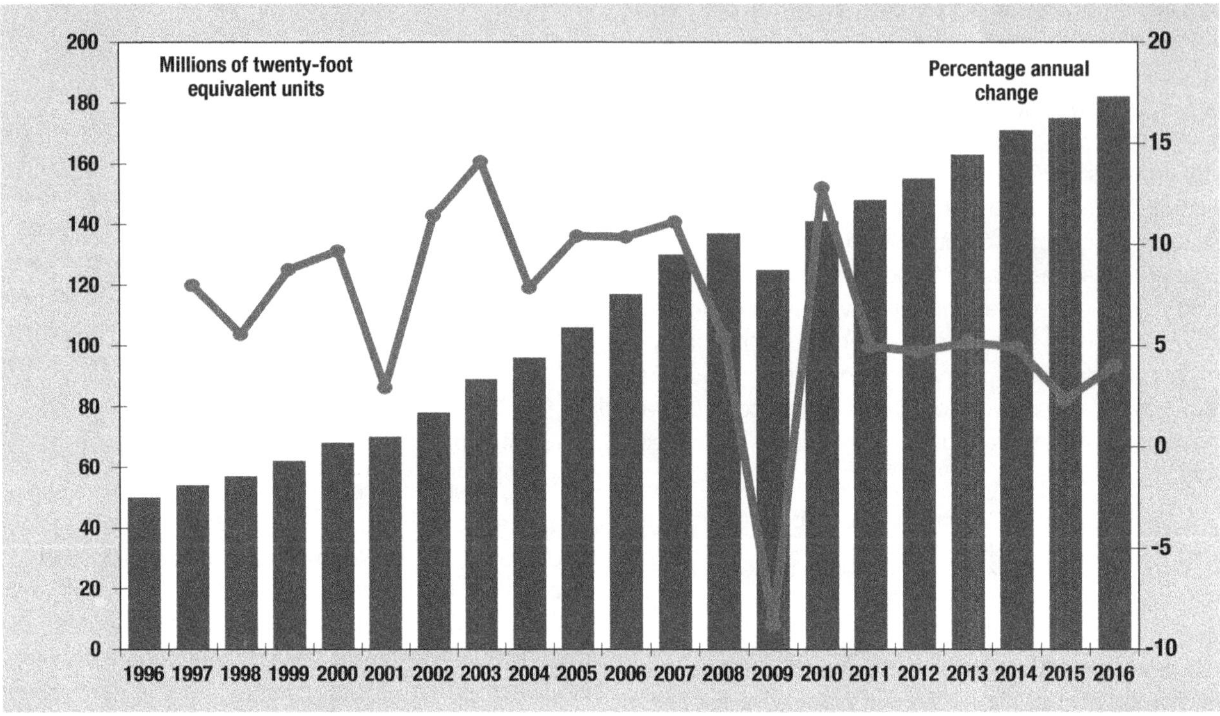

Source: UNCTAD secretariat calculations, based on Clarksons Research, Container Intelligence Monthly, various issues, and Drewry Shipping Consultants, 2008.

Table 1.7 Estimated containerized cargo flows on major East–West container trade routes, 2014–2015 (Millions of twenty-foot equivalent units)

	Trans-Pacific		*Europe–Asia*		*Transatlantic*	
	Eastern Asia–North America	*North America–Eastern Asia*	*Asia–Europe*	*Europe–Asia*	*Europe–North America*	*North America–Europe*
2014	15.8	7.4	15.2	6.8	3.9	2.8
2015	16.8	7.2	14.9	6.8	4.1	2.7
Percentage change, 2014–2015	6.6	-2.9	-2.2	0.0	5.4	-2.4

Source: UNCTAD secretariat calculations, based on the MDS Transmodal world cargo database.

Volumes on the mainlane East–West route increased by about 1.2 per cent in 2015, reaching 52.5 million TEUs (figure 1.7). Growth was constrained by negative performance (-2.2 per cent) on the headhaul of Europe–Asia trade, which reflected weaker import demand in Europe, adjustments in retail inventories, a weak euro and the negative impact of unilateral coercive measures on import volumes into the Russian Federation.

The decline in 2015 of European containerized trade seems inconsistent with data indicating that, during the year, intra-European trade growth outpaced the growth of trade between the European Union and the rest of the world. While intraregional imports grew by 1.4 per cent, imports from the rest of the world remained flat. The share of intraregional imports of total European imports increased from 60 per cent in 2007 to 65 per cent in 2015 (Danish Ship Finance, 2016). Combined with statistics showing a relatively strong demand in Europe for consumer goods during the year, it has been argued that a shift may be unfolding towards regional and closer-to-end-market sourcing of goods.

On the trans-Pacific trade route, firm demand in the United States supported trade volumes, with an overall growth of 3.6 per cent in 2015. However, while growth on the headhaul was particularly strong – estimated at 6.6 per cent – trade on backhauls declined by 2.9 per

Figure 1.7 Estimated containerized cargo flows on major East–West container trade routes, 1995–2015 (Millions of twenty-foot equivalent units)

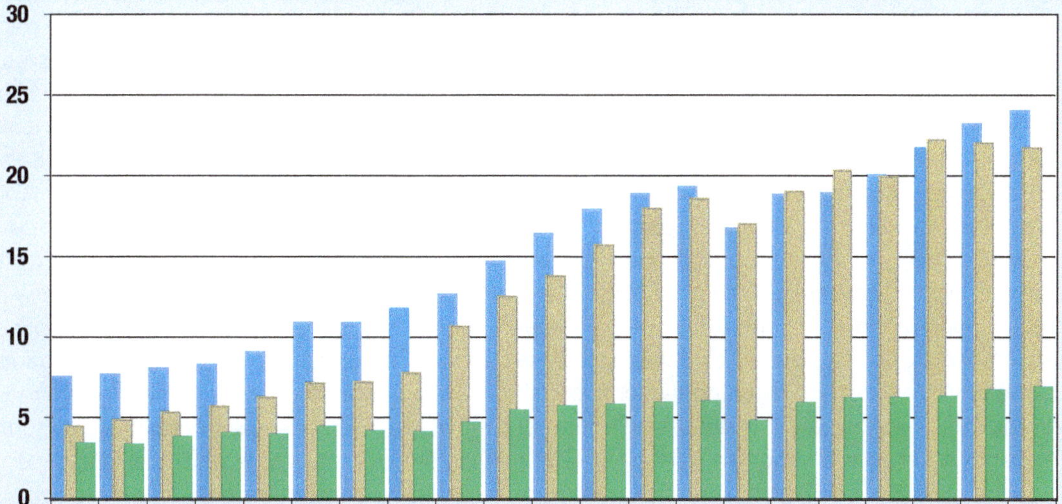

	1995	1996	1997	1998	1999	2000	2001	2002	2003	2004	2005	2006	2007	2008	2009	2010	2011	2012	2013	2014	2015
Trans-Pacific	8	8	8	8	9	11	11	12	13	15	16	18	19	19	17	19	19	20	22	23	24
Europe–Asia	4	5	5	6	6	7	7	8	11	12	14	16	18	19	17	19	20	20	22	22	22
Transatlantic	3	3	4	4	4	4	4	4	5	5	6	6	6	6	5	6	6	6	6	7	7

Source: UNCTAD secretariat calculations, based on Clarksons Research (2009–2013), Container Intelligence Monthly, MDS Transmodal world cargo database (2009–2015 figures) and United Nations Economic Commission for Latin America and the Caribbean, 2010.

cent. A strong dollar and rising consumer spending boosted United States imports from China and Viet Nam. Key developments affecting this route in 2015 included the opening of the new Panama Canal and congestion in ports on the west coast of the United States. The congestion in 2015 caused delays and a drop in container port throughput, which in turn resulted in cargo diversion benefiting ports on the east coast (Clarksons Research, 2015b).

Volumes on the North–South trade route increased by 1.4 per cent in 2015, reaching 30.8 million TEUs. Limited growth reflected the weak container import demand in Africa and Latin America resulting from, among other factors, political unrest in a number of North African countries, the recession in Brazil and the negative impact of eroding terms of trade on the purchasing power of commodity-exporting developing economies in the two regions (Danish Ship Finance, 2016).

Intraregional container trade expanded at an estimated 3.1 per cent in 2015. Intra-Asian trade – accounting for over two thirds of the total – expanded by 2.9 per cent, down from 6 per cent in 2014. The deceleration reflected the situation in China and the decline in imports in other economies in Asia, such as Indonesia and Japan. Intra-Asian trade continued to be supported, however, by the relocation of manufacturing centres from China to other areas in Asia and by increased imports to the Philippines, the Republic of Korea and Viet Nam, as well as by robust growth on the Asia–South Asia route (Clarksons Research, 2016g).

Overall, in 2015, containerized trade continued to face the upsizing of container ships (see chapters 2 and 3). The average ship size in the global fleet increased at a cumulative annual growth rate of 1.9 per cent in 2001–2009 and 18.2 per cent in 2010–2015 (Davidson, 2016).

One study has noted that container ship size increases of up to 18,000 TEUs were likely to result in maximum cost savings for shipping and ports by only 5 per cent of total network costs, and that the economics of scale diminished as vessel sizes increased beyond 18,000 TEUs (Batra, 2016).

Some observers maintain that the costs of ever-larger ships may outweigh their benefits. The disadvantages include reduced service frequency, higher peaks in container traffic, greater pressure on the operations of cargo-handling services, rising terminal capital and operational costs, reductions in options available to shippers and higher supply chain risks with the concentration of trade in larger but fewer ships, as well as environmental effects arising from dredging deeper channels and expanding yard area. There will likely be a need for ports and lines to further cooperate, including, for example, through terminal operator alliances, mergers and acquisitions, and joint ventures between the shipping industry and port terminals (Davidson, 2016). In 2015, consolidation activity heightened in the container shipping sector, leading to greater speculation about the future (see chapter 2). An immediate consequence of consolidation is the tendency for alliances to focus on reducing transit times and increasing reliability to attract shippers, at the expense of services and port calls (King, 2016).

With regard to containerized trade, on 1 July 2015, a weight verification requirement was adopted under the International Convention for the Safety of Life at Sea (SOLAS), requiring shippers to verify the gross mass of shipped containers by weighing either the containers and contents combined or individual items in a container (see chapter 5). Some observers expect the charges associated with the new requirement to increase ocean freight transport costs by over 10 per cent (Waters, 2016).

Finally, while speculating about the impact of the decision by the United Kingdom to leave the European Union may be premature, some analysts contend that the effects on container shipping will not be dramatic, as the United Kingdom accounts for only 1.4 per cent of global container volumes and its share of global container port throughput has declined, from 3 per cent in 2000 to 1.2 per cent in 2013. Its importance as a maritime centre for container shipping has gradually diminished, and its shares with regard to controlled container ships and capacity operated are marginal (Baker, 2016).

C. OTHER DEVELOPMENTS AFFECTING SEABORNE TRADE, AND POTENTIAL OPPORTUNITIES FOR DEVELOPING COUNTRIES

Maritime transport and seaborne trade face other developments that involve both challenges and opportunities and could redefine the sector's operating landscape. In addition to the already noted continued macroeconomic uncertainty and apparent shift in the trade–GDP relationship, demand for maritime transport as measured by seaborne trade is subject to other fast-evolving trends. A number of observed developments have the potential to stimulate growth, boost merchandise trade, lift seaborne trade volumes and generate opportunities for developing countries, both as users and providers of maritime transport services. Such developments are increasing and may potentially be game-changing for the maritime transport sector in the long term. They include infrastructure development initiatives, developments in trade policy and liberalization, population growth and urbanization and the growing use of e-commerce. The implications for maritime transport of other parallel trends, such as the fourth industrial revolution, shared and circular economy concepts and reduced fossil fuel use, may be less certain. The fourth industrial revolution involves, in particular, the expansion of the digital revolution into production processes, including technology, innovation, big data and the Internet of Things (UNCTAD, 2016c). While such developments may benefit trade and shipping through improved efficiencies and productivity gains, they may also bring about a shift in global production, consumption and transportation structures and patterns, and potentially reduce demand for maritime transport services and constrain seaborne trade volumes.

1. Transport infrastructure investment, development and expansion

In 2015, a number of infrastructure development and expansion projects were announced, launched or completed, with a view to improving connectivity, enhancing access to suppliers and consumers and enabling trade and regional integration. Such initiatives included the construction, expansion and improvement of logistics infrastructure and physical assets such as the Panama Canal and Suez Canal, as well as the One Belt, One Road Initiative in China and the joint Japan–Asian Development Bank Partnership for Quality Infrastructure. The latter two initiatives have the potential to stimulate growth, boost trade and drive up demand for transport and logistics services.

(a) Panama Canal and Suez Canal

A landmark development in 2015 was the completion of the $8.2 billion expansion project of the Suez Canal, from the original 60 km to 95 km. The expanded Canal is expected to allow for the transit of 97 ships per day, for two-way traffic in some parts and for larger ships in others. The aim is also to cut transit and waiting times. Another milestone was reached in June 2016 when the expanded Panama Canal opened for operations (see chapter 2 and UNCTAD, 2014a). The Canal will allow for the passage of larger neo-Panamax ships that, in turn, may result in Panamax ships being redeployed on intraregional routes.

(b) One Belt, One Road Initiative

A recent development with potentially significant implications for seaborne trade is China's One Belt, One Road Initiative. Launched in 2013, this initiative aims to establish new trading routes, links and business opportunities by further connecting China, Asia, Europe, Africa and countries with economies in transition along five routes. The implementation process was initiated in 2015, and full implementation across all the countries involved is a long-term endeavour (China–Britain Business Council, 2015). If the initiative is fully implemented, the expected benefits are likely to be broad-based and to span a number of areas and various countries and regions. The initiative envisages the construction of a trade and transport infrastructure network involving 60 countries (table 1.8), accounting for 60 per cent of the world's population and representing a collective GDP equivalent to 33 per cent of the world's total (China–Britain Business Council, 2015). The surface transport component focuses on linking China to Europe through Central Asia and the Russian Federation; China with Western Asia through Central Asia; and China with South-East Asia, South Asia and the Indian Ocean, while the maritime transport component focuses on linking China with Europe through the Indian Ocean and China with the southern Pacific Ocean (Hong Kong [China] Trade Development Council, 2016). Six international economic cooperation corridors have been identified.

In China, the initiative is expected to help revitalize domestic industries; bring higher returns for Chinese capital and higher demand for Chinese goods and services; absorb China's labour; and use China's excess industrial capacity, such as cement for ports and roads and steel for rails and trains, among others (Zhu and Hoffman, 2015). China's western region is expected to benefit through the building of hinterland connections and infrastructure, and the generation of demand for high value-added steel products, such as for pipelines and high-speed railways (Zhu and Hoffman, 2015). Greater energy security for China may also be achieved by making use of alternative routes to the Straits of Malacca though Pakistan, Myanmar and Thailand.

Beyond China, the initiative may help reduce transport costs, increase trade flows and open new markets to all involved countries, as well as promote the development of emerging industries (China–Britain Business Council, 2015). Another important expected contribution is to closing the persistent infrastructure gap in developing regions, especially in transport. Infrastructure investment needs for Asia are estimated at $50 billion per year through 2020 and for Africa are estimated to exceed $93 billion (*Bloomberg Brief*, 2015). Beyond the initiative, China has already committed over $10 billion in investment to develop the Bagamoyo port in the United Republic of Tanzania and has contracts to build railways connecting the ports of Dar es Salaam and Mombasa, with inland countries (Bohlund and Orlik, 2015). Such investments may stimulate trade, as shown in Africa, where a tripling of China's investment value in 2008–2013 was associated with a doubling of exports, from $55 billion in 2008 to $116 billion in 2014 (Bohlund and Orlik, 2015).

From the transport sector perspective, the success of the initiative rests heavily on optimization of the transport infrastructure and services, including shipping and logistics, required to support connectivity in China and beyond. In turn, the transport sector may benefit from the trade growth opportunities generated by the initiative and growth in volumes stemming from reduced transport costs, greater market access and connectivity, and infrastructure and industrial development. With regard to shipping, these may provide an additional boost to lift volumes and reverse the recent trends of weak demand and slowly growing trade, and help bring balance to the market, which currently faces a mismatch between supply and demand, as well as continued excess capacity (see chapter 2). Maritime connections linking China to the Port of Piraeus, Greece, through the Indian Ocean and Suez Canal are expected to provide an alternative to ports such as Antwerp, Belgium; Hamburg, Germany; and Rotterdam, the Netherlands, while cutting 10 days off the journey to Central or Eastern Europe (Pong, 2015). The expanded Suez Canal is likely to benefit from the new traffic to be generated by the initiative, the trade flows from the Islamic Republic of Iran stemming from the removal of international sanctions and the oil trade expected to result from the growing importance of the refinery market in India (*Safety4Sea*, 2016). Surface transport offers alternative logistics options for business and trade, especially for high value added and time-sensitive goods (Pong, 2015). Several railways that already operate between China

Table 1.8	One Belt, One Road Initiative: Projected infrastructure investments by China
Bangladesh	Studies for Bangladesh–China–India–Myanmar corridor; deepwater port, Payra
Belarus	Mining and processing infrastructure, Starobinskoye ($1.4 billion); Sino-Belarus Industrial Park, Minsk ($5 billion)
Fiji	Hydroelectric plant ($158 million)
Georgia	International economic zone, Tbilisi ($150 million); deepwater port, Anaklia ($5 billion)
India	High-speed rail cooperation; industrial parks, Gujarat and Maharashtra
Indonesia	Jakarta–Bandung high-speed railway; coal mining and transport infrastructure, Papua and Kalimantan ($6 billion); road and port infrastructure, Kalimantan ($1.1 billion); ferronickel plant, Sulawesi ($5.1 billion)
Kazakhstan	China–Kazakhstan oil pipeline; development of special economic zone Khorgos-East Gate at Kazakhstan–China border
Kyrgyzstan	China–Kyrgyzstan–Uzbekistan highway; China–Uzbekistan railway ($2 billion); power grid upgrades, southern Kyrgyzstan; power plant refurbishment, Bishkek; transport and logistics cooperation
Lithuania	Encouraging investment in joint railway and port projects; China Merchants Group letter of intent with port of Klaipeda
Malaysia	Malaysia–China Kuantan Industrial Park, including deepwater container port, steel and aluminium plants and palm oil refinery ($3.4 billion)
Myanmar	Bangladesh–China–India–Myanmar transport network, including roads, railways, waterways and airports; Kyaukphyu–Kunming oil and gas pipelines; Myanmar–Yunnan optical cable
Pakistan	China–Pakistan economic corridor, roads and railway ($46 billion); Lahore–Karachi highway; port upgrades, including airport, power plant and roads, Gwadar; coal mine and power plant, Gadani; 720,000 kW Karot Hydropower Plant; soft loans for two nuclear power plants near Karachi ($6.5 billion)
Sri Lanka	Deepwater port in Hambantota ($600 million); China Merchants Holdings International investment in Port of Colombo ($500 million)
Russian Federation	Kazan–Moscow high-speed railway; Siberian gas pipelines to supply China
Thailand	Kra Isthmus Canal ($28 billion); Kunming–Bangkok highway; railway between Nong Kahi, Bangkok and proposed China–Lao People's Democratic Republic railway
Tajikistan	Central Asia–China gas pipeline; 500kV power substation reconstruction, Tursunzoda; Dushanbe–Chanak highway upgrades ($280 million)
Turkmenistan	Islamic Republic of Iran–Kazakhstan–Turkmenistan road and rail network
Uzbekistan	Uzbekistan–China gas pipeline
Viet Nam	Port upgrades, Haiphong; Lang Son–Hanoi highway
Africa	Agreement with African Union to help build railways, roads and airports; coastal road, Nigeria ($13 billion); Nairobi–Mombasa railway, Kenya ($3.8 billion); Addis Ababa–Djibouti railway ($4 billion)
Central and South America	Pledged investment to region ($250 billion); proposed transcontinental railway between coasts of Brazil and Peru ($10 billion); natural gas development, pipelines, power generation facilities, highways, ports and telecommunications
Europe	Upgrade of Port of Piraeus, Greece ($260 million); Hungary–Serbia high-speed railway ($3 billion); China–Spain cargo railway (12,875 km)

Source: UNCTAD secretariat calculations, based on Australia Department of Foreign Affairs and Trade, 2015; and Hong Kong [China] Trade Development Council, 2016.

and Europe provide an advantage with regard to average travel days, which hover at 15 compared with 30–40 by sea. In addition, rail compares favourably with air with regard to shipping costs, and constitutes a more environmentally friendly mode of transport.

(c) Partnership for Quality Infrastructure

The Partnership for Quality Infrastructure aims to promote infrastructure investment in collaboration with other countries and international organizations. Japan, through its economic cooperation tools, including official development assistance, as well as by collaborating with the Asian Development Bank, is expected to provide $110 billion to finance quality infrastructure development in Asia over the next five years (Japan Ministry of Foreign Affairs, 2015). The initiative is expected to meet infrastructure demand and achieve quality and quantity in infrastructure by mobilizing further financial resources and know-how from the private sector. Examples of related projects include the Delhi Metro, India; Ulaanbaatar railway fly-over, Mongolia; and Viet Nam–Japan Friendship Bridge.

2. Trade policy and liberalization developments

Government policies and interventions contribute to shaping international trade patterns, including seaborne trade. While addressing the weakness in global demand caused largely by stagnant real wages is essential to boosting trade, a number of actions may potentially support a recovery in global aggregate demand and support trade, including, for example, a rollback on restrictive measures and implementation of the Agreement on Trade Facilitation, which could potentially increase trade by up to $1 trillion (World Trade Organization, 2016). Efforts to further liberalize trade through regional agreements are being pursued. Some initiatives have the potential to create large markets and cover a large share of global GDP when fully implemented. For example, the Trans-Pacific Partnership adopted in 2015, which brings together 12 countries, is expected to create a market of 800 million people with over 40 per cent of world GDP (United Nations Department of Economic and Social Affairs, 2016). In addition, negotiations are ongoing for the Regional Comprehensive Economic Partnership, which would cover more than 3 billion people (The Economist Intelligence Unit, 2016b). Negotiations are also ongoing for the Transatlantic Trade and Investment Partnership, which, together with other broad economic agreements among a group of countries that together have significant economic weight, is likely to have a major impact on investment patterns; the three regional groupings each account for a quarter or more of global flows of foreign direct investment (UNCTAD, 2014b). In addition, the Association of Southeast Asian Nations Economic Community, launched in December 2015, could generate a market covering over 622 million people and worth $2.6 trillion (King, 2015). As part of the One Belt, One Road Initiative, China is also reported to be planning to negotiate a free trade agreement with 65 countries. According to the Ministry of Commerce, by the end of 2015, China had established 53 economic cooperation zones in 18 countries along One Belt, One Road Initiative routes, with associated investments of over $14 billion, and had signed free trade agreements with 11 countries and bilateral investment agreements with 56 countries. China is also pursuing trade facilitation initiatives through customs cooperation with neighbouring countries.

3. Population growth and urbanization

Seaborne trade continues to be influenced by growth in the global population and urbanization, and is likely to be further defined by demographic shifts, such as the ageing population in traditional consumer markets in developed regions (including in the United States and Europe) and China, as well as the rise of consumers with lower purchasing power in developing regions (Danish Ship Finance, 2016).

4. Growing cross-border e-commerce trade

Asia–Pacific is the world's biggest and fastest growing business-to-consumer e-commerce region, recording $877.61 billion in retail e-commerce sales in 2015. E-commerce in the region is expected to grow to over $1.89 trillion by 2018 (DHL, 2016). In 2015, China surpassed the United States as the world's largest e-commerce market, with online revenue projected to double to $1.1 trillion by 2020. India's e-commerce turnover, on a par with that of Australia and the Republic of Korea, is projected to grow fivefold by 2020 (DHL, 2016). E-commerce provides a significant growth opportunity, as it enables trade, supply chain capacity and logistics. In developing countries, potential business opportunities and gains may be considerable, as e-commerce alters consumption patterns and consumer shopping behaviour and allows access to a wider selection of goods and brands at a relatively reasonable cost. By boosting and reshaping consumption patterns and enabling small and medium-sized enterprises to reach new markets overseas, e-commerce also generates greater trade volumes. While such developments have the potential to generate higher demand for shipping, ports and logistics services, the actual impact on maritime transport has yet to be fully assessed, as e-commerce may pose some challenges to the shipping sector. For example, shipping may not be able to capture the full trade potential arising from e-commerce, as large retailers (such as Amazon and Wal-Mart Stores) increasingly optimize travel distances, including by expanding their networks of warehouses, positioning inventory and warehouse centres closer to consumption markets and developing their own ship-carrying capacities to avoid the costs of external shipping companies (Subramanian, 2015).

5. Fourth industrial revolution

The fourth industrial revolution, through digitization and the leveraging of innovation, technology, data and the Internet of Things to shift established modes of production and consumption, may generate welfare and productivity gains and offer new opportunities (UNCTAD, 2016c). Innovation, technology and big data may help increase efficiency and productivity, reduce transport costs, enhance the performance of supply chains and shorten travel distances. However, they may disrupt production processes based on vertical specialization and the international fragmentation of production. By cutting the length of supply chains and potentially limiting (such as through the use of three-dimensional printing and robotics) the ability of countries to generate employment opportunities on the scale experienced in China, which in turn may hinder the emergence of a middle-income class, the fourth industrial revolution has the potential to reduce demand for maritime transport services and constrain growth in world seaborne trade volumes (Danish Ship Finance, 2016).

6. Shared or circular economy

The concepts of shared economy (for example, renting and swapping) and circular economy are increasingly attracting attention. A shared economy through, among others, new technology and platforms that allow for asset management, service delivery and information access, could alter demand as well as supply chains and modify patterns of feedback loops across connected industries (Danish Ship Finance, 2015). A circular economy, by promoting the effective use of resources, greater resource conservation and a reduced reliance on fossil fuels and raw materials, allows for sustainable production and consumption patterns in line with the Sustainable Development Goals. However, the associated savings and efficiency gains could also lower demand for maritime transport services. For example, applying circular economy principles in the automotive industry, where the trend is reported to be gaining traction, may affect demand for automobile carriers (Danish Ship Finance, 2015).

7. Reduced global use of fossil fuels

While the global climate action agenda is expected to further shape tanker trade patterns, advances in renewable energy and energy storage could affect global end-user oil demand (Danish Ship Finance, 2016). Related technologies may reduce demand for crude oil and petroleum products, as well as coal and liquid natural gas, and thereby affect demand for tankers, gas carriers and bulk carriers (Danish Ship Finance, 2015). The attractiveness of gas as a possibly more environmentally friendly alternative to oil and coal implies that trade in liquid natural gas may be expected to benefit, at least in the short and medium terms, from global action on climate change-related effects. In addition, in the renewable energy market, developing countries have the opportunity to increase their importance, as both users and producers. The potential for growth is significant. In 2015, globally, wind energy, which remained the largest source of renewable electricity throughout the year, increased by 17.4 per cent, while solar power generation grew by 32.6 per cent (British Petroleum, 2016). Most developing countries are endowed with renewable energy resources, including for solar energy, wind power, geothermal energy and biomass, as well as the human resources required to manufacture the relatively labour-intensive systems associated with renewable energy production.

D. OUTLOOK

The outlook for seaborne trade remains uncertain and subject to downside risks, including weak global demand and investment, political uncertainties, such as the ongoing migration crisis, doubts about the future pace and direction of European integration and a further loss of momentum in developing economies. UNCTAD forecasts world GDP growth to dip below the 2.5 per cent recorded in 2014 and 2015 and grow by 2.3 per cent in 2016. According to World Trade Organization data, world merchandise trade volumes are projected to remain steady and expand at the same pace as in 2015.

Prospects in developing countries remain generally weak. Lower commodity prices are estimated to cut almost 1 percentage point annually in 2015–2017 from the average rate of economic growth in commodity-exporting countries, compared with the rate in 2012–2014. The negative impact on the growth of energy-exporting countries is estimated to be greater, at about 2.25 percentage points on average over the same period (International Monetary Fund, 2015). In developed economies, the weak performance recorded since the 2008–2009 economic and financial crisis is set to continue. In addition, the long-term consequences of the decision by the United Kingdom to leave the European Union have yet to be fully understood.

Negative signals in the macroeconomic framework are increasingly dampening maritime cargo volumes. While some estimates indicate a slight improvement in 2016, the projected growth rates remain below the UNCTAD estimated average of over 3 per cent in 1970–2014. Major dry bulk commodities are projected to grow marginally, reflecting a continued drop in coal trade, while containerized trade volumes are expected to recover marginally in 2016. Tanker trade, including gas trade, is projected to grow by an estimated 3.6 per cent in 2016, supported in part by growth in China's crude oil imports and refineries and continued stock-building activity (Clarksons Research, 2016a). Although positive, this rate remains below the level in 2015, reflecting the diminishing positive effect of lower oil prices on demand, lower trading activity and moderation in stock-building. In addition to the potential impact of China's ongoing economic transition and geopolitical tensions in various parts of the world and the potential disruptions to oil supply, tanker trade is also shaped by infrastructure developments such as the expansion by 2020 of the Eastern Siberia–Pacific Ocean pipeline that links China and the Russian Federation (Danish Ship Finance, 2015).

Although many signals are negative, seaborne trade continues to grow, with volumes exceeding an estimated 10 billion tons in 2015. While a slowdown in China is bad news for shipping, developing countries other than China are increasingly entering the shipping scene and have the potential to drive further growth. The lifting of some sanctions on the Islamic Republic of Iran is expected to stimulate crude oil trade, as well as non-oil sectors.

With the continued observed shift in the trade–GDP relationship, it is increasingly evident that projecting seaborne trade flows based on a linear extrapolation from GDP and merchandise trade growth may no longer be valid. Forecasting methods need to be reconsidered, and to reflect variables other than GDP, including fiscal and environmental policies, as well as transport costs and regulatory aspects. Such considerations should be taken into account when projecting future growth and trade flows with a view to planning future transport infrastructure and capacity development, and devising strategies and policies aimed at supporting supply chains and industrialization through manufacturing and greater participation in regional and global value chains. Additionally, better understanding of the new trade–GDP relationship provides an opportunity for developing countries to consider ways in which they may increase participation in global production processes and trade networks. While vertical specialization and the fragmentation of production in China and the United States may have peaked, there remains scope to enhance the international division of labour by integrating regions that have been at the margin of global supply chains, such as Africa, South America and South Asia. Developing countries may benefit by exploring untapped potential and opportunities.

At the same time, and while South–South trade is gaining momentum and regional trade liberalization agreements are being negotiated or concluded, planned initiatives, such as the One Belt, One Road Initiative and Partnership for Quality Infrastructure, and the expansion of transit passages and sea bridges, such as the Panama Canal and Suez Canal, also have the potential to stimulate trade and reshape world shipping networks and trade routes, as well as to redefine hubs and networks. The growth potential associated with such developments may be significant. If fully implemented, the One Belt, One Road Initiative, for example, may boost trade, increase demand for maritime transport services, raise seaborne trade volumes and provide opportunities for developing countries to strengthen their position both as users and providers. Globally, developing countries already account for 60 and 62 per cent, respectively, of goods loaded and unloaded.

Technology, innovation, the data revolution and e-commerce can significantly transform and disrupt the shipping industry, generating both challenges and opportunities, including with regard to efficiency gains, new business models, use of the Internet, digitization, efficient logistics, effective asset management and the greater integration of small and medium-sized enterprises. Developing countries may leverage related trends to cut costs, raise productivity, develop capacity – including skills and knowledge – and enable access to new businesses opportunities.

How these trends will materialize on a broader scale remains unknown, yet it is nevertheless important for all countries – in particular in developing regions – and their transport industries to keep these developments in mind, monitor their evolution and assess their particular implications for their transport and logistics sectors and, more broadly, for their economies, societies and environments. An improved understanding of the trends and their implications may help countries ensure that these are effectively integrated into relevant planning and investment-related decision processes, and aligned with the 2030 Agenda for Sustainable Development.

Finally, the international climate agenda can be expected to further shape the maritime transport operating landscape, as the sector faces the dual challenge of climate change mitigation and adaptation (for a more detailed discussion of the climate change–maritime transport nexus, see the *Review of Maritime Transport*, 2012, 2013, 2014 and

2015). Future trends in emissions from international shipping remain uncertain and subject to international efforts and commitments to curb greenhouse gas emissions including the efforts under the frameworks of the International Maritime Organization (IMO) and the Conference of the Parties to the United Nations Framework Convention on Climate Change. Curbing greenhouse gas emissions from international shipping is an imperative, as freight transport, including maritime transport, grows in tandem with the global population, consumption needs, industrial activity, urbanization, trade and economy. Despite the current slowdown in the growth of world seaborne trade, maritime freight volumes and demand for maritime transport services are expanding. At the same time, shipping's heavy reliance on oil for propulsion translates into significant emissions of airborne pollutants and greenhouse gases. According to IMO data, carbon dioxide (CO_2) emissions from international shipping were estimated at 2.2 per cent of total emissions in 2012 and are projected to increase by 50–250 per cent by 2050, depending on economic growth and the global energy demand. As the Paris Agreement under the United Nations Framework Convention on Climate Change does not refer to emissions from international shipping, continued work under the frameworks of IMO and the United Nations Framework Convention on Climate Change is of critical importance. The twenty-second session of the Conference of the Parties, to be held from 7 to 18 November 2016, offers a renewed opportunity for shipping to advance the work on climate change mitigation. This, in turn, entails both challenges and opportunities for the sector, as it can emerge as a key player in implementing effective climate change policy action and the sustainable development agenda. Supporting this objective, UNCTAD has been increasingly considering climate change, as part of its ongoing work in the field of trade logistics, and carrying out substantive work to improve the understanding of issues at the interface of maritime transport and the climate change challenge (see http://unctad.org/en/Pages/DTL/TTL/Legal.aspx and http://unctad.org/en/Pages/DTL/TTL/Infrastructure-and-Services/Sustainable-Transport.aspx).

REFERENCES

Australia Department of Foreign Affairs and Trade (2015). China's one belt, one road: Economic implications for Australia. Business Envoy. Available at http://dfat.gov.au/about-us/publications/trade-investment/business-envoy/Pages/business-envoy-july-2015.aspx (accessed 15 September 2016).

Baker J (2016). Brexit vote to have limited impact on box shipping. *Lloyd's List Intelligence*. 29 June.

Batra A (2016). Container mega-ships may not deliver the promised economies of scale. *Shipping and Finance*. 237.

Bloomberg Brief (2015). One belt, one road: Assessing the economic impact of China's new silk road. 2 July.

Bohlund M and Orlik T (2015). China's road to Africa lifts investment, adds debt risk. *Bloomberg Intelligence*. 18 June.

British Petroleum (2016). *Statistical Review of World Energy 2016*. London.

Catlin J (2015). Analysis on the factors affecting dry bulk shipping. *Shipping and Finance*. 233.

China–Britain Business Council (2015). One belt one road: A role for United Kingdom companies in developing China's new initiative – new opportunities in China and beyond. Available at http://www.cbbc.org/sectors/one-belt,-one-road/ (accessed 15 September 2016).

Clarksons Research (2015a). *LNG Trade and Transport*.

Clarksons Research (2015b). *Container Intelligence Monthly*. 17(12).

Clarksons Research (2016a). *Seaborne Trade Monitor*. 3(7).

Clarksons Research (2016b). *Container Intelligence Monthly*. 18(7).

Clarksons Research (2016c). *Dry Bulk Trade Outlook*. 22(7).

Clarksons Research (2016d). *China Intelligence Monthly*. 11(7).

Clarksons Research (2016e). *Shipping Market Outlook*. Spring.

Clarksons Research (2016f). *Dry Bulk Trade Outlook*. 22(5).

Clarksons Research (2016g). *Container Intelligence Quarterly*. First quarter.

Constantinescu C, Mattoo A and Ruta M (2015). The global trade slowdown: Cyclical or structural? International Monetary Fund Working Paper No. 15/6.

Danish Ship Finance (2015). Shipping market review – November. Available at http://www.shipfinance.dk/en/shipping-research/~/media/PUBLIKATIONER/Shipping-Market-Review/Shipping-Market-Review---November-2015.ashx (accessed 15 September 2016).

Danish Ship Finance (2016). Shipping market review. Available at http://www.shipfinance.dk/en/shipping-research/~/media/PUBLIKATIONER/Shipping-Market-Review/Shipping-Market-Review---May-2016.ashx (accessed 15 September 2016).

Davidson N (2016). Juggling bigger ships, mega-alliances and slower growth. Presented at the Terminal Operations Conference Europe. Hamburg, Germany. 14 June.

DHL (2016). DHL demystifies Asian trade trends and uncovers supply chain implications. Available at http://www.dhl.com/en/press/releases/releases_2016/all/dhl_demystifies_asian_trade_trends_and_uncovers_supply_chain_implications.html (accessed 15 September 2016).

Drewry Shipping Consultants (2008). *Container Market Review and Forecast: Annual Report 2008–2009*. London.

European Central Bank (2015). Understanding the weakness of world trade. Economic Bulletin No. 3.

Hong Kong [China] Trade Development Council (2016). The belt and road initiative. Available at http://china-trade-research.hktdc.com/business-news/article/One-Belt-One-Road/The-Belt-and-Road-Initiative/obor/en/1/1X000000/1X0A36B7.htm (accessed 15 September 2016).

IHS Markit (2016). Maritime and trade. Available at http://www.ihs.com/index.html (accessed 15 September 2016).

International Grains Council (2016). Grain market report. No. 467.

International Monetary Fund (2015). *World Economic Outlook*. October.

International Monetary Fund (2016). *World Economic Outlook Update*. January.

Japan Ministry of Foreign Affairs (2015). Summary of Partnership for Quality Infrastructure. Available at http://www.mofa.go.jp/policy/oda/page18_000076.html (accessed 15 September 2016).

King M (2015). Association of Southeast Asian Nations Economic Community launch milestone event. *Lloyd's Loading List*. 31 December.

King M (2016). Alliances to cut port calls to reduce transit times. *Lloyd's Loading List*. 7 June.

Miller G (2016). How United States crude exports will redraw the map. *IHS Fairplay*. 5 January.

Organization for Economic Cooperation and Development (2016). Main economic indicators. Available at http://www.oecd.org/std/oecdmaineconomicindicatorsmei.htm (accessed 15 September 2016).

Pong LK (2015). One belt one road – implications for the European Union. European Union Academic Programme. Available at http://euap.hkbu.edu.hk/main/one-belt-one-road-implications-for-the-european-union/ (accessed 15 September 2016).

Safety4Sea (2016). New Suez Canal to benefit from one belt one road. 24 February.

Subramanian R (2015). How will e-commerce transform the shipping industry? *Yale Insights*. 7 April.

The Economist Intelligence Unit (2016a). *Country Forecast – Global Outlook*. May.

The Economist Intelligence Unit (2016b). *Country Forecast – Global Outlook*. January.

Tusiani M (2016). India to replace China as centre of world's oil demand growth. *Shipping and Finance*. 237.

UNCTAD (2014a). *Review of Maritime Transport 2014*. United Nations publication. Sales No. E.14.II.D.5. New York and Geneva.

UNCTAD (2014b). *World Investment Report 2014*. United Nations publication. Sales No. E.14.II.D.1. New York and Geneva.

UNCTAD (2015a). *Key Statistics and Trends in International Trade 2015*. United Nations publication. Geneva.

UNCTAD (2015b). *Review of Maritime Transport 2015*. United Nations publication. Sales No. E.15.II.D.6. New York and Geneva.

UNCTAD (2016a). *Trade and Development Report, 2016*. United Nations publication. Sales No. E.16.II.D.5. New York and Geneva.

UNCTAD (2016b). Development and globalization: Facts and figures. Available at http://stats.unctad.org/Dgff2016/ (accessed 15 September 2016).

UNCTAD (2016c). Harnessing emerging technological breakthroughs for the 2030 Agenda for Sustainable Development. Policy Brief No. 45.

United Nations Department of Economic and Social Affairs (2016). *World Economic Situation and Prospects*. United Nations publication. Sales No. E.16.II.C.2. New York.

United Nations Economic Commission for Latin America and the Caribbean (2010). Fal Bulletin. No. 288(8). Available at http://www.cepal.org/en/node/33845 (accessed 15 September 2016).

United States Department of the Interior and United States Geological Survey (2016). Mineral commodity summaries 2016. Available at http://minerals.usgs.gov/minerals/pubs/mcs/ (accessed 15 September 2016).

Waters W (2016). Box-weighing changes could raise freight costs more than 10 per cent. *Lloyd's Loading List*. 23 March.

World Bank (2016). *Global Economic Prospects – Divergences and Risks*. Washington, D.C.

World Nuclear Association (2016). Nuclear power in Japan. Available at http://www.world-nuclear.org/information-library/country-profiles/countries-g-n/japan-nuclear-power.aspx (accessed 15 September 2016).

World Steel Association (2016). World crude steel output decreases by 2.8 per cent in 2015. Press release. 25 January.

World Trade Organization (2014). *International Trade Statistics 2014*. Geneva.

World Trade Organization (2016). Trade growth to remain subdued in 2016 as uncertainties weigh on global demand. Press release 768. 7 April.

Zhu Y and Hoffman K (2015). Steel demand may improve on one belt one road. *Bloomberg Intelligence*. 23 June.

ENDNOTES

1 Breakdown by cargo type and related growth rates (unless otherwise indicated) based on Clarksons Research, 2016a, 2016b and 2016c.

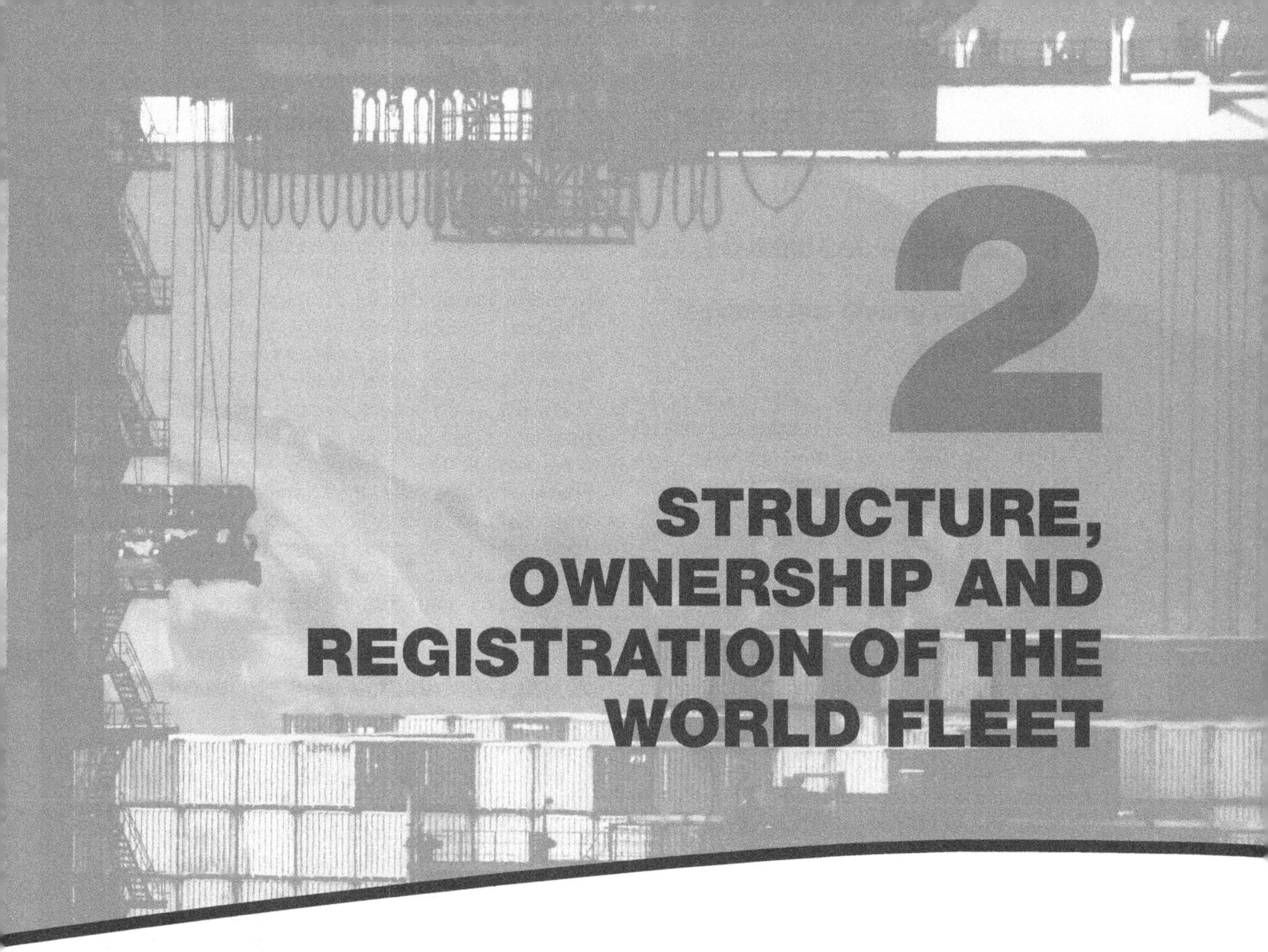

2

STRUCTURE, OWNERSHIP AND REGISTRATION OF THE WORLD FLEET

The world fleet in terms of dwt grew by 3.5 per cent in the 12 months to 1 January 2016. This is the lowest growth rate since 2003, yet still higher than the 2.1 per cent growth in demand, leading to a continued situation of global overcapacity.

The position of countries within global container shipping networks is reflected in the UNCTAD liner shipping connectivity index. In May 2016, the best-connected countries were Morocco, Egypt and South Africa in Africa; China and the Republic of Korea in Eastern Asia; Panama and Colombia in Latin America and the Caribbean; Sri Lanka and India in South Asia; and Singapore and Malaysia in South-East Asia.

Different countries participate in different sectors of the shipping business, seizing opportunities to generate income and employment. As at January 2016, the top five shipowning economies in terms of dwt were Greece, Japan, China, Germany and Singapore, while the top five economies by flag of registration were Panama, Liberia, the Marshall Islands, Hong Kong (China) and Singapore. The largest shipbuilding countries are China, Japan and the Republic of Korea, accounting for 91.4 per cent of gross tonnage constructed in 2015. Most demolitions take place in Asia; four countries – Bangladesh, India, Pakistan and China – accounted for 95 per cent of ship scrapping gross tonnage in 2015. The largest suppliers of seafarers are China, Indonesia and the Philippines. As countries specialize in different maritime subsectors, a process of concentration of the industry occurs. As each maritime business locates in a smaller number of countries, most countries host a decreasing number of maritime businesses, albeit with growing market shares in the subsectors.

Despite uncertainties, the long-term growth prospects for seaborne trade and maritime businesses are positive (see chapter 1). There are ample opportunities for developing countries to generate income and employment and help promote foreign trade. Policymakers are advised to identify and invest in maritime sectors in which their countries may have a comparative advantage. Supporting the maritime sector "as a whole" is no longer a policy choice. Rather, the challenge is to identify and support selected maritime businesses. Policymakers need to carefully assess the competitive environment for each maritime subsector they wish to develop, and to consider the value added of a sector for the State economy, including possible synergies and spillover effects to other sectors – maritime and beyond. Policymakers should also take into account the fact that the port and shipping business is a key enabler of a country's foreign trade. Apart from possibly generating income and employment in the maritime sector, it is generally even more important to ensure that a country's traders have access to fast, reliable and cost-effective port and shipping services, no matter who is the provider.

A. STRUCTURE OF THE WORLD FLEET[1]

1. World fleet growth and principal vessel types

The global commercial shipping fleet in terms of dwt grew by 3.48 per cent in the 12 months to 1 January 2016 (figure 2.1), the lowest growth rate since 2003. Yet the world's cargo-carrying shipping capacity still increased faster than demand (2.1 per cent; see chapter 1), leading to a continued situation of global overcapacity.

In total, as at 1 January 2016, the world commercial fleet consisted of 90,917 vessels, with a combined 1.8 billion dwt. The highest growth was recorded for gas carriers (+9.7 per cent), followed by container ships (+7.0 per cent) and ferries and passenger ships (+5.5 per cent), while general cargo ships continued their long-term decline, with the lowest growth rate of major vessel types (table 2.1). Their share of the world's tonnage is currently only 4.2 per cent, down from 17 per cent in 1980 (figure 2.2).

In 2015, there were 211 new container ships delivered, less than half the number (436 ships) delivered in the peak year of 2008. However, as vessel sizes in this market segment have increased significantly, in terms of container-carrying capacity, 2015 set a historical record in the building of container ships. Globally, shipyards produced 1.68 million TEUs in 2015, an increase of 12.7 per cent over 2014 and 12.4 per cent over the previous peak number of deliveries in 2008. The average size of container ship newbuildings has risen by 132 per cent over the last seven years. Only 5 per cent of TEUs built in 2015 were geared ships (that is, ships that carry their own container-handling equipment), compared with 12 per cent in 2008. Large container ships invariably depend on the availability of ship-to-shore container cranes in terminals, still a challenge for some smaller seaports in developing countries.

2. Age distribution of world merchant fleet

At the start of 2016, the average age of commercial ships had reached 20.3 years, a slight increase over the previous year (table 2.2). Following additions to the fleet over the last 10 years, the current average age remains low, compared with previous decades. There were slightly fewer newbuildings and somewhat reduced scrapping activity, as many ships are too new to be demolished. Among the main vessel types,

Figure 2.1 Annual growth of world fleet, 2000–2015 (Percentage of dead-weight tonnage)

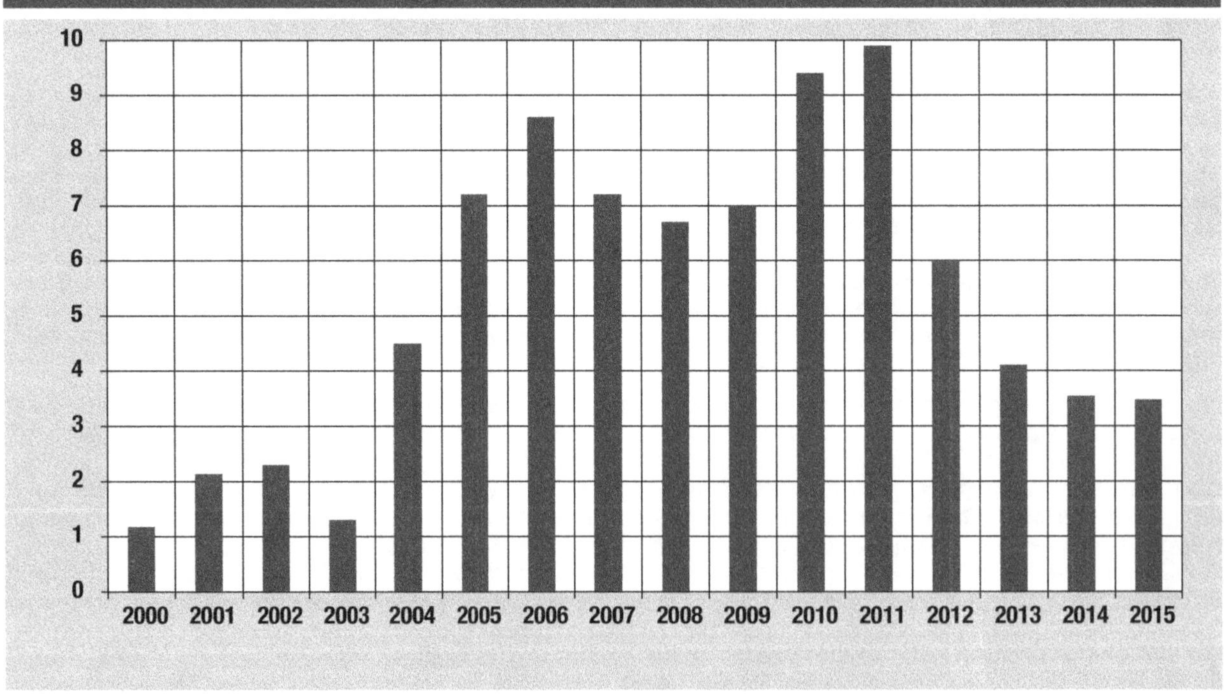

Source: UNCTAD, *Review of Maritime Transport*, various issues.

Table 2.1 World fleet by principal vessel type, 2015–2016 (Thousands of dead-weight tons and percentage share)

	2015	*2016*	*Percentage change, 2015–2016*
Oil tanker	488 308	503 343	
	28.0	27.9	3.08
Bulk carrier	761 776	778 890	
	43.6	43.1	2.25
General cargo ship	74 158	75 258	
	4.2	4.2	1.48
Container ship	228 224	244 274	
	13.1	13.5	7.03
Other:	193 457	204 886	
	11.1	11.3	5.91
Gas carrier	49 669	54 469	
	2.8	3.0	9.67
Chemical tanker	42 467	44 347	
	2.4	2.5	4.43
Offshore	72 606	75 836	
	4.2	4.2	4.45
Ferry and passenger ship	5 640	5 950	
	0.3	0.3	5.49
Other (not applicable)	23 075	24 284	
	1.3	1.3	5.24
World total	1 745 922	1 806 650	
	100	100	3.48

Source: UNCTAD secretariat calculations, based on data from Clarksons Research.

Note: Propelled seagoing merchant vessels of 100 gross tons and above, as at 1 January.

Figure 2.2 World fleet by principal vessel type, 1980–2016 (Percentage share of dead-weight tonnage)

	1980	1990	2000	2010	2016
Other	4.5	7.5	9.4	7.2	11.3
Container ship	1.6	3.9	8.0	13.3	13.5
General cargo ship	17.0	15.6	12.7	8.5	4.2
Dry bulk carrier	27.2	35.6	34.6	35.8	43.1
Oil tanker	49.7	37.4	35.4	35.3	27.9

Source: UNCTAD secretariat calculations, based on data from Clarksons Research and UNCTAD, Review of Maritime Transport, various issues.

Note: Propelled seagoing merchant vessels of 100 gross tons and above, as at 1 January.

Table 2.2. Age distribution of world merchant fleet by vessel type, 2016

		Years					Average age		Percentage change, 2015–2016
		0–4	5–9	10–14	15–19	20+	2015	2016	
World									
Bulk carriers	Percentage of total ships	42.83	25.46	11.97	9.86	9.89	9.04	8.83	-0.21
	Percentage of dead-weight tonnage	46.40	25.95	11.48	8.14	8.04	8.06	7.95	-0.11
	Average vessel size (dwt)	78 988	74 330	69 988	60 182	59 281			
Container ships	Percentage of total ships	19.47	33.45	19.36	17.15	10.57	10.86	11.21	0.35
	Percentage of dead-weight tonnage	33.42	33.94	17.94	10.51	4.19	8.23	8.41	0.18
	Average vessel size (dwt)	79 877	7 220	43 141	28 516	8 425			
General cargo ships	Percentage of total ships	9.67	15.93	8.66	8.41	57.33	23.99	24.72	0.73
	Percentage of dead-weight tonnage	18.97	22.10	10.09	10.72	38.12	17.46	17.97	0.52
	Average vessel size (dwt)	7 985	5 659	5 005	5 188	2 620			
Oil tankers	Percentage of total ships	17.12	22.41	14.09	8.26	38.12	18.02	18.49	0.47
	Percentage of dead-weight tonnage	24.93	33.65	23.92	12.57	4.92	8.95	9.54	0.59
	Average vessel size (dwt)	77 324	79 850	90 878	82 949	7 125			
Other	Percentage of total ships	15.02	18.22	9.72	8.80	48.23	22.12	22.52	0.41
	Percentage of dead-weight tonnage	19.06	27.43	12.55	10.47	30.49	15.47	15.60	0.13
	Average vessel size (dwt)	6 853	8 288	7 649	6 912	4 000			
All ships	Percentage of total ships	13.47	17.03	9.11	7.53	52.86	19.92	20.31	0.39
	Percentage of dead-weight tonnage	34.42	29.18	15.89	10.07	10.45	9.55	9.74	0.19
	Average vessel size (dwt)	42 284	32 314	33 772	24 657	5 963			
Developing economies – all ships	Percentage of total ships	18.59	19.54	9.91	8.63	43.33	19.34	19.74	0.40
	Percentage of dead-weight tonnage	37.56	24.68	11.80	10.51	15.44	10.29	10.42	0.13
	Average vessel size (dwt)	35 457	23 339	23 307	22 663	6 571			
Developed economies – all ships	Percentage of total ships	18.21	22.92	13.15	11.24	34.48	18.30	18.67	0.36
	Percentage of dead-weight tonnage	32.98	32.38	18.55	9.68	6.41	10.29	9.06	-1.23
	Average vessel size (dwt)	52 482	41 256	42 608	26 585	6 940			
Countries with economies in transition– all ships	Percentage of total ships	6.73	8.41	4.59	3.48	76.79	28.35	29.04	0.69
	Percentage of dead-weight tonnage	15.92	26.13	16.96	11.84	29.15	15.37	15.75	0.38
	Average vessel size (dwt)	15 029	21 080	24 561	21 427	2 389			

Source: UNCTAD secretariat calculations, based on data from Clarksons Research.
Note: Propelled seagoing merchant vessels of 100 gross tons and above, as at 1 January.

only dry bulk carriers were newer in early 2016 than in early 2015; 42.8 per cent of dry bulk ships are 0–4 years old. The oldest ships are general cargo carriers (24.7 years). The age distribution of the fleet also reflects the growth in vessel sizes over the last two decades. In particular, container ships have increased their average carrying capacity; those built 15–19 years previously have an average size of 28,516 dwt, while those built in the last four years are on average 2.8 times larger, with an average size of 79,877 dwt. In the early 2000s, a typical dry or liquid bulk ship was 2–3 times larger than a container ship newbuilding, while at present new container ships are the vessel type with the largest average tonnage.

B. DEVELOPING COUNTRY PARTICIPATION IN MARITIME BUSINESS

Throughout most of the twentieth century, the maritime business was concentrated in developed countries, with national fleets that were generally built, owned, operated and staffed by nationals of the same countries whose flag the ships flew. Today, few countries maintain their participation in all maritime businesses, but instead specialize in selected maritime subsectors. The process of specialization has provided opportunities for developing countries, which are increasing their participation in practically all maritime businesses. Policymakers have an interest in identifying those maritime sectors in which their countries currently participate or may in future participate.

To assist policymakers in depicting their country's market shares and trends in maritime sectors, UNCTAD, in March 2016, launched a set of maritime country profiles on a dedicated website (http://stats.unctad.org/maritime). A total of 230 maritime country profiles are available; each profile consists of six blocks, as follows:

- Basic data: Core data on the economy, trade and maritime sectors
- Market shares: Share in selected maritime sectors (ship registration, owning, building and demolition and container port traffic), population, GDP and coastline and merchandise trade
- Merchandise trade: Commodities traded (all transport modes), trade balance and main partners
- Trade in transport services: Basic trade in services data, including trade in transport services, and trade balance in such services
- Nationally flagged fleet: Trends, and composition with regard to types of ships
- Liner shipping connectivity: Position in global liner shipping network, including timeline of national liner shipping connectivity index, and list of States with greatest bilateral connectivity.

In interpreting the sample maritime country profile shown in figure 2.3, the following may be inferred about Chile: it has a GDP per capita above the world average, and its share of the world's GDP (0.33 per cent) is higher than its share of the world's population (0.24 per cent); it is an open economy, as it has a higher share in international trade than GDP; it has a merchandise trade surplus and its main export markets are China, the United States and Japan; it depends highly on containerized shipping, accounting for 0.55 per cent of the world's container port traffic; its nationally owned fleet is mostly foreign flagged, as its share in fleet ownership (0.14 per cent) is higher than its share in the nationally flagged fleet (0.05 per cent); and there is no significant shipbuilding or demolition taking place.

In comparing the maritime country profiles of different countries, specializations in different subsectors may be noted. It is usually not possible to remain in business in all port and shipping-related activities, and certain choices must be made. Three such choices and possible trade-offs are illustrated in the following paragraphs.

Do policymakers favour national shipowners or national seafarers? To remain competitive, a national shipowner may wish to employ foreign seafarers, due to the lower costs involved, to the detriment of national seafarers. To be allowed to do so, the owner may need to register ships under a foreign flag. Policymakers can make it more or less attractive to register under national flags, for example through the tax system, or through cargo reservation regimes.

Does national policy prioritize the facilitation of international trade or the provision of transport services? In some countries, liner shipping companies are still allowed to engage in conferences, which may include the joint setting of freight rates. Shippers (that is, users of transport services) consider such price fixing as detrimental to their interests, while shipping companies that enjoy such a conference regime state that this helps them

Figure 2.3 Sample UNCTAD maritime country profile: Chile

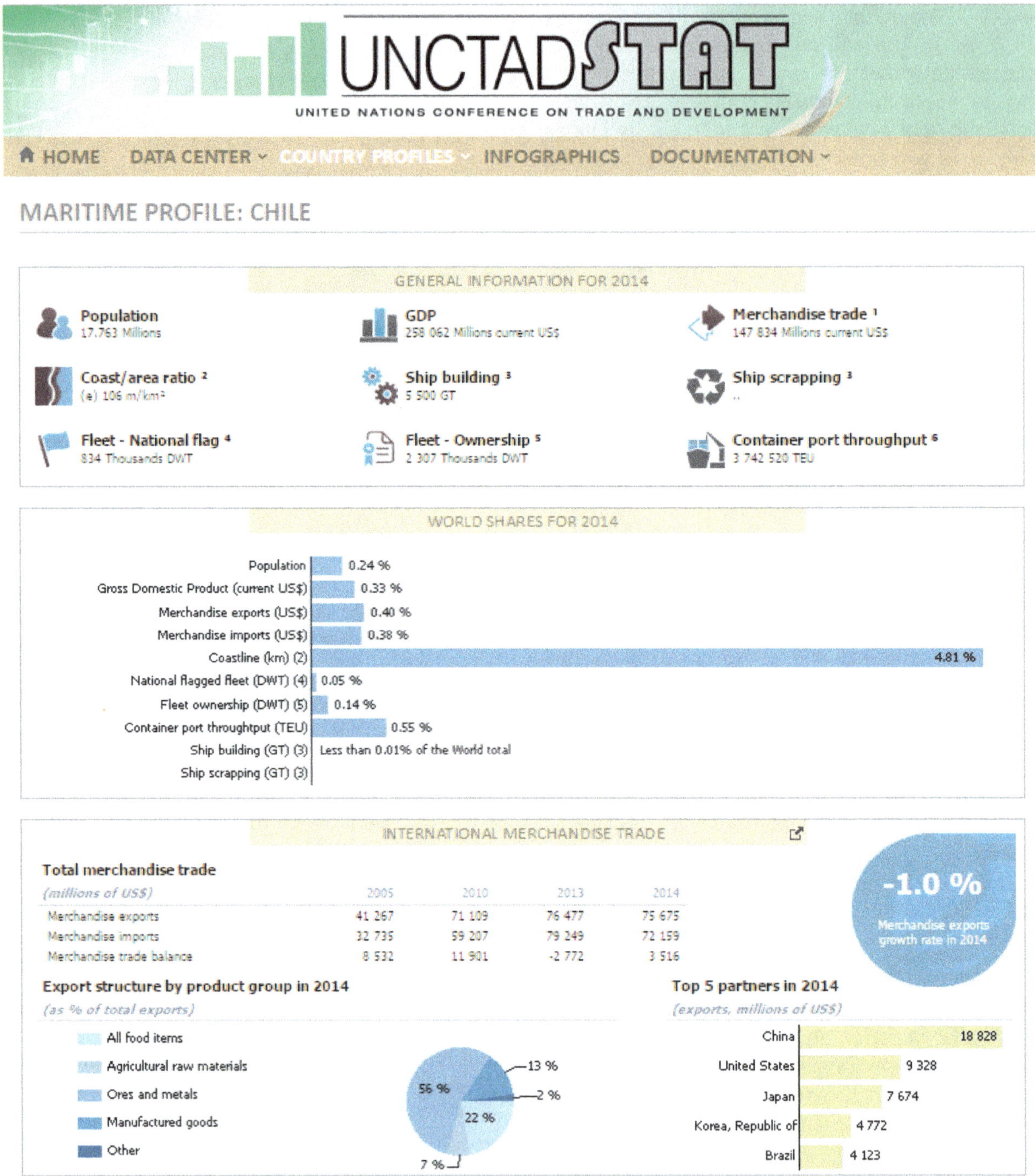

Figure 2.3 Sample UNCTAD maritime country profile: Chile *(continued)*

INTERNATIONAL TRADE IN TRANSPORT SERVICES

-19.5 %
Transport services exports growth rate in 2014

Services exports by main category [7]

(as % of total services)	2005	2010	2013	2014
Transport	60.0	57.4	48.7	43.9
Travel	15.5	14.8	17.6	20.5
Other services	24.5	27.9	33.7	35.6

Total trade in transport services [7]

(millions of US$)	2005	2010	2013	2014
Transport services exports	4 301	6 394	6 013	4 838
Transport services imports	4 135	6 571	7 090	6 110
Transport services trade balance	166	-177	-1 077	-1 272

NATIONAL FLEET

+5.0 %
Fleet growth rate in 2014

Carrying capacity by type of ship [4]

(Thousands DWT)	2005	2010	2013	2014
Total fleet	1 143.0	1 095.8	794.3	833.7
Oil tankers	493.0	395.6	404.3	336.1
Bulk carriers	318.0	381.4	236.6	346.4
General cargo	104.0	75.4	71.5	65.7
Container ships	21.0	21.2	38.4	38.4
Other types of ships	207.0	222.2	43.5	47.1

Fleet by type of ship [4]

(Number of ships)

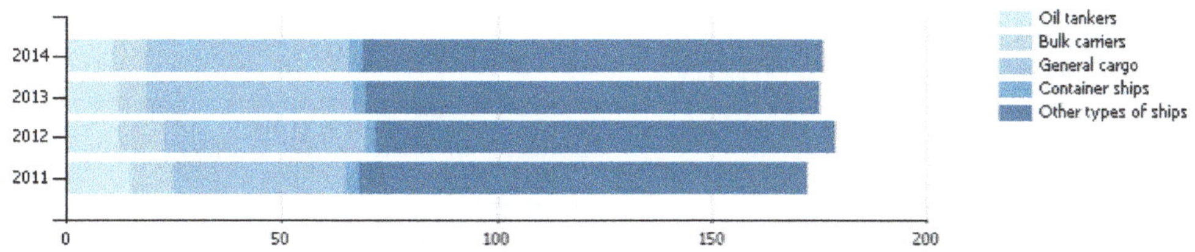

LINER SHIPPING CONNECTIVITY INDEX

Bilateral connectivity index - Top 10 partners in 2014 [8]

Can only take values between 0 (minimum) and 1 (maximum)

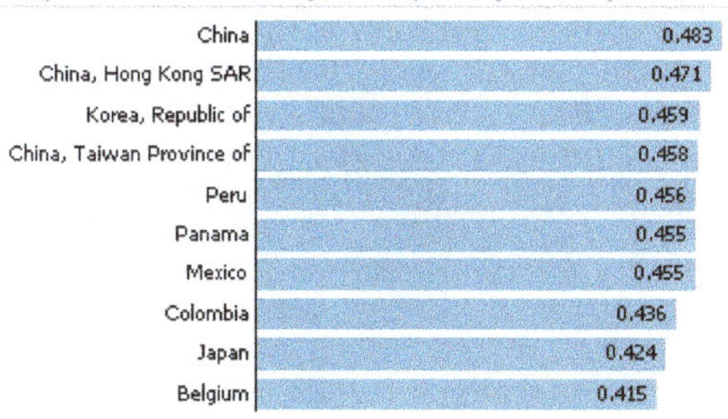

National connectivity index [8]

Maximum 2004=100 for China

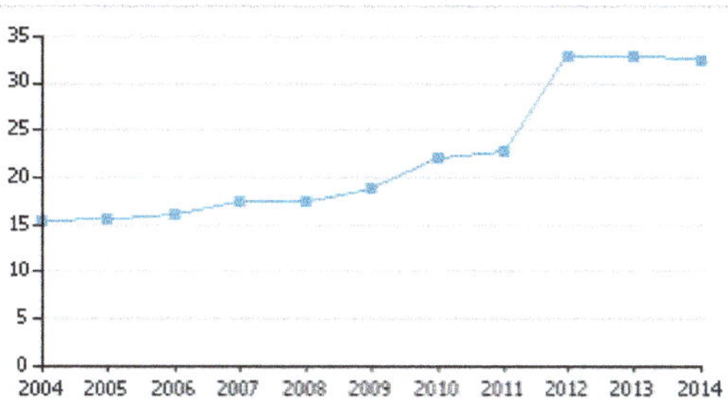

Source: UNCTADstat (http://unctadstat.unctad.org)

Notes:

1 Sum of exports and imports.
2 Coastline length based on data calculated in 2000 from the World Vector Shoreline database at 1:250,000 scale.
3 Propelled seagoing merchant vessels of 100 GT and above. Source: Clarksons Research.
4 Propelled seagoing merchant vessels of 100 GT and above, on 1 January. Source: Clarksons Research.
5 Propelled seagoing merchant vessels of 1000 GT and above, on 1 January. Source: Clarksons Research.
6 TEU: Twenty Foot Equivalent Unit. Source: UNCTAD Secretariat, derived from various sources including Dynamar B.V. Publications, terminal operators and port authorities.
7 Statistics presented correspond to the 6th edition of the IMF Balance of Payments and International Investment Position Manual, 2009 (BPM6, 2009).
8 Source: UNCTAD Secretariat, generated from data provided by Lloyds List Intelligence.
e Estimated.

Symbols for missing values:

0 Zero means that the amount is nil or negligible
.. Not available or not separately reported
_ Not applicable
... Not available, including no quotation
Non-relevant calculation
. Not publishable
Negative accumulation of flows; Value included in regional and global totals

Note: GT, gross tons.

provide better services at a more stable freight rate. In the European Union, for example, the anti-trust immunity of liner shipping conferences has been abolished, with a view to increasing competition and reducing freight rates, bearing in mind the interests of shippers.

Are policymakers more concerned about the nationally flagged fleet or the attractiveness of national seaports? In many countries, maritime cabotage (shipping between two national seaports) remains reserved for nationally flagged ships, at times for reasons of national security. Such a cargo reservation regime also protects national shipowners and seafarers employed on nationally flagged ships from foreign competition, and may help generate business for national shipyards, if legislation includes an obligation to deploy nationally built vessels on cabotage services. At the same time, such a limitation puts national ports at a disadvantage when competing for trans-shipment services. For example, cabotage restrictions in Argentina, India, Malaysia and the United States have effectively enhanced the competitiveness of trans-shipment services in, respectively, Uruguay, Sri Lanka, Singapore and the Bahamas.

In the following sections, the participation of developing countries in ship registration, owning, building, demolition and operation and in seafaring are addressed in greater detail.

C. OWNERSHIP AND OPERATION OF WORLD FLEET

1. Shipowning countries

The leading shipowners among developing countries are in Asia, led by China and Singapore (table 2.3). Developed countries still account for almost 60 per cent of global vessel ownership (figure 2.4), although the share of developing countries has been increasing. Among the top 35 shipowning economies, 18 are in Asia, 13 in Europe and 4 in the Americas. By subregion, the largest shipowning countries in Africa are Angola (5.4 million dwt), Nigeria and Egypt; in South America, Brazil (15.8 million dwt), the Bolivarian Republic of Venezuela and Chile; in South Asia, India (21.7 million dwt), Bangladesh and Pakistan; and in South-East Asia, Singapore (95.3 million dwt), Indonesia and Malaysia (for details of all shipowning countries and a complete listing of nationally owned fleets, see http://stats.unctad.org/fleetownership).

Different shipowning countries also specialize in different vessel types (figure 2.5). Countries with economies in transition have the highest share of oil tankers, many of which are owned by the Russian Federation. A high share of offshore supply vessels is owned by developing countries in Africa and the Americas, notably Angola, Brazil, Mexico and Nigeria.

2. Container ship operators

Among the different vessel types, container ships are the most frequently operated by companies that do not own the ships. Ship deployment and services are decided not by a shipowner but by a liner shipping company that may charter ships from owners and managers. Charter-owning companies, such as Anglo-Eastern, NSB and V.Ships, are often less well known by the public compared with liner operators, such as Maersk and Evergreen, whose names are visible on the ships they operate and who offer their services to traders. Liner companies decide on service patterns and vessel deployment, and an analysis of container shipping services thus needs to focus on operators rather than on owners.

As at end-July 2016, Maersk was the largest liner shipping company (table 2.4) in terms of operated container ship capacity by TEU, with a market share of 15.1 per cent, followed by Mediterranean Shipping Company (13.4 per cent), CMA CGM (9.2 per cent),[2] China Ocean Shipping (Group) Company (7.8 per cent) and Hapag-Lloyd (4.8 per cent). Four of the top five carriers are European, with the majority of the remaining top 20 based in Asia, and none in Africa or the Americas (as Compañía Sud Americana de Vapores, based in Chile, has merged with Hapag-Lloyd).

In 2016, the average size of ships in the order book is 8,508 TEUs, more than double the existing average vessel size. That is, ships entering the market in the coming months and years will be far larger than those currently in use. In total, the order book is at 18 per cent of existing capacity (as at July 2016).

Since 2015, there has been a further process of concentration among container ship operators. Recent and expected mergers include those between China Ocean Shipping Company and China Shipping Container Lines (both from China) and between Hapag-Lloyd (Germany) and United Arab Shipping Company (Kuwait), and the acquisition by CMA

Table 2.3 Ownership of world fleet, 2016

	Country or territory	Number of vessels			Dead-weight tonnage				
		National flag	Foreign flag	Total	National flag	Foreign flag	Total	Foreign flag as percentage of total	Total as percentage of world
1	Greece	728	3 408	4 136	64 704 141	228 383 091	293 087 231	77.92	16.36
2	Japan	835	3 134	3 969	28 774 119	200 206 090	228 980 209	87.43	12.78
3	China	3 045	1 915	4 960	74 106 227	84 778 140	158 884 367	53.36	8.87
4	Germany	240	3 121	3 361	11 315 790	107 865 615	119 181 405	90.51	6.65
5	Singapore	1 499	1 054	2 553	61 763 603	33 548 770	95 312 373	35.20	5.32
6	Hong Kong (China)	854	594	1 448	67 522 162	19 853 100	87 375 262	22.72	4.88
7	Republic of Korea	795	839	1 634	16 107 565	62 726 629	78 834 194	79.57	4.40
8	United States	782	1 213	1 995	8 155 717	52 123 421	60 279 138	86.47	3.36
9	United Kingdom	332	997	1 329	5 247 009	46 194 091	51 441 100	89.80	2.87
10	Bermuda	14	404	418	503 077	47 950 084	48 453 161	98.96	2.70
11	Norway	858	996	1 854	17 576 954	30 610 893	48 187 847	63.52	2.69
12	Taiwan Province of China	122	776	898	5 094 232	41 047 112	46 141 345	88.96	2.58
13	Denmark	398	562	960	16 079 319	22 235 206	38 314 525	58.03	2.14
14	Monaco	-	320	320	-	29 892 471	29 892 471	100.00	1.67
15	Turkey	562	978	1 540	8 311 987	19 639 445	27 951 433	70.26	1.56
16	Italy	575	227	802	15 427 422	7 311 946	22 739 369	32.16	1.27
17	Belgium	93	156	249	7 522 451	14 575 301	22 097 752	65.96	1.23
18	India	815	132	947	15 699 868	5 977 855	21 677 723	27.58	1.21
19	Switzerland	47	320	367	1 523 873	18 956 258	20 480 131	92.56	1.14
20	Russian Federation	1 325	355	1 680	6 727 958	11 415 747	18 143 705	62.92	1.01
21	Islamic Republic of Iran	168	65	233	4 051 601	13 786 700	17 838 301	77.29	1.00
22	Netherlands	771	458	1 229	6 682 312	10 758 780	17 441 092	61.69	0.97
23	Indonesia	1 607	105	1 712	15 141 943	2 145 145	17 287 088	12.41	0.96
24	Malaysia	466	155	621	8 450 122	8 341 174	16 791 296	49.68	0.94
25	Brazil	236	151	387	3 695 541	12 087 869	15 783 410	76.59	0.88
26	United Arab Emirates	103	712	815	483 733	15 006 924	15 490 657	96.88	0.86
27	Saudi Arabia	100	146	246	2 905 434	11 084 021	13 989 455	79.23	0.78
28	France	179	283	462	3 484 683	8 707 221	12 191 904	71.42	0.68
29	Canada	208	154	362	2 582 779	7 283 792	9 866 571	73.82	0.55
30	Kuwait	43	37	80	5 318 686	3 902 986	9 221 672	42.32	0.51
31	Cyprus	128	144	272	3 332 921	5 717 105	9 050 026	63.17	0.51
32	Viet Nam	797	99	896	6 791 347	1 507 502	8 298 849	18.17	0.46
33	Oman	6	33	39	5 850	7 104 727	7 110 577	99.92	0.40
34	Thailand	327	62	389	5 066 934	1 659 327	6 726 261	24.67	0.38
35	Qatar	53	77	130	768 614	5 829 361	6 597 975	88.35	0.37
Total of top 35 shipowning countries		19 111	24 182	43 293	500 925 974	1 200 213 898	1 701 139 872	70.55	94.95
All others		2 727	2 495	5 222	30 447 669	51 631 975	82 079 644	59.70	4.58
Total with known country of ownership		21 838	26 677	48 515	531 373 643	1 251 845 873	1 783 219 516	70.20	99.53
Others of unknown country of ownership		-	-	708	-	-	8 364 884	-	0.47
World total		-	-	49 223	-	-	1 791 584 400	-	100.00

Source: UNCTAD secretariat calculations, based on data from Clarksons Research.

Note: Propelled seagoing merchant vessels of 1,000 gross tons and above, as at 1 January, ranked by dwt.

Figure 2.4 Share of vessel ownership by country grouping, 2016 (Percentage)

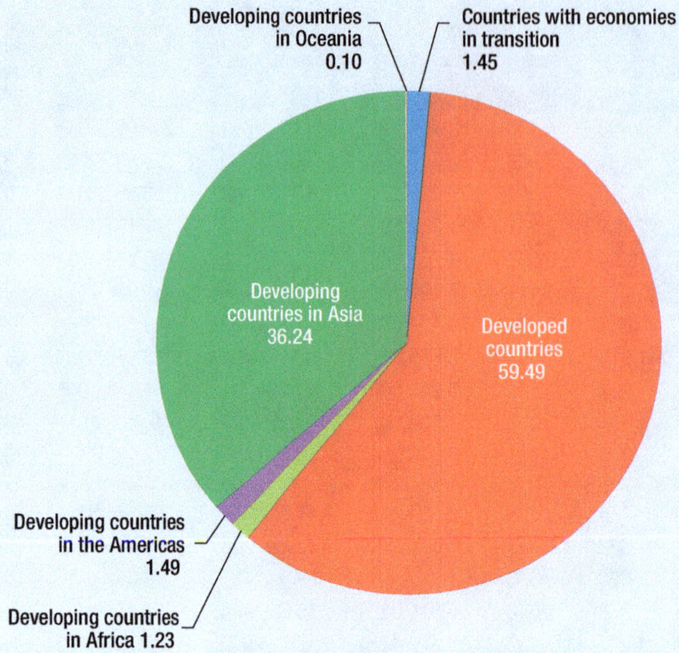

Source: UNCTAD secretariat calculations, based on data from Clarksons Research.
Note: Propelled seagoing merchant vessels of 1,000 gross tons and above, as at 1 January.

Figure 2.5 Nationally owned fleets by principal vessel type and country grouping, 2016 (Percentage share of dead-weight tonnage)

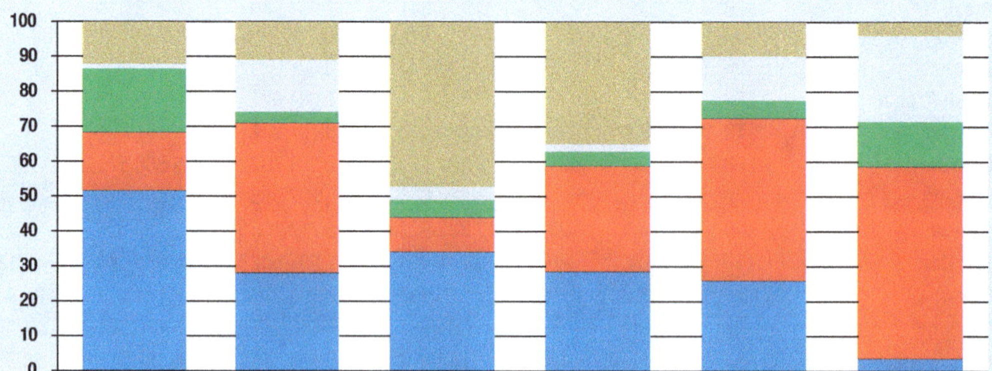

	Countries with economies in transition	Developed countries	Developing countries in Africa	Developing countries in the Americas	Developing countries in Asia	Developing countries in Oceania
Other	12.1	10.9	47.2	34.9	9.8	3.9
Container ship	1.4	14.9	3.8	2.2	12.6	24.7
General cargo ship	18.0	3.1	4.9	4.0	5.1	12.7
Bulk carrier	16.8	42.9	9.9	30.3	46.6	55.1
Oil tanker	51.6	28.2	34.2	28.5	26.0	3.7

Source: UNCTAD secretariat calculations, based on data from Clarksons Research.
Note: Propelled seagoing merchant vessels of 1,000 gross tons and above, as at 1 January.

CGM (France) of Neptune Orient Lines (Singapore). In addition, the main operators continue to extend their collaboration in the form of alliances. During the most recent adjustments, the top 16 carriers joined forces in three global alliances, down from four at the beginning of the year, and Hyundai Merchant Marine will reportedly join the alliance between Maersk and Mediterranean Shipping Company (Murphy, 2016). Sanchez and Mouftier (2016) estimate that the level of concentration, with the most recent mergers and alliance arrangements taken into account, as captured by the commonly used Herfindahl Hirschman index, increased by more than 70 per cent in 2014–2016. Despite this increase, the index level suggests a moderately concentrated market. An alternative way to consider the level of concentration is by market share in terms of actual container carryings rather than container ship capacity. DynaLiners (2016) reported the following figures for 2015: Maersk was the leading carrier, with 19,044,000 carryings, giving it a market share of 12.3 per cent; China Ocean Shipping Company and China Shipping Container Lines (separate companies in 2015) together ranked second, with 17,637,100 carryings (a market share of 11.4 per cent); Mediterranean Shipping Company ranked third, with 15,311,600 carryings. In 2015, the top 25 companies increased carryings by 4 per cent over 2014, while those of smaller companies declined by 27 per cent. This also reflects a global process of concentration.

3. How big is too big?

Container ships have never been bigger than at present, and container freight rates have rarely been lower (see chapter 3). In March 2016, the idle container ship fleet stood at 1.6 million TEUs (see http://www.alphaliner.com). In June 2016, for example, a shipper could pay less than $800 for a forty-foot container shipped from Shanghai to the west coast of North America (Clarksons Research, 2016). In addition, in 2016, the largest bankruptcy ever to take place in container shipping unfolded, after the board of Hanjin Shipping voted unanimously to file for court receivership (*The Load Star*, 2016).

The oversupply of tonnage is the result of past investment decisions and slower-than-expected demand growth. When the ships currently entering the market were ordered, the owners placing the orders had expected the economy in 2016 to be stronger. Individual carriers typically respond to such a situation by trying to reduce costs and raise market shares, often by investing in modern large container ships to save fuel costs and achieve economies of scale, and seeking mergers to better control the market, which is necessary to fill the new large ships. This makes sense from an individual company perspective, yet a bigger picture outlook also shows three further considerations, as addressed in the following paragraphs.

First, old ships may be replaced, but do not exit the market. Overcapacity usually remains, unless scrapped, and most of the container ship fleet is too new to be demolished. In the end, all carriers are confronted with historically low freight rates. Overinvestment is not in the interest of the liner business.

Second, larger ships may cut unit costs for carriers, but total system costs are not reduced and might actually rise. The costs of mega-ships to the logistics system may outweigh the benefits. The additional costs for ports, insurance companies, onward transport providers and the overall network structure (that is, with more transhipments but fewer direct services) lead to higher total system costs as vessel sizes grow. This applies not only to those ports and routes that have to accommodate the largest ships but, due to a cascading effect, is also relevant in many smaller and developing country markets. Overinvestment is not in the interest of carrier logistics partners.

Third, as ships get bigger they need be filled with cargo. As a result, there is space for fewer carriers in individual markets, leading to a continued process of concentration. While lower freight rates may be beneficial for shippers in the short term, in the long term there is a danger of more markets with oligopolistic market structures. Overinvestment is not in the long-term interest of shippers, at least in smaller markets.

These reasons for not investing in more and larger container ships are not relevant for individual carriers. As a commercial entity, such a carrier must consider its returns and will not accept staying behind competitors. Still, for some carriers, diseconomies of scale have certainly been reached, as they cannot cover their fixed costs if ships are not reasonably full.

In the long term, there is scope for further consolidation. Logistics partners (ports and rail and trucking service providers) will do their best to adapt to growing vessel sizes, and the optimal vessel size for the logistics system will become larger. In the meantime, the pressure on maritime freight rates will continue, and the resulting low trade costs may help the global economy recover.

Table 2.4 Leading 50 liner shipping companies by number of ships and total shipboard capacity deployed in twenty-foot equivalent units

	Ships	*End-2014*		*End-2015*		*End-July 2016*			
		Ships	*Capacity*	*Ships*	*Capacity*	*Ships*	*Capacity*	*Average vessel size*	*Market share (percentage)*
1	**Maersk**	592	2 792 124	619	3 059 984	616	3 007 392	4 882	15.1
2	**Mediterranean Shipping Company**	477	2 495 439	479	2 703 404	465	2 661 135	5 723	13.4
3	**CMA CGM**	454	1 691 290	459	1 873 439	435	1 829 951	4 207	9.2
4	**China Ocean Shipping (Group) Company**	272	1 524 588	283	1 608 456	268	1 554 434	5 800	7.8
5	**Hapag-Lloyd**	186	974 430	182	978 663	174	956 194	5 495	4.8
6	**Evergreen**	199	947 159	194	949 492	189	937 957	4 963	4.7
7	**Hamburg Süd**	126	584 944	138	670 029	132	651 549	4 936	3.3
8	**Hanjin Shipping**	98	595 056	110	648 043	101	617 665	6 115	3.1
9	**Orient Overseas Container Line**	103	527 827	109	571 429	111	589 476	5 311	3.0
10	**Neptune Orient Lines – American President Lines**	99	604 073	90	567 635	89	564 028	6 337	2.8
11	**Mitsui Osaka Shosen Kaisha Lines**	106	560 678	98	542 909	93	531 376	5 714	2.7
12	**Yang Ming Marine Transport**	85	389 614	100	542 127	97	520 580	5 367	2.6
13	**United Arab Shipping Company**	53	338 532	51	452 510	54	510 296	9 450	2.6
14	**Nippon Yusen Kaisha**	104	508 801	101	493 443	100	500 165	5 002	2.5
15	**Hyundai Merchant Marine**	63	385 753	56	381 728	57	401 152	7 038	2.0
16	**Kawasaki Kisen Kaisha Limited – K Line**	69	340 347	71	397 557	68	380 851	5 601	1.9
17	**Zim Integrated Shipping Services**	83	350 255	85	368 884	79	343 598	4 349	1.7
18	**Pacific International Lines**	171	410 512	135	336 699	129	332 403	2 577	1.7
19	**Wan Hai Lines**	85	195 481	92	217 847	98	255 124	2 603	1.3
20	**X-Press Feeders**	81	127 021	75	116 709	82	131 686	1 606	0.7
21	**Republic of Korea Marine Transport Company**	65	103 130	65	109 012	66	112 659	1 707	0.6
22	**Islamic Republic of Iran Shipping Lines**	28	93 372	27	92 674	27	92 674	3 432	0.5
23	**Shandong International Transportation Corporation**	65	76 254	76	98 573	73	90 909	1 245	0.5
24	**Arkas Container Transport**	40	58 498	45	67 237	45	68 388	1 520	0.3
25	**T S Lines**	38	70 245	44	91 308	33	61 512	1 864	0.3
26	**Simatech Shipping**	15	36 269	20	55 984	20	58 802	2 940	0.3
27	**Regional Container Lines**	30	52 096	30	54 771	30	56 790	1 893	0.3
28	**Sinokor Merchant Marine**	29	41 656	36	45 121	40	56 636	1 416	0.3
29	**Nile Dutch**	30	95 296	16	48 867	15	49 866	3 324	0.3
30	**Transworld Group of Companies**	23	34 730	24	40 256	28	46 379	1 656	0.2
31	**Heung-A Shipping**	33	41 263	35	49 199	34	39 777	1 170	0.2
32	**Matson**	24	52 223	20	40 952	19	39 484	2 078	0.2
33	**Unifeeder**	56	57 856	40	43 395	37	39 259	1 061	0.2
34	**China Merchants Group**	27	39 471	29	37 238	29	38 508	1 328	0.2

Table 2.4 Leading 50 liner shipping companies by number of ships and total shipboard capacity deployed in twenty-foot equivalent units *(continued)*

	Ships	*End-2014*		*End-2015*		*End-July 2016*			
		Ships	*Capacity*	*Ships*	*Capacity*	*Ships*	*Capacity*	*Average vessel size*	*Market share (percentage)*
35	**Emirates Shipping Line**	3	7 867	9	41 611	8	36 267	4 533	0.2
36	**Samudera**	23	22 116	26	31 480	28	33 280	1 189	0.2
37	**Seaboard Marine**	23	27 096	25	35 767	20	27 121	1 356	0.1
38	**Salam Pacific Indonesia Lines**	33	23 404	34	24 162	34	25 687	756	0.1
39	**Namsung Shipping Company**	32	28 275	29	26 437	28	24 857	888	0.1
40	**Meratus Line**	26	24 067	25	22 504	26	24 613	947	0.1
41	**Shipping Corporation of India**	8	25 574	7	23 252	6	22 517	3 753	0.1
42	**Quanzhou Ansheng Shipping Company**	8	22 307	8	21 721	8	21 721	2 715	0.1
43	**Tanto Intim Line**	31	20 329	31	20 485	31	20 485	661	0.1
44	**Zhonggu Shipping**	1	4 113	6	19 912	6	19 912	3 319	0.1
45	**Western European Container Lines**	17	15 782	17	16 018	21	19 693	938	0.1
46	**Log-in Logistica Intermodal**	8	19 399	8	19 005	8	19 005	2 376	0.1
47	**Turkon Line**	11	15 492	10	15 509	10	15 509	1 551	0.1
48	**Temas Line**	18	11 194	18	11 194	23	14 849	646	0.1
49	**Dole Fresh Fruit**	7	8 829	9	11 465	10	14 776	1 478	0.1
50	**Far Shipping**	15	19 783	13	19 085	10	14 499	1 450	0.1
	Top 50	4 273	17 491 910	4 309	18 715 181	4 210	18 483 446	4 390	93.1
	All others	838	761 375	921	1 020 292	1 014	1 371 289	1 352	6.9
	World total	5111	18 253 285	5 230	19 735 473	5 224	19 854 735	3 801	100.0

Source: UNCTAD secretariat calculations, based on data from Clarksons Research.

Note: Includes all container ships known to be operated by liner shipping companies ranked by total TEUs. Source: UNCTAD secretariat calculations, based on data from Clarksons Research.

Note: Includes all container ships known to be operated by liner shipping companies ranked by total TEUs.

D. CONTAINER SHIP DEPLOYMENT AND LINER SHIPPING CONNECTIVITY

1. Country-level connectivity

The trend towards consolidation in the industry is also reflected in the data on fleet deployment. Container ship sizes per country – both average and maximum – are rising, while the number of companies providing services to and from the average country's seaports is falling (figure 2.6).

The number of carriers competing for the average country's cargo has declined by 34 per cent in 12 years, from 21.1 carriers in 2004 to 14.6 carriers in 2016. While 14.6 companies per country would usually suffice to guarantee a competitive market, the average does not reveal the growing number of countries in which there are only a few providers offering container services, leading to potentially oligopolistic markets. In 2004, there were 44 countries with five or fewer providers, compared with 56 such countries in 2016; an increase of 27 per cent. In the same period, UNCTAD recorded a doubling in the number of countries with only one provider, from 5 countries in 2004 to 10 countries in 2016.

The overall position of a country in global container shipping networks is reflected in the liner shipping connectivity index. In May 2016, the best-connected countries, that is, those with the highest index LSCI, were Morocco, Egypt and South Africa in Africa; China and the Republic of Korea in Eastern Asia; Panama and Colombia in Latin America and the Caribbean; Sri Lanka and India in South Asia; and Singapore and Malaysia in South-East Asia (for the index for all coastal countries in 2004–2016, see http://stats.unctad.org/maritime). While the average index LSCI has increased continuously since first generated in 2004, several countries have not improved their connectivity over the last decade. Experience suggests that there are three main policy areas that, if focused on, can help to improve a country's index LSCI, as detailed in the following paragraphs.

Figure 2.6 Averages per country, 2004–2016: Number of liner shipping companies, container ship size and maximum ship size

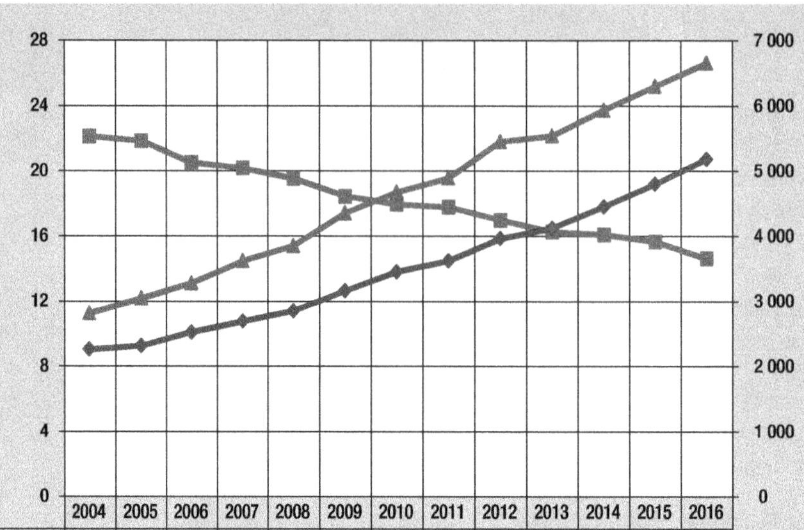

	2004	2005	2006	2007	2008	2009	2010	2011	2012	2013	2014	2015	2016
Number of liner shipping companies	22.1	21.8	20.5	20.2	19.5	18.4	17.9	17.8	17.0	16.3	16.1	15.7	14.6
Container ship size (twenty-foot equivalent units)	2 259	2 312	2 520	2 689	2 848	3 161	3 452	3 622	3 962	4 121	4 449	4 798	5 184
Maximum ship size (twenty-foot equivalent units)	2 812	3 045	3 279	3 620	3 847	4 353	4 673	4 889	5 452	5 540	5 937	6 298	6 656

Source: UNCTAD secretariat calculations, based on data from Lloyd's List Intelligence.
Note: Data represent averages per country based on vessel deployment in 160 countries.

The first policy area is increasing the volume of cargo in port hinterlands. To widen the hinterland (that is, expand the market for a port's services), it is important to facilitate international trade and transit, in order that cargo from clients from neighbouring countries may more easily reach the port. For example, in Western Africa, the ports of Benin, Côte d'Ivoire, Ghana, Nigeria and Togo compete for cargo from neighbouring landlocked countries. However, inland transport is expensive, and inefficient border-crossing procedures combined with roadblocks make it difficult to expand the hinterland. One way to improve shipping connectivity in countries in Western Africa would be by improving intermodal inland transport and trade connectivity.

The second policy area is ensuring that markets are competitive. Ideally, shippers should have a choice among different terminals and trucking and shipping companies. Any restriction on transport services, such as cargo reservation regimes in trucking or cabotage restrictions in shipping, leads to lower maritime connectivity.

The third policy area is fulfilling liner company demand for efficient and modern seaports. This includes physical infrastructure to accommodate ever-larger vessels, with the necessary water depth and ship-to-shore container handling cranes. Modern port operations and customs are also necessary to avoid delays and uncertainties, which in turn help to improve transport connectivity.

2. Bilateral connectivity

The highest bilateral connectivity is found in intraregional services, notably intra-Asian and intra-European. Among the top 10 routes in terms of TEU-carrying capacity, only one is intercontinental, namely, China–United States (table 2.5). The largest ships are deployed on Asia–Europe services, including the corresponding intraregional connections. North America is not yet served by the largest mega-vessels, either on the North Atlantic route or services from China. This is not likely to change in the foreseeable future as, even after the opening of the expanded Panama Canal, the new neo-Panamax ships carry only up to 13,000–14,000 TEUs, less than the 19,224 TEUs of the largest existing container ships.

Table 2.5 Container ship deployment on top 10 routes, 1 May 2016

Direct services	*Total twenty-foot equivalent units deployed*	*Number of companies (vessel operators)*	*Largest vessel (twenty-foot equivalent units)*
China–Republic of Korea	5 408 608	43	19 224
China–Singapore	5 277 023	34	19 224
China–Hong Kong (China)	4 289 451	43	16 652
China–Malaysia	4 270 653	29	19 224
Germany–Netherlands	3 645 488	35	19 224
Germany–United Kingdom	3 598 791	31	19 224
Netherlands–United Kingdom	3 311 277	40	19 224
China–United States	3 095 080	25	14 036
Malaysia–Singapore	2 787 121	47	19 224
Belgium–Germany	2 717 078	30	19 224
China–Taiwan Province of China	2 694 478	34	14 080

Source: UNCTAD secretariat calculations, based on data from Lloyd's List Intelligence.

3. Connecting through the Panama Canal

In June 2016, successfully concluding a nine-year project estimated to have cost $5.4 billion, the Panama Canal inaugurated an expanded set of longer and deeper locks. Before the expansion, vessels with a beam exceeding 32.3 m could not pass; the new locks allow the passage of ships with a beam of up to 49 m. Several services on the Asia–United States East Coast route via the Panama Canal have already been upsized to neo-Panamax vessels (Clarksons Research, 2016). As a result, as at June 2016, 85 per cent of the global fleet of container ships in terms of TEUs is neo-Panamax or smaller and can thus offer services through the Canal. This is a significant increase compared with the situation before the expansion, when only 37 per cent of the global container ship fleet was Panamax or smaller (Clarksons Research, 2016). The change in the order book is similar, that is, before the expansion, only 15 per cent of the ships in the order book were small enough to pass through the former Canal, and this share has now increased to more than 50 per cent. There are also plans for the conversion of existing ships. NSB (2016) has reported plans to widen container ships by enlarging ships of 4,880 TEUs to 6,330 TEUs, to match the dimensions of the new Panama Canal; cargo capacity may thereby be increased by 30 per cent, and fuel consumption per 14-ton average container load decreased by 50 per cent.

The expansion provides opportunities, both for Panama and for the countries whose international trade passes through the Canal. For Panama, there are three main benefits. First, the additional capacity will generate additional direct transit fees and open up additional markets, for example, by allowing for the passage of large gas carriers for the first time. Second, ports in Panama will generate additional trans-shipment business. Third, importers and exporters from Panama will benefit from additional connectivity and lower trade costs, as larger ships and more competition may help ensure that carrier savings due to economies of scale are passed on to clients in the form of lower freight rates. For clients of the Canal, in absolute terms, the largest impact will be the improved competitiveness of services between Asia and the east coast of North America. The all-water route through the Panama Canal gains in competitiveness against its main rivals, namely, the land bridge across North America and the Suez Canal. From a client perspective, importers and exporters on the west coast of South America may be among the major beneficiaries, as they will have more options to connect with Europe and North America through the Canal. Finally, further opportunities also arise for Caribbean and Latin American ports, which may expect to attract some of the trans-shipment business as far larger ships will be employed on routes passing near Colombia, Cuba, Jamaica and other countries. As the difference in size between the largest and smallest container ships widens, so does the economic incentive to trans-ship cargo, with a view to ensuring that the optimal size of vessel is used on each leg of a trade route.

E. REGISTRATION

The tonnage registered under a foreign flag (that is, where the nationality of an owner differs from the flag flown by a vessel) is 70.2 per cent of the world total (table 2.3). The system of open registries (that is, where the owner and flag are from different countries) has been an opportunity for many developing countries – including many small island developing States, such as the Marshall Islands, and least developed countries, such as Liberia – to provide the services of vessel registries. At the same time, the majority of shipowners remain in developed countries, and it is due to the system of open registries that they may remain competitive against fleets owned by companies based in developing countries. For example, under the flags of Liberia, the Marshall Islands or Panama, an owner from Germany or Japan can employ third-country seafarers, for example from Indonesia or the Philippines, who work for lower wages than their German or Japanese colleagues. As at 1 January 2016, Panama, Liberia and the Marshall Islands continued to be the largest vessel registries, together accounting for 41.0 per cent of world tonnage, with the Marshall Islands recording the highest growth among major registries, at 12 per cent over 2015 (table 2.6). The top 10 registries account for 76.8 per cent of the world fleet in terms of dwt.

More than 76 per cent of the world fleet is registered in developing countries (including many open registries), a further increase over 2015 (table 2.7). Some nationally flagged fleets are also nationally owned. Notably, in countries with long coasts and important cabotage and interisland traffic, national legislation often limits the options of shipowners to flag out. For example, many of the ships flying the flags of China, India, Indonesia and the United States are deployed on cabotage services (for a complete list see http://stats.unctad.org/fleet). With regard to the share of regional groups among the national flags of the world fleet, 11.42 per cent of the 12.97 per cent of tonnage registered in Africa flies the flag of Liberia and 11.07 per cent of the 11.49 per cent of tonnage registered in Oceania flies the flag of the Marshall Islands (table 2.7). Put differently, 88 per cent of the African-registered fleet flies the flag of Liberia and more than 96 per cent of the Oceania-registered fleet flies the flag of the Marshall Islands.

Different registries focus on different vessel types. Antigua and Barbuda has the largest market share of general cargo multipurpose vessels, while Liberia is the most important registry for container ships, the Marshall Islands for oil tankers and Panama for dry bulk carriers. One reason for such specialization is traditional linkages with shipowning countries. Japan – with a large share of dry bulk carriers – often registers its ships in Panama. Germany – specializing mostly in container ships – has a close relationship with Liberia; the two States have an income tax treaty or double taxation agreement, which is beneficial for German officers employed on ships flagged in Liberia (German Federal Ministry of Finance, 1975).

F. SEAFARERS

The world fleet provides approximately 1,545,000 jobs for seafarers in international shipping (Baltic and International Maritime Council and International Chamber of Shipping, 2016). Approximately 51 per cent of positions are for officers, compared with 49 per cent for ratings, that is, non-officer sailors such as able seafarer or ordinary seafarer (in 2005, the ratio was 45 per cent officers compared with 55 per cent ratings). For the first time in history, the proportion of officers is higher than that of ratings, reflecting technological advances and lower demand for manual on-board work. On-board employment provides an example of the importance of economies of scale in shipping. For example, a crew of 14 or 15 seafarers is required for a container ship or dry bulk carrier of 10,000 gross tons. A ship of 10 times the size (100,000 gross tons) does not require 10 times more seafarers, but can operate well with 19 or 20 seafarers.

In 2005–2015, global demand for seafarers increased by 45 per cent, roughly in line with the growth of the world fleet in the same period. The highest numbers of seafarers are provided by China (243,635), followed by the Philippines (215,500), Indonesia (143,702), the Russian Federation (87,061), India (86,084) and Ukraine (69,000) (Baltic and International Maritime Council and International Chamber of Shipping, 2016). Taking into account population sizes, remittances from seafarers working abroad are significantly more important for the Philippines than for the other major suppliers. For example, as a share of the population, almost 2 of every 1,000 nationals of the Philippines work on board a ship, compared with fewer than 1 of every 10,000 nationals of India. In the Philippines, seafarer remittances in 2015 reportedly amounted to $5.8 billion, an increase of 5.3 per cent over 2014 (*The Seafarer Times*, 2016). The Government pursues its overseas employment programme with the general objective of

Table 2.6 Flags of registration with largest registered fleets, 2016

	Number of vessels	Vessel share of world total (percentage)	Thousands of dead-weight tons	Share of world total dead-weight tonnage (percentage)	Cumulated share of dead-weight tonnage (percentage)	Average vessel size (dead-weight tons)	Dead-weight tonnage growth, 2015–2016 (percentage)
Panama	8 153	8.97	334 368	18.51	18.51	42 768.99	-0.53
Liberia	3 185	3.50	206 351	11.42	29.93	64 869.88	2.21
Marshall Islands	2 942	3.24	200 069	11.07	41.00	68 073.98	12.03
Hong Kong (China)	2 515	2.77	161 787	8.96	49.96	65 553.85	7.63
Singapore	3 605	3.97	127 193	7.04	57.00	37 028.53	7.50
Malta	2 101	2.31	94 992	5.26	62.26	45 867.66	8.90
Bahamas	1 450	1.59	79 541	4.40	66.66	55 545.18	7.61
China	4 052	4.46	75 850	4.20	70.86	19 845.66	-0.96
Greece	1 386	1.52	73 568	4.07	74.93	63 640.19	-2.49
Cyprus	1 053	1.16	33 313	1.84	76.77	32 405.97	0.46
Japan	5 320	5.85	31 869	1.76	78.54	7 435.49	3.55
Isle of Man	389	0.43	22 539	1.25	79.79	57 940.94	-8.36
Norway	1 561	1.72	20 697	1.15	80.93	15 308.45	3.00
Indonesia	7 843	8.63	18 117	1.00	81.93	3 858.78	3.41
Denmark	671	0.74	17 185	0.95	82.88	27 540.26	4.57
Republic of Korea	1 906	2.10	16 820	0.93	83.82	9 899.83	-5.42
Italy	1 376	1.51	16 470	0.91	84.73	14 296.63	-2.14
India	1 625	1.79	16 338	0.90	85.63	10 439.41	4.58
United Kingdom	1 167	1.28	15 192	0.84	86.47	15 360.50	7.59
United Republic of Tanzania	265	0.29	13 255	0.73	87.21	54 771.44	6.84
United States	3 570	3.93	11 841	0.66	87.86	5 773.27	4.16
Antigua and Barbuda	1 080	1.19	11 506	0.64	88.50	10 723.20	-7.38
Germany	618	0.68	11 402	0.63	89.13	21 675.88	-8.37
Bermuda	156	0.17	10 610	0.59	89.72	69 346.29	-3.17
Malaysia	1 662	1.83	9 612	0.53	90.25	6 787.80	2.19
Turkey	1 276	1.40	8 635	0.48	90.73	8 271.34	2.37
Belgium	200	0.22	8 479	0.47	91.20	45 103.65	-3.24
Portugal	373	0.41	8 398	0.46	91.66	25 295.14	65.12
Russian Federation	2 546	2.80	8 390	0.46	92.13	3 364.06	5.94
Netherlands	1 245	1.37	8 252	0.46	92.58	7 387.92	-2.80
Viet Nam	1 786	1.96	7 670	0.42	93.01	4 488.03	7.24
France	543	0.60	6 856	0.38	93.39	15 870.14	6.84
Philippines	1 462	1.61	6 390	0.35	93.74	5 263.61	4.82
Thailand	782	0.86	5 397	0.30	94.04	7 787.59	0.38
Kuwait	165	0.18	5 364	0.30	94.34	36 995.92	0.08
Top 35 total	70 029	77.03	1 704 316	94.34	94.34	27 697.39	3.70
Rest of world	20 888	22.97	102 334	5.66	5.66	4 899.19	-0.18
World total	90 917	100.00	1 806 650	100.00	100.00	22 757.36	3.48

Source: UNCTAD secretariat calculations, based on data from Clarksons Research.

Note: Propelled seagoing merchant vessels of 100 gross tons and above, as at 1 January, ranked by share of dwt.

Table 2.7 Vessel type capacity by registration country grouping, 2016 (Percentage)

		Total fleet	Oil tankers	Bulk carriers	General cargo	Container ships	Other
Developed countries	Share of dead-weight tonnage	22.75	18.70	27.05	28.20	25.09	25.25
	Annual growth	-0.30	-0.09	-0.14	0.11	-1.07	0.12
Countries with economies in transition	Share of dead-weight tonnage	0.69	0.18	0.04	5.34	0.89	1.24
	Annual growth	-0.02	-0.03	0.00	-0.08	0.03	-0.05
Developing countries	Share of dead-weight tonnage	76.30	81.08	72.87	65.44	73.93	72.00
	Annual growth	0.30	0.11	0.12	-0.08	1.02	-0.08
Of which:							
Africa	Share of dead-weight tonnage	12.97	9.91	19.47	5.87	17.03	9.52
	Annual growth	-0.45	-0.22	-1.37	-0.09	-0.52	-0.56
Americas	Share of dead-weight tonnage	25.01	29.74	18.95	21.38	19.01	30.35
	Annual growth	-0.71	-1.07	-0.52	-0.51	-0.24	-0.51
Asia	Share of dead-weight tonnage	26.82	29.80	28.78	35.00	22.79	20.05
	Annual growth	0.30	0.05	0.51	0.46	0.55	0.53
Oceania	Share of dead-weight tonnage	11.49	11.64	5.66	3.19	15.10	12.08
	Annual growth	0.83	1.09	0.53	0.08	0.88	0.47
Unknown and other	Share of dead-weight tonnage	0.26	0.04	0.05	1.02	0.08	1.51
	Annual growth	0.02	0.01	0.02	0.05	0.03	0.01

Source: UNCTAD secretariat calculations, based on data from Clarksons Research.
Note: Propelled seagoing merchant vessels of 100 gross tons and above, as at 1 January.

Table 2.8 Delivery of newbuildings by principle vessel type and country of build, 2015 (Thousands of gross tons)

	China	Japan	Republic of Korea	Philippines	Rest of world	World total
Oil tankers	2 872	892	4 781	—	425	8 970
Bulk carriers	13 310	10 767	1 588	869	226	26 760
General cargo ships	697	200	329	—	388	1 614
Container ships	4 982	188	9 331	995	639	16 135
Gas carriers	119	667	3 426	—	14	4 227
Chemical tankers	150	193	185	—	116	644
Offshore	860	48	1 488	—	996	3 391
Ferries and passenger ships	103	28	6	—	790	926
Other	47	392	838	—	193	1 470
Total	23 140	13 375	21 971	1 865	3 787	64 137

Source: UNCTAD secretariat calculations, based on data from Clarksons Research.
Note: Propelled seagoing merchant vessels of 100 gross tons and above.

achieving social and economic benefits for migrants from the Philippines, their families, communities and the country as a whole. Remittances have become a constant source of income, superseding even foreign direct investment and overseas development assistance funds received by the Philippines (De Vries, 2011). In some smaller countries, employment as seafarers is even more important. In Kiribati, for example, more than 1 of every 50 nationals works on board a ship.

Countries also differ with regard to the proportion of officers and ratings that work on board ships. Nationals from Greece and Japan that work as seafarers, for example, largely do so as officers, while seafarers from Indonesia, Pakistan and the Philippines are more likely to be employed as ratings (UNCTAD secretariat calculations, based on Baltic and International Maritime Council and International Chamber of Shipping, 2016).

Overall, the market for employment on board is increasingly separate from the country of vessel ownership. Once a ship is registered in one of the major open registries, such as Liberia, the Marshall Islands and Panama, the shipowner may employ foreign nationals at wage levels that depend more on seafarer nationality than on country of ownership or registration.

G. SHIPBUILDING, DEMOLITION AND NEW ORDERS

1. Deliveries of newbuildings

In 2015, 91.3 per cent of shipbuilding by gross tonnage took place in only three countries, namely, China (36.1 per cent), the Republic of Korea (34.3 per cent) and Japan (20.9 per cent) (table 2.8; for more detailed data on other countries see http://stats.unctad.org/shipbuilding). These shares are similar to those in 2014, with a slight increase in the share of China and a slight decline in the share of Japan. China had its largest shares in dry bulk carriers and general cargo ships, the Republic of Korea was strongest in container ships, gas carriers and oil tankers and Japan mostly built dry bulk carriers. The rest of the world – including shipbuilders in Europe – maintained a lead in the construction of ferries and passenger ships, including cruise ships. The Philippines further established its share in the market for container ships.

2. Demolitions

Most demolitions of old ships take place in Asia (table 2.9). Four countries - Bangladesh, China, India and Pakistan – accounted for approximately 95 per cent of known ship scrapping in 2015 (for more detailed data on other countries see http://stats.unctad.org/shipscrapping). In 2015, the most tonnage demolished was of dry bulk carriers (73 per cent of gross tonnage). Among the other vessel types, Pakistan had the highest share of oil tankers, India of container ships and Bangladesh of offshore.

Table 2.9 Tonnage reported sold for demolition by principle vessel type and country of demolition, 2015 (Thousands of gross tons)

	Bangladesh	*China*	*India*	*Pakistan*	*Unknown South Asia*	*Turkey*	*Other or unknown*	*World total*
Oil tankers	311	92	110	540	—	24	93	1 169
Bulk carriers	5 758	2 895	3 136	3 559	671	235	563	16 816
General cargo ships	202	134	259	5	—	138	80	818
Container ships	640	415	1 008	—	—	188	35	2 285
Gas carriers	10	203	61	—	—	7	8	289
Chemical tankers	26		98	15	—	23	4	166
Offshore	386	26	147	24	—	131	229	943
Ferries and passenger ships	19		86	—	—	91	15	212
Other	67	204	34	—	—	16	17	338
Total	7 419	3 970	4 940	4 143	671	852	1 044	23 037

Source: UNCTAD secretariat calculations, based on data from Clarksons Research.
Note: Propelled seagoing merchant vessels of 100 gross tons and above.

3. Tonnage on order

In line with falling shipyard capacity and the stretched finances of owners and banks, the world order book continued to decline for most vessel types in 2015–2016, with the exception of container ships (figure 2.7). Compared with their peak values in 2008 and 2009, the order book for container ships declined by 46 per cent, for oil tankers by 51 per cent, for dry bulk carriers by 61 per cent and for general cargo vessels by 82 per cent (the largest decline recorded). To date in 2016, demolitions have increased and there has been a slowdown in new orders. However, this has not sufficed to reduce existing overcapacity. With low oil prices, there is less pressure for operators to apply slow steaming to save fuel, and if ships are faster, additional vessels are potentially released from service, increasing overcapacity. Another effect of low oil prices is that there is less incentive to scrap old, inefficient capacity.

Figure 2.7 World tonnage on order, 2000–2016 (Thousands of dead-weight tons)

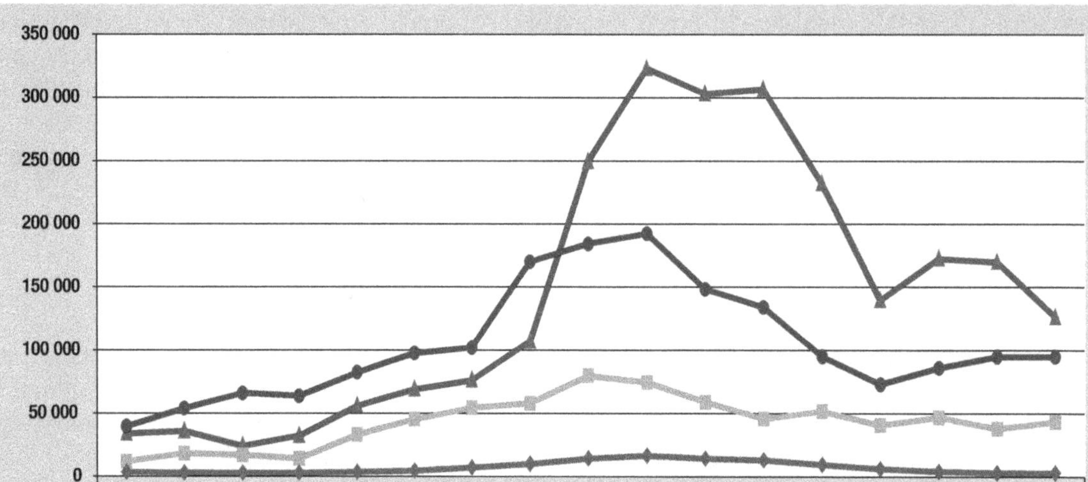

	2000	2001	2002	2003	2004	2005	2006	2007	2008	2009	2010	2011	2012	2013	2014	2015	2016
Dry bulk carriers	33 721	35 757	24 144	32 066	55 850	68 878	75 988	106 896	249 289	322 903	302 797	306 458	232 138	139 516	172 539	169 734	126 280
Oil tankers	39 546	53 919	65 896	63 678	82 258	97 474	102 010	169 883	184 196	192 252	148 307	134 044	94 936	72 843	85 844	94 851	94 716
Container ships	11 922	18 348	17 121	14 225	33 004	45 241	54 351	57 938	79 665	74 408	58 821	45 860	51 614	40 685	46 795	37 977	43 259
General cargo ships	3 325	3 053	2 984	2 881	3 587	4 638	7 139	10 070	14 389	16 657	14 315	13 051	9 526	6 172	4 226	3 058	2 979

Source: UNCTAD secretariat calculations, based on data from Clarksons Research.
Note: Propelled seagoing merchant vessels of 100 gross tons and above, as at 1 January.

H. OUTLOOK

Countries may specialize in different maritime subsectors, and this leads to a process of concentration of industries in a reduced number of countries. In other words, individual countries participate in different sectors of the shipping business, thereby seizing opportunities to generate income and employment in selected maritime subsectors. In shipbuilding, the top three countries together account for more than 90 per cent of global production, and in ship scrapping, the top four countries have a combined market share of 95 per cent. In shipowning, registration, port traffic and seafarer supply, about two fifths of world totals are provided by three countries in each area.

In past centuries, maritime nations benefited from synergies between different maritime businesses. Shipowners flew national flags and generally employed their compatriots; they called at home ports and had their ships built and repaired in national shipyards. An experienced captain could find land-based employment close to home, in maritime and port administrations or through a classification society that certified national shipbuilding. Later on, steel from recycled ships could be reused for new constructions.

In principle, such synergies remain valid. However, other aspects have gained in importance. There may be more synergies between shipbuilding and other industrial activities such as car manufacturing than between shipbuilding and shipowning. Labour costs and qualifications are of differing levels of importance in different sectors. Vessel registration is often provided by countries that may also be active in offshore financial and non-maritime services, while the clustering of insurance-related and legal services may be beneficial for trading and ship operations. Often, different types of clusters are not found in the same country.

Without the system of open registries, shipowners from, for example, Germany, Greece or Japan would be less competitive, as they would often have to pay higher taxes, and pay wages in line with national income levels. The system thus provides opportunities for newcomers – often developing countries – to enter maritime sectors such as shipbuilding, registration or staffing, while at the same time assisting traditional shipowners from developed countries remain competitive. Those who have lost market share are above all in labour-intensive sectors, such as shipbuilding and seafaring, in developed countries.

Shipping will continue to be the most important mode of transport for international trade, with the lowest environmental impact per ton–mile of transported cargo. The long-term perspectives for seaborne trade and maritime businesses are good. Policymakers are advised to identify and invest in maritime sectors in which their countries may have a comparative advantage.

In conclusion, it is no longer a policy choice to support the maritime sector "as a whole". The challenge is, instead, to identify and support selected maritime businesses. In order to identify opportunities for their countries in the port and shipping business, policymakers need to carefully assess the competitive environment for each of the maritime subsectors they wish to develop. New opportunities may arise in specific sectors, such as ship repair; as new mega-container ships have entered service, they will need to be dry-docked after 7.5 years. Policymakers need to consider the value added of a sector for a country's economy, including possible synergies and spillover effects to other sectors, whether maritime or not. Policymakers also need to consider that the port and shipping business is a key enabler of a country's foreign trade. Apart from opportunities to generate income and employment as a provider in the maritime sector, it is often even more important to ensure opportunities for a country's importers and exporters, as traders need access to fast, reliable and cost-effective port and shipping services, no matter who is the provider.

REFERENCES

Baltic and International Maritime Council and International Chamber of Shipping (2016). *Manpower Report*. London.

German Federal Ministry of Finance (1975). Agreement between the Federal Republic of Germany and the Republic of Liberia for the avoidance of double taxation with respect to taxes on income and on capital. Available at http://www.bundesfinanzministerium.de/Content/DE/Standardartikel/Themen/Steuern/Internationales_Steuerrecht/Staatenbezogene_Informationen/Laender_A_Z/Liberia/1973-09-06-Liberia-Abkommen-DBA.html (accessed 15 September 2016).

Clarksons Research (2016). *Container Intelligence Monthly*. 18(7).

De Vries S (2011). Mobilizing the use of remittances towards poverty reduction and economic and social development through government initiatives: The Philippine experience. Presented at the Expert Meeting on Maximizing the Development Impact of Remittances. Geneva. 14–15 February.

DynaLiners (2016). *The Millionaires*. July.

Murphy A (2016). 2M to become three. *Containerization International*. 49(6).

NSB (2016). Vessel efficiency. Presented at the European Marine Engineering Conference. Amsterdam. 13–14 April.

Sanchez R and Mouftier L (2016). The puzzle of shipping alliances in July 2016. PortEconomics. Available at http://www.porteconomics.eu/2016/07/29/the-puzzle-of-shipping-alliances-in-july-2016/ (accessed 15 September 2016).

The Load Star (2016). Alliance partners abandon ship as Hanjin applies for court receivership. 31 August.

The Seafarer Times (2016). Seafarers' 2015 remittances top $5.8 billion, up 5.3 per cent year on year. 21 February.

ENDNOTES

1 Underlying data on the world fleet based on Clarksons Research. The vessels covered in the UNCTAD analysis include all propelled seagoing merchant vessels of 100 gross tons and above, including offshore drillships, floating production, storage and offloading units and the Great Lakes fleets of Canada and the United States, which for historical reasons were excluded in earlier issues of the *Review of Maritime Transport*. Military vessels, yachts, inland waterway vessels, fishing vessels and offshore fixed and mobile platforms and barges are excluded. Data on fleet ownership cover only ships of 1,000 gross tons and above, as information on true ownership is often not available for smaller ships. For more detailed data on the world fleet (registration, ownership, building and demolition), as well as other maritime statistics, see http://stats.unctad.org/maritime.

2 Compagnie maritime d'affrètement–Compagnie générale maritime.

3

FREIGHT RATES AND MARITIME TRANSPORT COSTS

In 2015, most shipping segments, except for tankers, suffered historic low levels of freight rates and weak earnings, triggered by weak demand and oversupply of new tonnage. The tanker market remained strong, mainly because of the continuing and exceptional fall in oil prices.

In the container segment, freight rates declined steadily, reaching record low prices as the market continued to struggle with weakening demand and the presence of ever-larger container vessels that had entered the market throughout the year. In an effort to deal with low freight rate levels and reduce losses, carriers continued to consider measures to improve efficiency and optimize operations, as in previous years. Key measures included cascading, idling, slow steaming, and wider consolidation and integration, as well as the restructuring of new alliances.

The same was true of the dry bulk freight market, which was affected by the substantial slowdown in seaborne dry bulk trade and the influx of excess tonnage. Rates fluctuated around or below vessels' operating costs across all segments. As in container shipping, measures were taken to mitigate losses and alliances were reinforced, as illustrated by the formation in February 2015 of the largest alliance of dry bulk carriers, Capesize Chartering.

Market conditions in the tanker market, however, were favourable. The crude oil and product tanker markets enjoyed strong freight rates throughout 2015, mainly triggered by a surge in seaborne oil trade and supported by a low supply of crude tanker fleet capacity.

A. CONTAINER FREIGHT RATES

Container freight rates declined steadily, reaching record low prices as the market continued to struggle with weakening demand and the presence of ever-larger container vessels that had entered the market in 2015. As illustrated in figure 3.1, global container shipping demand slackened in 2015. The segment recorded its slowest growth rate since 2010 – 2 per cent, compared with 5 per cent in 2014. At the same time, sluggish demand was challenged by an accelerated massive global expansion in container supply capacity, estimated at 8 per cent in 2015 – its highest level since 2010. This represented a slight increase over 2014, when container supply capacity stood at 7 per cent.

The limited growth in container demand in 2015 can be attributed to several factors, including weak European demand, which had an impact on peak leg trade between Asia and Europe, and low commodity prices, in particular of iron ore and crude oil. This affected the economies, and in particular the imports, of commodity-dependent developing countries, mainly in Africa and Latin America. Another contributing factor was slower economic activity in China, which also had an impact on intra-Asian trade growth (Clarksons Research, 2016a) (see chapter 1).

Oversupply of fleet was mainly prompted by the use of larger vessels among major carriers striving for greater efficiency, economy of scale and market share, as well as by the new IMO Tier III requirements concerning sulphur oxides (SO_x) and nitrogen oxides (NO_x) that went into effect on 1 January 2016 in the North American and the United States Caribbean emission control areas (see chapter 5). As noted in chapter 2, 211 new container ship deliveries entered the market in 2015. These new ships added some 1.7 million TEUs to the global fleet (with 87 per cent of this volume increase in the 8,000+ TEUs sector) (Clarksons Research, 2016b). This put freight rates under massive pressure.

Both mainlane and non-mainlane freight rates struggled to cope with volatility and strong downward pressure, reaching a record low in 2015. Average spot freight rates on all trade lanes dropped significantly, some more than others, as shown in table 3.1. The Far East–Northern Europe trade route freight rates, for example, averaged as low as $629 per TEU in 2015, down by almost 46 per cent from the 2014 average and by 65 per cent, compared with rates in 2010. In contrast, Far East–Mediterranean spot rates fell by 41 per cent, reaching $739 per TEU, a decline of 41 per cent, compared with rates in 2014, and almost 58 per cent less than rates in 2010. Far East–South America

Figure 3.1 Growth of supply and demand in container shipping, 2001–2016 (Annual growth rates in percentage)

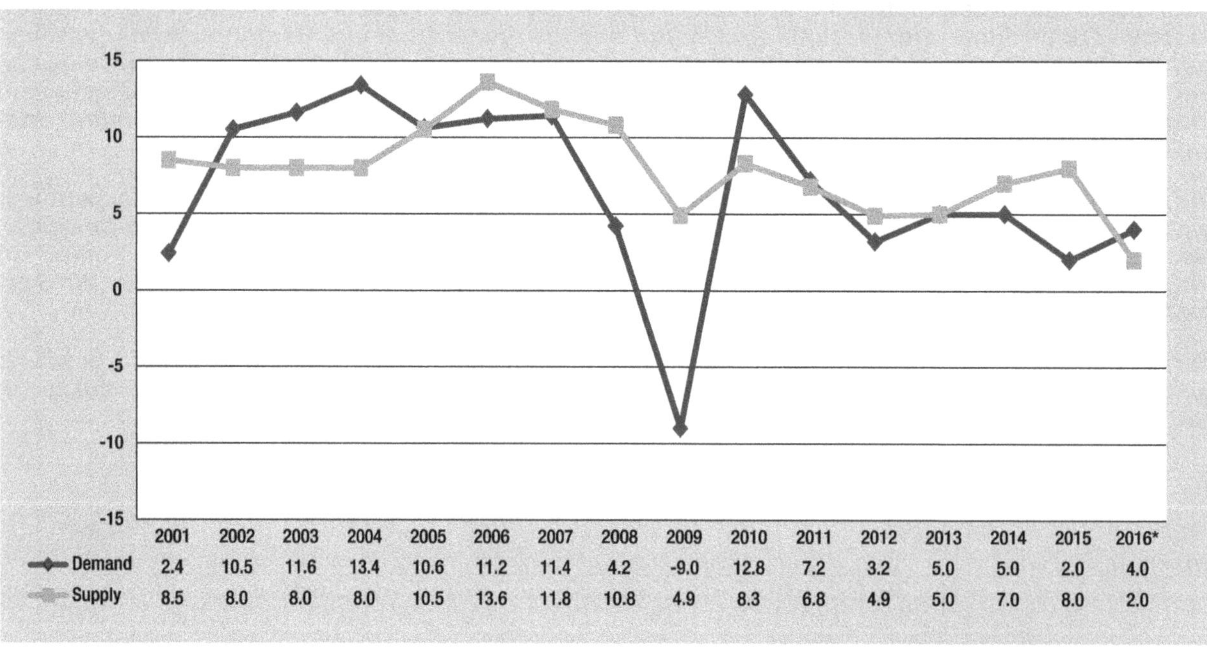

	2001	2002	2003	2004	2005	2006	2007	2008	2009	2010	2011	2012	2013	2014	2015	2016*
Demand	2.4	10.5	11.6	13.4	10.6	11.2	11.4	4.2	-9.0	12.8	7.2	3.2	5.0	5.0	2.0	4.0
Supply	8.5	8.0	8.0	8.0	10.5	13.6	11.8	10.8	4.9	8.3	6.8	4.9	5.0	7.0	8.0	2.0

Source: UNCTAD secretariat calculations, based on data from Clarksons Research Container Intelligence Monthly, various issues.

Notes: Supply data refer to total capacity of the container-carrying fleet, including multipurpose and other vessels with some container-carrying capacity. Demand growth is based on million TEU lifts. Data for 2016 are projected figures.

freight rates declined on average to $455 per TEU, a decrease of 59 per cent from 2014, less than 80 per cent, compared with prices in 2010. These low rates barely covered minimum operational costs.

Even those trade routes that had experienced stronger growth in demand were faced with low freight rates. For instance, the Transpacific Shanghai–United States West Coast annual rate averaged $1,506 per 40-foot equivalent unit, a drop of 23.55 per cent, compared with 2014, less than 35 per cent, compared with prices in 2010. Shanghai–United States East Coast spot rates fell by 14.45 per cent to reach an annual average of $3,182 per 40-foot equivalent unit in 2015, compared with $3,720 in 2014, 9 per cent less than in 2010. Given the challenging market conditions, the expected profits from the new large and more efficient ships that had entered the sector did not materialize and led to further financial distress for some major carriers. This resulted in a decline in revenues for the major shipping companies, from $204 billion in 2011 to $173 billion in 2015 (AlixPartners, 2016a).

Table 3.1 Container freight markets and rates, 2009–2015

Freight markets	*2009*	*2010*	*2011*	*2012*	*2013*	*2014*	*2015*
Trans-Pacific				**(Dollars per FEU)***			
Shanghai–United States West Coast	1 372	2 308	1 667	2 287	2 033	1 970	1 506
Percentage change		68.21	-27.77	37.19	-11.11	-3.10	-23.55
Shanghai– United States East Coast	2 367	3 499	3 008	3 416	3 290	3 720	3 182.41666666667
Percentage change		47.84	-14.03	13.56	-3.7	13.07	-14.45
Far East–Europe				**(Dollars per TEU)**			
Shanghai–Northern Europe	1 395	1 789	881	1 353	1 084	1 161	629
Percentage change		28.24	-50.75	53.58	-19.88	7.10	-45.82
Shanghai–Mediterranean	1 397	1 739	973	1 336	1 151	1 253	739
Percentage change		24.49	-44.05	37.31	-13.85	8.86	-41.02
North–South				**(Dollars per TEU)**			
Shanghai–South America (Santos)	2 429	2 236	1483	1 771	1 380	1 103	455
Percentage change		-7.95	-33.68	19.42	-22.08	-20.07	-58.75
Shanghai–Australia/New Zealand (Melbourne)	1 500	1 189	772	925	818	678	492
Percentage change		-20.73	-35.07	19.82	-11.57	-17.11	-27.43
Shanghai–West Africa (Lagos)	2 247	2 305	1 908	2 092	1 927	1 838	1 449
Percentage change		2.56	-17.22	9.64	-7.89	-4.62	-21.16
Shanghai–South Africa (Durban)	1 495	1 481	991	1 047	805	760	693
Percentage change		-0.96	-33.09	5.65	-23.11	-5.59	-8.82
Intra-Asian				**(Dollars per TEU)**			
Shanghai–South-East Asia (Singapore)	..	318	210	256	231	233	187
Percentage change			-33.96	21.84	-9.72	0.87	-19.74
Shanghai–East Japan	..	316	337	345	346	273	146
Percentage change			6.65	2.37	0.29	-21.10	-46.52
Shanghai–Republic of Korea	..	193	198	183	197	187	160
Percentage change			2.59	-7.58	7.65	-5.08	-14.44
Shanghai–Hong Kong (China)	..	116	155	131	85	65	56
Percentage change			33.62	-15.48	-35.11	-23.53	-13.85
Shanghai–Persian Gulf (Dubai)	639	922	838	981	771	820	525
Percentage change		44.33	-9.11	17.06	-21.41	6.36	-35.98

Source: Clarksons Research, Container Intelligence Monthly, various issues.
Note: Data based on yearly averages.
* Abbreviation: FEU, 40-foot equivalent unit.

Keys measures that shaped container shipping in 2015

High fleet growth proved to be difficult to manage because most trade lanes had been oversupplied with tonnage. The new megaships that entered service were deployed on the Far East–Northern Europe trade route at a time when trade was slowing down. In addition, their entry into service produced a cascading effect, with larger vessels replacing smaller ships on routes that were already struggling with oversupply. Large container ships that had formerly serviced the Far East–Northern Europe trade route were, for instance, deployed into the trans-Pacific trade route, and former trans-Pacific ships were reassigned to the transatlantic route. Despite efforts to increase the idling of container ship capacity, which soared to 1.36 million TEUs at the end of 2015, compared with 0.23 million TEUs at the beginning of 2016 (BRS Group, 2016), carriers were not able to absorb the new surplus capacity (see chapter 2). Global idle container ship capacity represented 6.8 per cent of existing fleet capacity in 2015, a record high, not seen since 2009, when idle fleets had reached 1.5 million TEUs, or11.6 per cent of fleet capacity) (BRS Group, 2016).

In an attempt to overcome supply and demand imbalance and low freight rate levels, carriers imposed several rounds of general rate increases in 2015, all of which were unsuccessful. Despite low fuel prices, slow steaming remained another key practice used by carriers to absorb excess tonnage – increasing voyage times, reducing ship call frequency at a given port and optimizing the operations of larger vessels by increasing their occupancy rate. Slow steaming is estimated to have absorbed some 2.5 million TEUs of nominal capacity since the end of 2008 (Clarksons Research, 2016c). Further, vessel scrapping helped somewhat to offset some of the influx of new tonnage by removing 201,000 TEUs of older ships from the global fleet. This figure accounted for only 11.7 per cent of the newbuilding deliveries (BRS Group, 2016).

On the other hand, low bunker prices allowed carriers to reduce operating costs and cover some of the losses incurred from falling freight rates in 2015. Bunker prices averaged $278 per ton, registering a 10-year low of $140 per ton in December 2015. This was a 49 per cent drop. compared with the average price of $547 per ton in 2014 (BRS Group, 2016). However, the benefits gained from low bunker prices, which allowed carriers to maintain unit costs below unit revenue, were not sustainable because of the persistent decline in freight rates throughout 2015. A case in point is Maersk, the world's largest container shipping company, which experienced a decline in net profit of 82 per cent. (JOC.com, 2016).

The severe market turmoil witnessed by the container shipping industry in 2015 led to wider consolidation as a means for shipping companies to effectively manage current and future tonnage capacity, increase scale and reduce costs and thus improve profitability in the face of low revenues. The beginning of 2015 was marked by the merger in December 2014 between Compañía Sud Americana de Vapores and Hapag-Lloyd, and the acquisition of Compañía Chilena de Navegación Interoceánica by Hamburg Süd in March 2015. This was followed by the merger of China Ocean Shipping Company and China Shipping Container Lines, as well as the announcement of the acquisition of Singapore-based Neptune Orient Lines and its American President Lines brand by the French line CMA CGM, in December 2015 (the transaction was concluded in June 2016). These two transactions paved the way for larger carriers to become even bigger. For instance, CMA CGM reinforced its position as a leader in the container shipping industry, reaching a capacity of approximately 2.35 million TEUs, with an estimated market share of 11.7 per cent and a fleet of some 540 vessels (American President Lines, 2016).

The reinforcement of alliances between carriers was a trend that continued throughout 2015. The top five carriers are expected to control more than 50 per cent of the market by the end of 2016, compared with only 23 per cent in 1996 (BRS Group, 2016). In this respect, the beginning of 2015 saw the consolidation of the five leading carriers into two new alliances (East–West): the 2M alliance (Maersk and the Mediterranean Shipping Company) and the Ocean Three alliance (CMA CGM, China Shipping Container Lines and the United Arab Shipping Company) (BRS Group, 2016). In early 2016, the Hyundai Merchant Marine, a major shipping line of the Republic of Korea, entered negotiations to join the 2M alliance (*The Wall Street Journal*, 2016).

Nevertheless, the rising level of industry concentration and consolidation failed to limit the severe market disarray and sharp drop in freight rates witnessed in 2015. The establishment of new alliances and rounds of restructuring may continue, as it is unlikely that the market will stabilize in the near future. Moreover, the global shipping infrastructure is facing deep challenges caused by the arrival of mega-container ships. Port infrastructure and hinterland connectivity need to expand and adapt to the new requirements of larger ships. This will entail investments in infrastructure – bridge height, river width/depth, quay walls, container yards – and port equipment, as well as the recruitment of more highly skilled staff to operate and handle increasing volumes efficiently and safely. It is estimated that transport costs related to mega-ships may increase by $0.4 billion per year (one third for extra equipment, one third for dredging and one third for port infrastructure and hinterland costs) (Organization for Economic Cooperation and Development and International Transport Forum, 2015). This may suggest that cooperation and consolidation between carriers could be further reinforced, taking various forms in the future, including through vertically integrated activities such as joint investments in land, port and hinterland transport operations to optimize their business and provide a comprehensive solution to remain competitive. However, growing concentration may squeeze out smaller carriers and result in an oligopolistic market structure.

Charter rates for container ships also followed the same patterns of fluctuation and downturn. Charter rates started 2015 on an upward trend until the charter market plunged again near the middle of the year, affected by weak trade growth, the availability of large quantities of chartered ships and increased container ship idling capacity. As illustrated by the Container Ship Time Charter Assessment Index (New ConTex) (figure 3.2), container ship time charter rates remained low in 2015, with an estimated average of 460 points, even when they appeared to have improved from the previous yearly average of 364 points. These rates continued to drop during the first half of 2016, reaching some of their lowest levels of the last five years and breaking below operating costs. The largest time charter segments, Panamax and Sub-Panamax, were especially affected, experiencing a decline of more than 50 per cent since May 2015. The one-year time charter for Panamax vessels was fixed at $6,000 per day at the end of 2015, compared with $10,150 per day at the end of 2014, and $15,000 per day in mid-2015. In contrast, the one-year time charter rate for a Sub-Panamax vessel dropped to $6,500 per day at the end of 2015, compared with $8,000 per day at the end of 2014, and $11,750 per day in mid-2015 (Clarksons Research, 2016c).

Conclusion

Problems affecting the container freight market in 2015 can be traced to diverging and persistent global supply-and-demand trends and growing imbalances. This situation is expected to continue throughout 2016 and 2017, when carriers with capacities of up to 21,100 TEUs will be in service. Despite weakening demand and low freight rates, carriers continued to invest in larger vessels in 2015. The global container

Figure 3.2 New ConTex, 2011–2016 (2007 =1,000 points)

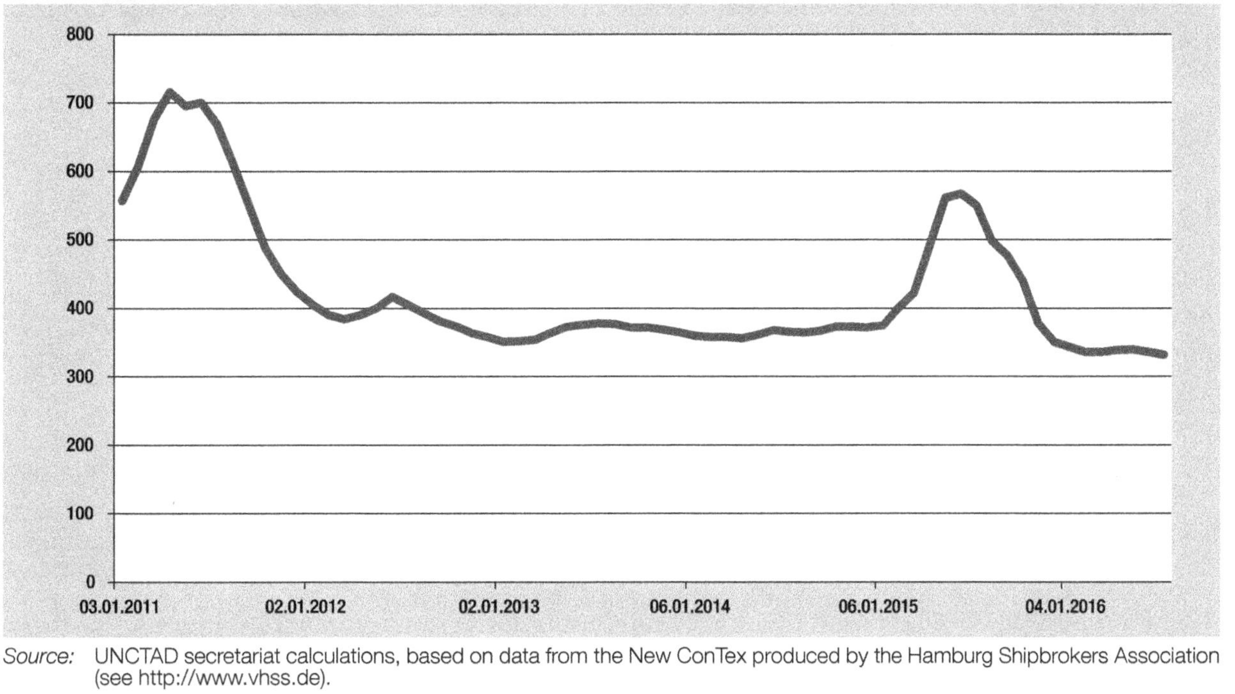

Source: UNCTAD secretariat calculations, based on data from the New ConTex produced by the Hamburg Shipbrokers Association (see http://www.vhss.de).

Note: The New ConTex is a time charter assessment index for container ships calculated as an equivalent weight of percentage change from six ConTex assessments, including the following ship sizes in TEUs: 1,100, 1,700, 2,500, 2,700, 3,500 and 4,250.

ship fleet is projected to grow by 4.6 per cent in 2016 and another 5.6 per cent in 2017 (AlixPartners, 2016a). Such a pace would continue to outstrip global container demand and exacerbate market fundamentals and in turn challenge container ship market conditions and freight rates in the short term, especially on the mainlanes (Clarksons Research, 2016c). Consequently, poor performance is also expected and may result in further consolidation and restructuring of the container shipping industry.

B. DRY BULK FREIGHT RATES

In 2015, the dry bulk market witnessed one of its worst years since 2008. Dry bulk freight rates plunged to a record low as weakening demand and strong supply created a high imbalance in market fundamentals. As noted in chapter 1, the dry cargo market was mainly affected by a substantial slowdown in seaborne dry bulk trade, with volumes contracting by 0.2 per cent as a result of limited growth in the iron ore trade and declining coal volumes. China, the largest player on the market, saw demand for dry bulk fall in 2015, the first time since the Great Recession.

On the other hand, excess supply-side tonnage remained high, although bulk carriers continued to cancel and push back newbuilding deliveries, while ship scrapping activity surged to high levels. As stated in chapter 2, dry bulk carriers accounted for 73 per cent of gross tonnage demolished in 2015. The increase in cancellation and scrapping activities helped to limit overall fleet growth to its slowest pace in 15 years (Clarksons Research, 2016b) but it was not enough to bridge the gap between supply and demand and bring the sector back into balance. Idling of vessels was another measure taken to limit supply but on a smaller scale (about 5 million dwt lay idle) (Danish Ship Finance, 2016).

Given these challenging market conditions, the Baltic Exchange Dry Index reached several low levels. As shown in figure 3.3, the Index dropped to 519 points in December 2015, its lowest average in the year, plunging by 43 per cent from its average in December 2014. The fall continued in early 2016, and the Index posted an average of 319 points in February.

Bulk carriers experienced weak earnings, marked by a decrease of 28 per cent. Earnings dropped to $7,123 per day in 2015, the lowest level since 1999 (Clarksons Research, 2016b). These carriers traded at rates fluctuating around or below vessels' operating costs across all segments. As illustrated in figure 3.4, the Capesize segment experienced the sharpest decline, with average time charter rates on four major routes falling by almost 50 per cent in 2015, greatly affected by the slowdown of the Chinese economy. The other segments

Figure 3.3 Baltic Exchange Dry Index, 2014–2016 (1985 = 1,000 points)

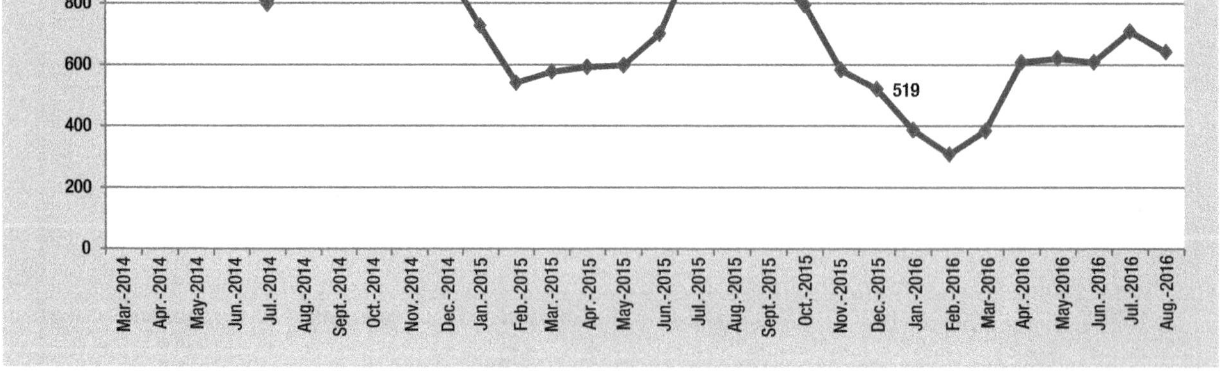

Source: *UNCTAD secretariat calculations, based on data from the Baltic Exchange.*

Note: *The Index is made up of 20 major dry bulk routes measured on a time charter basis and covers Capesize, Handysize, Panamax and Supramax dry bulk carriers, which carry commodities such as coal, iron ore and grain.*

Figure 3.4 Daily earnings of bulk carrier vessels, 2013–2016 (Dollars per day)

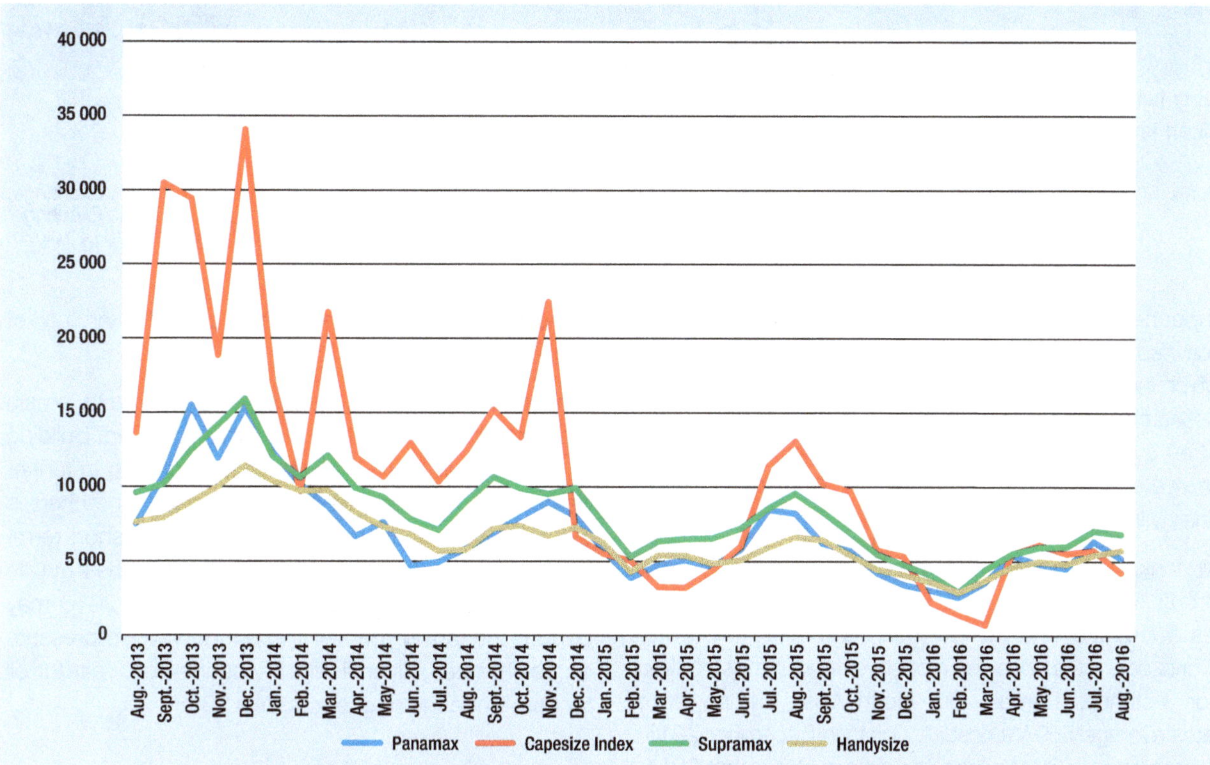

Source: *UNCTAD secretariat calculations, based on data from Clarksons Research and the Baltic Exchange.*
Note: *Capesize and Panamax, average of the four time charter routes; Handysize and Supramax, average of the six time charter routes.*

also declined by about 30 per cent each in 2015, with the time charter rates for Panamax-size vessels on four major routes reaching their lowest level, at an average of $3,450 per day in December 2015. As rates continued to undergo pressure with the cost of operations remaining high, many bulker carriers reported losses in 2015, four companies filed for protection and many others sought out-of-court restructurings (AlixPartners, 2016b).

As a reaction to depressed rates, dry bulk carriers followed an approach similar to that of the container shipping companies that had forged alliances to reinforce collaboration, coordinate chartering services and improve market conditions. In this respect, Capesize Chartering, the largest dry bulk alliance, was formed in February 2015 between Bocimar International, C transport maritime (commonly known by its acronym CTM), Golden Union Shipping, Golden Ocean Group and Star Bulk Carriers, as a means of sharing information and optimizing fleet deployment to reduce costs (AlixPartners, 2016b).

Weak demand for dry bulk, coupled with large vessel orders, could delay market recovery. Given the situation, it is expected that bulk carriers will take measures, such as further industry consolidation, vessel scrapping and cancellations of orders for vessels, to reduce imbalances and stabilize the market.

C. TANKER FREIGHT RATES

The tanker market, which encompasses the transportation of crude oil, refined petroleum products and chemicals, witnessed one of its best years since the market crisis in 2008. The crude oil tanker and oil product tanker markets enjoyed strong freight rates throughout 2015, prompted by the drop in oil prices that had begun in mid-2014 and had been sustained by relatively low supply-side growth in 2015.

As shown in table 3.2, the progression of the Baltic Exchange tanker indices was relatively moderate. The average Dirty Tanker Index increased by 5.6 per cent to 821 points in 2015, compared with 777 points in 2014. The average Clean Tanker Index reached 638 points in 2015, compared with 607 in 2014, a 5 per cent increase over the 2014 average.

Conditions in the crude oil market were favourable in 2015, enabled by a surge in seaborne crude oil trade, which grew by 3.8 per cent (see chapter 1). Such growth was

Table 3.2 Baltic Exchange tanker indices, 2008–2016

	2008	2009	2010	2011	2012	2013	2014	2015	Percentage change 2014–2015	2016 (first half)
Dirty Tanker Index	1 510	581	896	782	719	642	777	821	5.6	790
Clean Tanker Index	1 155	485	732	720	641	605	607	638	5	539

Source: Clarksons Research, 2016d.

Notes: The Dirty Tanker Index is an index of charter rates for crude oil tankers on selected routes published by the Baltic Exchange. The Clean Tanker Index is an index of charter rates for product tankers on selected routes published by the Baltic Exchange. Dirty tankers generally carry heavier oils, such as heavy fuel oils or crude oil. Clean tankers generally carry refined petroleum products such as gasoline, kerosene or jet fuels or chemicals.

supported by a sharp increase in floating and stocking activities, low oil prices and low crude tanker fleet capacity, which increased less than 1 per cent in 2015 (Clarksons Research, 2016b). For example, the price of Brent crude oil fell by 47 per cent from $98.89 per barrel in 2014, to an average of $52.32 per barrel in 2015 (United States Energy Information Administration, 2016).

All tanker segments performed well, benefiting from strong freight rates and low bunker prices, which resulted in strong tanker earnings. As shown in table 3.3, Worldscale rates observed a positive trend in most routes. For instance, Persian Gulf–North-West Europe spot rates averaged 59 Worldscale points in December 2015, compared with 32 Worldscale points in December 2014, an increase of 84 per cent. Persian Gulf–United States Gulf Coast rates were equally firm and stood at 49 Worldscale points in December 2015, compared with 34 Worldscale points in December 2014 (44 per cent), whereas Cross Mediterranean rates averaged 97 Worldscale points in December 2015, compared with 84 Worldscale points in December 2014. In contrast, clean tanker spot freight achieved mixed results. In an annual comparison, average clean tanker freight rates were significantly lower than in 2014, despite average monthly rate variations (table 3.3).

Overall, average tanker earnings per vessel rose to an average of $31,036 per day, an increase of 73 per cent over 2014, the highest level since 2008 (Clarksons Research, 2016b). The largest gains were observed in the very large crude carrier segment. Average earnings more than doubled to reach $64,846 per day in 2015 and exceeded $100,000 per day in December, for the first time since mid-2008. Suezmax average earnings rose by 68 per cent to $46,713 per day, while average Aframax earnings increased by 54 per cent to $37,954 per day. Dirty Panamax earnings also improved, reaching an average of $26,548 per day in 2015, the highest level since 2008 (Clarksons Research, 2016b).

Product tankers also recorded some progress. An expansion in refinery capacity and product exports from the Middle East, as well as firm naphtha import demand in Asia, triggered demand in the clean tanker market (Clarksons Research, 2016b).

Tanker markets and freight rates are expected to remain the same as in 2016. However, the significant building of oil stocks in 2015 may slow down growth in tanker demand. At the same time, while demand for tankers is expected to increase at a slow pace in the short term, the entry into market of new tanker deliveries (crude tankers and products) towards the end of 2016 may perturb the tanker market and put downward pressure on freight rates. Overall, 2015 was the best year for oil tankers since the market crash in 2008.

D. OUTLOOK

In 2015, maritime freight rates in most shipping segments endured volatility and downward movements that saw record low levels in container and dry bulk markets, breaking well below operating costs. Weak demand and high fleet growth pushed fleet utilization down further and intensified deflationary pressure on freight rates in most markets, except for tankers.

This pattern of low rates may have benefited shippers by translating into lower freight costs. The net impact of lower freight costs on trade, especially on developing countries with higher transport costs, could be positive to some extent.

Low freight rates have led to increases in insolvencies and liquidations among shipping companies, as well as to wider consolidation and integration in the shipping industry, namely in the container and dry bulk segments, which in turn may squeeze out smaller carriers and result in an oligopolistic market structure.

In 2016, the shipping industry is likely to face yet another challenging year in most segments because of the persistent mismatch between supply capacity and demand. With an uncertain global outlook for seaborne trade, freight rates will therefore continue to be determined by the way supply capacity management is handled.

Table 3.3 Tanker market summary: Clean and dirty spot rates, 2010–2015 (Worldscale 100)

Vessel type	Routes	2010 Dec.	2011 Dec.	2012 Dec.	2013 Dec.	2014 Dec.	2015 Jan.	Feb.	Mar.	Apr.	May	June	July	Aug.	Sept.	Oct.	Nov.	Dec.	Percentage change Dec. 2014–Dec. 2015
Very large crude carried/ultralarge crude carrier (200 000 dwt+)																			
	Persian Gulf–Japan	61	59	48	64	77	67	61	53	63	64	66	76	37	52	70	67	90	16.9%
	Persian Gulf–Singapore					71	69	68	54	61	66	66	59	36	56	71	66	83	16.9%
	Persian Gulf–United States Gulf Coast	36	37	28	37	34	39	31	27	61	38	35	35	22	30	37	42	49	44.1%
	Persian Gulf–North-West Europe	57	59	26	..	32	38	33	27	27	46	40	40	27	35	54	39	59	84.4%
	West Africa-United States Gulf Coast	..	..	..	..	68	73	70	61	69	73	80	74	52	70	82	80	90	32.4%
	West Africa–China	..	58	47	61	63	59	57	52	5	65	65	66	45	54	68	69	77	22.2%
Suezmax (120 000–200 000 dwt)																			
	West Africa–North-West Europe	118	86	70	102	76	86	86	91	73	90	91	83	69	63	81	89	80	5.3%
	West Africa–Caribbean/East Coast, North America	103	83	65	97	79	86	72	93	77	94	87	74	67	65	80	91	81	2.5%
	Mediterranean–Mediterranean	113	86	67	99	84	94	94	102	85	99	124	84	64	81	84	101	97	15.5%
Aframax (70 000–120 000 dwt)																			
	North-West Europe–North-West Europe	162	122	93	135	113	122	102	95	124	125	150	101	95	86	102	115	113	0.0%
	Caribbean–Caribbean/East Coast North America	146	112	91	155	108	135	159	168	126	111	155	111	115	103	115	175	130	20.4%
	Mediterranean–Mediterranean	138	130	85	100	106	113	137	116	106	118	134	97	101	74	91	112	97	-8.5%
	Mediterranean–North-West Europe	133	118	80	107	108	114	127	117	104	108	124	98	97	70	100	112	115	6.5%
	Indonesia–Far East	111	104	90	99	116	108	104	104	99	112	167	121	98	96	93	96	126	8.6%
Panamax (40 000–70 000 dwt)																			
	Mediterranean–Mediterranean	168	153	168	113	..	162	150	..	125	125	135	..	..	130	120	143	150	..
	Mediterranean–Caribbean/East Coast North America	146	121	160	105	130	..	153	125	115	120	135	158	..	87	90	150	..	..
	North-West Europe–Caribbean	..	..	..	..	118	146	148	120	118	123	135	141	101	88	88	133	129	9.3%
	Caribbean–East Coast, North America	..	..	..	..	113	..	159	148	126	111	149	151	109	94	115	163	160	41.6%
Clean tankers																			
70 000–80 000 dwt	**Persian Gulf–Japan**	..	..	..	81	102	90	100	103	95	104	125	148	166	84	78	72	90	-11.8%
50 000–60 000 dwt	**Persian Gulf–Japan**	..	..	..	93	110	118	106	117	107	119	140	162	148	108	79	83	94	-14.5%
35 000–50 000 dwt	**United States Gulf Coast–North-West Europe**	..	..	..	..	142	92	72	129	93	104	117	125	93	104	74	94	105	-26.1%
25 000–35 000 dwt	**Singapore–East Asia**	193	..	220	167	120	123	117	123	124	149	138	148	160	134	120	115	110	-8.3%

Source: UNCTAD secretariat calculations, based on data from Drewry Shipping Insight, various issues.

Note: The figures are indexed according to voyage charter rates per ton for a 75,000 dwt tanker.

REFERENCES

AlixPartners (2016a). *Container Shipping Outlook 2016: Overcapacity Catches Industry in Undertow. Outlook Transportation and Logistics*. Available at http://legacy.alixpartners.com/en/LinkClick.aspx?fileticket=F8t292 19hJg%3d&tabid=635 (accessed 20 September 2016).

AlixPartners (2016b). *Dry Bulk Shipping Outlook: Already-Troubled Waters Get Rougher*. Available at http://legacy.alixpartners.com/en/LinkClick.aspx?fileticket=CcmHGpd3EQc%3d&tabid=635 (accessed 20 September 2016).

American President Lines (2016). CMA CGM S.A. launches all-cash voluntary conditional general offer to acquire NOL. 6 June. Available at http://www.apl.com/wps/portal/apl/apl-home/news-media/press-releases/press-release/pressrelease-detailedpage-2016/cma+cgm+s.a.+launches+all-cash+voluntary+conditional+general +offer+to+acquire+nol (accessed 15 September 2016).

Baltic Exchange (2004–2016). Available at http://www.balticexchange.com/ (accessed 5 October 2016).

BRS Group (2016). 2016 *Annual Review: Shipping and Shipbuilding Markets*. Available at http://www.brsbrokers.com/flipbook_en2016/files/downloads/BRS-ANNUAL-REVIEW.pdf (accessed 15 September 2016).

Clarksons Research (2016a). *Container Intelligence Monthly*. 18(1).

Clarksons Research (2016b). *Shipping Review and Outlook*. Spring.

Clarksons Research (2016c). *Container Intelligence Quarterly*. First quarter.

Clarksons Research (2016d). Shipping Intelligence Network – Timeseries.

Danish Ship Finance (2016). Shipping market review. Available at http://www.shipfinance.dk/en/SHIPPING-RESEARCH/~/media/PUBLIKATIONER/Shipping-Market-Review/Shipping-Market-Review---May-2016.ashx (accessed 10 August 2016).

Drewry Maritime Research (2010–2015). *Shipping Insight*. Various issues.

Hamburg Shipbrokers Association (2016). Available at http://www.vhss.de (accessed 4 October 2016).

JOC.com (2016). Maersk profit plunges on freight rate, oil price collapse. 10 February. Available at http://www.joc.com/maritime-news/maersk-profits-plunge-82-per cent-freight-rate-oil-price-collapse_20160210.html (accessed 15 September 2016).

Organization for Economic Cooperation and Development and International Transport Forum (2015). *The Impact of Mega-Ships: Case-Specific Policy Analysis*. Available at http://www.itf-oecd.org/sites/default/files/docs/15cspa_mega-ships.pdf (accessed 15 September 2016).

The Wall Street Journal (2016). Hyundai Merchant Marine in talks to join 2M alliance. 23 June. Available at http://www.wsj.com/articles/hyundai-merchant-marine-in-talks-to-join-2m-alliance-1466657851 (accessed 15 September 2016).

United States Energy Information Administration (2016). Short-term energy outlook. 7 September. Available at https://www.eia.gov/forecasts/steo/report/prices.cfm (accessed 15 September 2016).

4 PORTS

This issue of the Review of Maritime Transport *sets out to describe the work of UNCTAD in helping developing countries improve port performance in order to lower transport costs and achieve better integration into global trade. The Review explores new datasets in port statistics and presents an overview of what these reveal about the port industry in 2015.*

The overall port industry, including the container sector, experienced significant declines in growth, with growth rates for the largest ports only just remaining positive. The 20 leading ports by volume experienced an 85 per cent decline in growth, from 6.3 per cent in 2014 to 0.9 per cent in 2015. Of the seven largest ports to have recorded declines in throughput, Singapore was the only one not located in China. Nonetheless, with 14 of the top 20 ports located in China, some ports posted impressive growth, and one (Suzhou) even grew by double digits. The top 20 container ports, which usually account for about half of the world's container port throughput and provide a straightforward overview of the industry in any year, showed a 95 per cent decline in growth, from 5.6 per cent in 2014 to 0.5 per cent in 2015.

A. OPPORTUNITIES FOR DEVELOPING COUNTRIES TO IMPROVE PORT PERFORMANCE

The organization of the maritime transport sector significantly affects trade volumes, transport costs and economic competitiveness, making it crucial for ports to adapt to the growing complexities of modern port management. In that context, the methodology developed by the TrainForTrade Port Management Programme,[1] which links performance indicators to strategic objectives, can be a valuable asset to port communities of developing countries.

Thirty-four countries currently participate in the Port Management Programme, nine of which are involved in the port performance initiative: Angola, Benin, the Dominican Republic, Ghana, Indonesia, Namibia, Peru, the Philippines and the United Republic of Tanzania. These represent 21 port entities, which are divided into four language networks: English, French, Portuguese and Spanish.

The indicators are included as part of a port performance scorecard containing 23 benchmarks. The participating ports are in charge of gathering these data, based on a set of recommendations generated from capacity-building workshops (Philippines, 2015; Indonesia, 2016) to maintain comparability across ports.

Port surveys provide valuable information about the type of ports in a network: historical context, legislative background, functional model and insights into port service management. The Port Performance Scorecard contains four strategic dimensions: finance, operations, human resources and market. Financial data are drawn from balance sheets, cash flow statements and profit-and-loss accounts, and are recorded by cargo mode, type of port dues and service charge category. Human resources data are based on labour-related financial measures and proxies for labour productivity. Other valuable indicators for port stakeholders include measures of vessel capacity, berth size, market share by cargo mode and dwell time.

The data suggest that ports belonging to the Programme share many characteristics and that they perform relatively well, according to their size and service profile. The Programme highlights the following key performance measures. The average container dwell time is seven days, the average operating margin is 38 per cent, the ratio of vessel dues to cargo dues is on average 1:2 and the average waiting time for a vessel to berth is 17 hours. In addition, port authority employees earn a yearly average of $23,863, and average training expenditure is less than 1 per cent of total payroll costs. No port authorities are privatized, and State contributions to long-term public interest assets, such as breakwaters, are common.

In addition to capacity-building, the UNCTAD port network provides a good opportunity to conduct research on port performance to identify best practices from which others may learn. UNCTAD research in port performance dates back to as early as the 1970s and is outlined in a number of publications (UNCTAD, 1976, 1979, 1983, 1987a and 1987b).

In 2012, UNCTAD held an expert meeting on assessing port performance that brought together leading scholars in the field (see http://unctad.org/en/pages/MeetingDetails.aspx?meetingid=175). In 2016, UNCTAD published a separate study detailing the ongoing global efforts in assessing port performance (UNCTAD, 2016). This chapter also highlights other types of work undertaken by UNCTAD on port statistics and shows how these complement each other in improving port efficiency and driving down the cost of international trade.

B. PORT STATISTICS

Scholars and bright minds have helped coin the adage, "if you can't measure it, you can't manage it"; therefore, you cannot improve it. Galileo (1564–1642) is attributed to saying, "Count what is countable: Measure what is measurable. What is not measurable, make measurable" (Kozak, 2004). Ports were often the sole gateway into and out of a country, which has made it easy for Governments to record trade data and levy taxes. Port statistics have traditionally been within the realm of terminal operators, local port authorities or national associations. To a large extent, these entities decided what data were collected and, more importantly, how and when the data were disseminated. In some cases, the figures would take months – even years – before they became widely available for scrutiny. Nowadays, the share of national income derived from the taxation of imports (tariffs) has dwindled in most countries, as it has become easier to raise taxes elsewhere. For instance, the share of import duties in tax revenue is estimated at 18 per cent (and in some cases more than 50 per cent) of the total revenue of many low-income countries (Kowalski,

2005). For example, in India, the average tariff rate was reduced from 55 per cent in the early 1990s to a little over 25 per cent by the end of the decade (United Nations Department of Economic and Social Affairs, 2002). While tariffs in the United States accounted for 30 per cent of government revenue in 1912, it now stands at 1 per cent (Progressive Economy, 2013) .

Today, most ports are characterized by a mixed ownership between private terminal operators and public port authorities. Ports are still prolific generators of statistics, providing details about labour employed, equipment usage, cargo throughput and vessel port calls. However, most of that data are for internal use and not for public scrutiny. Even data collected by public institutions are not always made publicly available. Further, available data for some ports are not always homogeneous or easily comparable with that of other ports.

Global or regional port statistics are difficult to ascertain because there is no global organization responsible for collecting these data; even the leading global terminal operators tend to operate in one market segment – container ports – and this industry is still relatively fragmented. The private sector also tends to publish terminal performance as marketing tools, not as a part of unbiased research. Thus data are selective, and their coverage is patchy. There is no global publication that is issued by a group of port authorities, and the International Association of Ports and Harbours, the only international group of port authorities, does not have either the necessary remit or the resources to conduct annual surveys on port statistics.

Further, it is not an advantage for ports to be compared globally, since competition for cargo is usually a regional issue. For years, port authorities have maintained that every port is different and therefore cannot and should not be compared. This is true to some extent, but academics have found ways to overcome limitations through various techniques. Data envelopment analysis, for example, takes into account the different inputs and outputs of ports, while cluster analysis combines similar items for comparison. The main advantage of a global comparison lies in identifying best practices for learning purposes. Port directors may ask themselves why their port should be compared with distant ports, with high volume throughput and greater economies of scale, when their main competitor is a familiar port in a neighbouring country.

While this may be true, this attitude will not drive ever-more needed innovation and change. On the one hand, having details on global ports could make it easier for ports to find suitable partner ports for a meaningful comparison. On the other hand, if a direct comparison between ports on different continents is not considered beneficial, there should be no fear of revealing data, since it would not result in the loss of business to a competitor. In reality, the main reason behind the reluctance of ports to be more transparent seems most likely the fear of being labelled "underperforming".

Researchers working in this area and wishing to compare global port performance have a difficult task in obtaining the inputs and outputs to be computed. Essentially, ports have to agree to be studied for the data to be collected and analysed, and whether to publish the findings. Even when there is an agreement to be studied, the relevant report is not always available to the public. Studies by regional associations, for example, the 2015 study of the Standing Committee for Economic and Commercial Cooperation of the Organization of Islamic Cooperation titled *Evaluating the Ownership, Governance Structures and Performances of Ports in the OIC Member Countries*, are not always widely publicized.

In 2015, UNCTAD, in association with the Port Management Association for West and Central Africa, organized a regional workshop in Ghana on identifying key performance indicators for ports from 11 countries. Port representatives expressed a desire to be transparent yet were concerned about being compared unfairly. For instance, any partial metric – that is, one that is not complete, such as a time element within a larger operation – that includes travel times from the point of waiting for a berth to completion of operations would give vastly different efficiency ratings for sea ports and fluvial ports, the latter having farther to travel to reach a berth. In addition, loading bulk cargo tends to be quicker than discharging, and differs by product type; therefore, care should be taken in assessing port performance. Also, not all indicators fit all ports, and a matrix of measurements is needed to reflect ports with different characteristics engaged in different market segments. This need led to the development of the aforementioned UNCTAD balance scorecard methodology.

One of the main reasons businesses tend to congregate around ports is to reduce their exposure to losses in the labour force, component suppliers or service providers. Being close to labour and other business suppliers often outweighs the cheaper costs of land and labour at inland locations. Poor transport links impede reliability, predictability and certainty. On a national scale, other factors such as the rule of law separate from government, secure property rights and the ability to repatriate capital, are also important for businesses wishing to establish a long-term view. However, transparent and readily available trade and transport data could help alleviate investors' concerns. Initially the publication of data helps to quantify risk, then manage it and later reduce it to provide certainty and build business confidence. Without data, businesses could underestimate the risks involved and thereby increase their chance of failure; alternatively, financial backers could significantly exaggerate their potential exposure and overcharge, thus making a business unprofitable. Either choice could lead to business failure, and while data are not a panacea, they can help avoid these pitfalls if used properly. A clear indication that a Government intends to create transparency in one area could spread to other aspects of government. The publication of trade and transport data should be a priority for policymakers wishing to promote international trade. The data should be publicly available and free to access. For this to be effective on a global scale, the data should emanate from a partnership involving a data provider, a host organization that collates and publishes the data – UNCTAD for example – and an academic institution responsible for providing one interpretation (or the first interpretation). As the data would be freely available, analysis by other interested parties would also be possible.

Observational data, the recording of specific actions that have been observed as having occurred, are the result of counting specific occurrences of individual actions without any analysis, for example, the number and type of vehicles, trains or vessels arriving and departing from a particular point. Individually, these data indicate very little, but when aggregated and analysed, may reveal patterns not previously visible. This chapter presents some observational data from two different sources to show what they reveal about the port sector. As with any data analysis, there are caveats. Owing to the large quantity of data required, the analysis must be automated in order to reduce analysts' labour time and costs, and automation may lead to errors. This research focuses on the descriptive data, rather than the analytics of that data, in an attempt to understand the dataset and establish proof of concept or possible limitations.

Information on ship arrivals and departures from ports may not reveal much in itself, but when analysed along with weather data or the number of patients treated for severe asthma in local hospitals, may indicate a pattern through which minor readjustments in operational matters could achieve major benefits for society. Governments and local authorities should not be dissuaded from providing data on the assumption that such data may bring about litigation, as the benefits in the long term will lead to a better life for as many people as possible. Exactly what big data on international trade will reveal is not yet known. Perhaps this will lead to cargo and vessels being matched more easily, thus leading to high fleet utilization rates and lower transport costs. Perhaps ports will be able to plan better for a ship's arrival, avoiding the need to buy expensive and underutilized equipment. Perhaps environmentalists will be able to anticipate periods of increased animal migration with peaks in vessel arrivals to lessen any negative factors. In reality, the opening of big data is likely to create new jobs and opportunities not previously imagined.

UNCTAD receives automatic identification system (AIS) observational data from MarineTraffic, a London-based private-sector maritime data provider (see http://www.marinetraffic.com, 2007–2016). AIS data are explained in box 4.1 and how the data work, in box 4.2. Box 4.3 looks at the validity of the data. MarineTraffic supplied UNCTAD with details on AIS data for 2.8 million vessel calls made at 661 ports in 151 countries in 2015 (figure 4.1). The dataset of 2.8 million vessels calls is not a complete picture of all vessel movements. As reported in chapter 2, the world merchant fleet consists of 90,917 vessels, but the AIS data in this sample pertain to 36,665 vessels (40 per cent). There are thousands of ports worldwide; some estimates put the figure at over 10,000, but monitoring all would be burdensome. UNCTAD experts have narrowed down the number of observations to 1.66 million signals, which they believe represents much of the estimated 80 per cent of the world's merchandisable trade carried by seagoing vessels. The four types of cargo-carrying vessels are dry cargo or passenger ships, container ships, tankers and bulk carriers. Their definitions should be interpreted with care, as a dry cargo ship or passenger ship may be either a passenger ferry that services commuters across a narrow strait or a large ocean-going vessel that carries merchant trade.

Figure 4.1 Sample of automatic identification system data signals by type of vessel, 2015

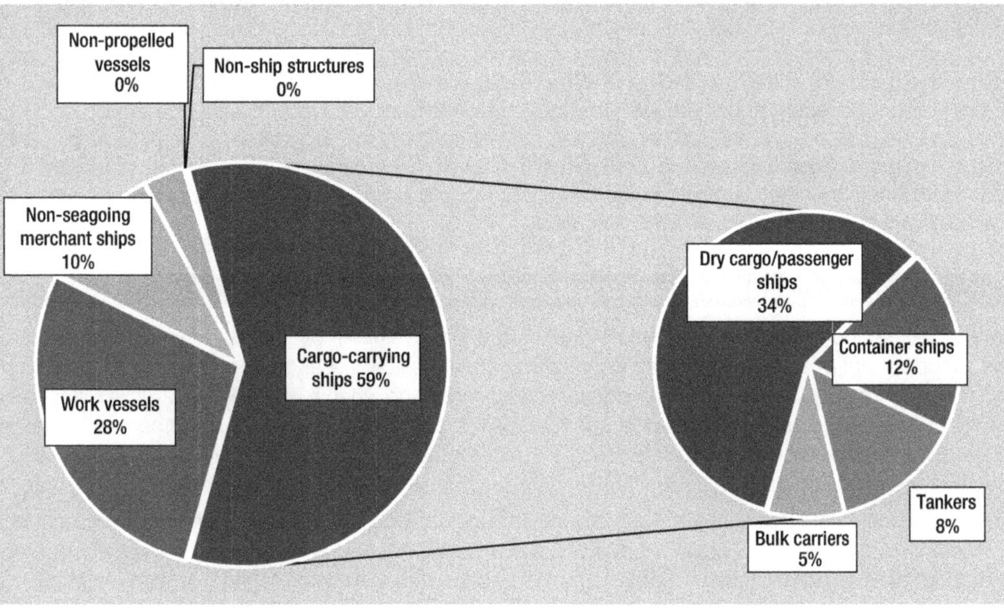

Source: UNCTAD secretariat calculations, based on raw observational data provided by MarineTraffic.

Note: The large pie chart relates to the 2.8 million signals received and the small one, to the 1.66 million signals pertaining to cargo-carrying vessels as defined by UNCTAD.

Box 1. What are automatic identification systems?

Since 2002, SOLAS requires that internationally bound ships with gross tonnage of 300 or more, and all passenger ships regardless of size, be fitted with AIS. AIS data are automatically and electronically broadcast by vessels through very high frequency radio at regular intervals. AIS data include items such as the following: IMO identification number, maritime mobile service identity, call sign, ship name, ship dimensions, position, course, speed and draft. The data are transmitted continuously at irregular intervals, providing a comprehensive and detailed dataset of the passage of a vessel. The AIS data transmission rate is usually about three minutes for anchored or moored vessels, and up to two seconds for fast-moving or manoeuvring vessels. Typically, the data range is limited by the very high frequency signal strength and topological features such as islands, mountain ranges and the earth's curvature. The horizontal range is thus around 75 km, whereas the vertical range can be up to 400 km, making satellite-mounted AIS receivers capable of providing extra coverage at sea. In 2010, the International Space Station was successfully fitted with an AIS receiver, and global coverage has increased. Nonetheless, the industry is still in its infancy as commercial products derived from the data are being explored.

AIS data are transmitted and received by other suitably equipped vessels and by the vessel traffic service located in and around ports and sea lanes, which is a part of a nation's maritime collision avoidance system. There are essentially two types of AIS transmitters and receivers on vessels: Class A is fully integrated into the ship's main systems for merchant vessels over 300 gross tons, and Class B is a more affordable less integrated version for smaller craft. In June 2016, one AIS data provider reported on the 69,726 vessels in range. Of these, 84 per cent were fitted with Class A transponders and 16 per cent, with Class B transponders (VT Explorer, 2006–2013). Much like radio signals, AIS data are picked up by multiple listening stations on land and in space; as a result, there is no restriction as to who may tune in and record what is broadcasted. Duplicate recordings of data are common where overlapping base stations in adjacent countries may pick up the same signal. Duplicated AIS data signals also provide valuable confirmation of a vessel's position from multiple sources.

Maritime safety authorities tend to save AIS data for incident investigation, traffic analysis or further research (Xiao et al., 2015). The data tend to be stored regionally by many national maritime authorities, not centrally by an international organization in one global hub. The volume of data can be very large. In the United States, the Nationwide Automatic Information System receives 92 million such messages per day from approximately 12,700 vessels (United States Coast Guard, 2016). It is therefore conceivable that the world fleet of merchant vessels of around 90,000 vessels could transmit several hundred billion signals yearly.

A number of private companies and at least one organization are building their own networks of listening stations and storing the received signals in their own databases.

In the fishing sector, for example, data providers and conservationists work together to increase transparency as to where fishing vessels catch their cargo. However, for the most part, AIS datasets on merchant fleets tend to have restricted access rights and cannot be easily analysed by the public. Either the information is restricted to the sole view of the data provider membership or, to individual users for one ship or one port or region at a time. Thus without a prearranged agreement, the data cannot be analysed on a global scale. A partial exception are communities of individual enthusiasts and professionals who record and share AIS broadcasts they have received from devices installed in or connected to their personal computers (see www.AISHub.net, AISHub data-sharing centre, which boasts nearly 500 global base stations). Membership is open to those possessing their own AIS receivers and who agree to share their data. Seemingly, interested parties in landlocked countries far from the sea or, those located in busy areas where others are already providing data, may find it difficult to join communities and share data.

Box 2. How do automatic identification systems work in practice?

AIS data on vessel port calls are automatically generated from vessel movements. MarineTraffic AIS data signals are triggered upon receipt of an arrival notification indicating when a ship crosses the boundary of an invisible predetermined polygon and, conversely, upon receipt of an exit notification indicating when a vessel leaves. While manoeuvring, a vessel's signal may be interpreted as a duplicate port call. Likewise, a port authority may, on the other hand, only include in their official statistics vessels that have been serviced through cargo handling, not those that have sailed close to a port to take a person or package on board.

The recordings of AIS data originating in ports can be considered to be the minimum number of vessel port calls for those ports. Broadcasts from ship AIS signals may not always be transmitted or captured for a variety of reasons, such as power outage linked to transmitters or receivers, technical difficulties with data management (for example, multiple signals generated simultaneously) or simple human errors or omissions. MarineTraffic data relate to 69 different vessel types, from anchor-handling vessels and search-and-rescue vessels, to military vessels and pleasure yachts. While the number of vessel types is difficult to interpret, data from a leading ship classification lists over 300 different vessel categories. Thus the first challenge with the dataset is to filter it down into working vessels (for example, tugs and cable-laying vessels) and cargo-carrying vessels (for example, vessels engaged in trading goods) and then into the aforementioned four broad categories of cargo-carrying vessels.

Table 4.1 Vessel port calls by region and type, 2015

Vessels	Africa	Asia	Caribbean	Europe	North America	Oceania	South America	Grand total
Cargo-carrying ships								
Bulk carriers	9 486	69 150	3 684	17 048	10 553	14 051	13 403	137 375
Container ships	20 418	180 705	16 729	64 900	14 620	7 188	17 669	322 229
Dry cargo/passenger ships	36 915	375 134	13 035	431 849	48 834	40 651	19 780	966 198
Tankers	9 160	127 312	6 599	62 721	10 387	3 306	10 312	229 797
Grand total	75 979	752 301	40 047	576 518	84 394	65 196	61 164	1 655 599

Source: UNCTAD secretariat calculations, based on raw observational data provided by MarineTraffic.

Note: The regions listed have been defined by UNCTAD; for the purpose of this research, the Caribbean region also includes Mesoamerican countries.

Box 3. Validity of automatic identification systems data

To check the validity of the AIS data figures, the data provided by a small multipurpose port were compared with those of the AIS dataset from MarineTraffic. The Mauritius Port Authority was chosen because it handles a mixture of vessel types and has a sound reputation for regular and timely publication of port statistics. The AIS database showed 537 container vessel calls at Port Louis in 2015, compared with 568 posted on the port website, which means that 95 per cent of port calls were registered. For bulk carriers. the figures are 55 AIS signals, compared with 52 port calls registered by the port (106 per cent). General cargo vessels generated 131 AIS signals, compared with103 recorded by the Port Authority (127 per cent). Cruise vessels generated 24 AIS signals, as opposed to 23 recorded by the Port Authority (104 per cent). Yet variations in fishing vessels show 126 AIS signals, compared with 953 recorded by the Port Authority (13 per cent). The significant variation in the figures relating to fishing vessels can be explained by the fact that many of the fishing vessels reported by the Port Authority may have been small (below 300 gross tons) and were not fitted with AIS transponders. In all, 2,090 AIS individual vessel signals were received, compared with 2,947 vessels calls recorded by the Port Authority (71 per cent). If fishing vessels are excluded, the alignment between the two sources would be much greater (98.5 per cent).

Next, the data concerning the port of Tangier, Morocco, were examined. Initially the AIS data did not show any vessels other than roll-on/roll-off passenger ships. This caused some concern, as Tangier is a well-known port of call for container liner companies, as demonstrated by the 3 million TEUs handled at the port in 2015. The error could be traced to an interpretation of the name of the port. The initial AIS data pertained to the old port of Tangier, not the new container port, Tanger Med, or its second phase, Tanger Med II, located 40 km to the east of the old port. Once rectified, the total number of vessel port calls from AIS signals quadrupled to 15,575. Although detailed by port and cargo category, however, the data from the website Agence nationale des ports (http://www.anp.org.ma/) mainly cover volume amounts and percentage increases, as opposed to the number of vessel arrivals. This does not make a direct comparison possible.

Lastly, the large multipurpose Port of Rotterdam was chosen for comparison with the AIS dataset of MarineTraffic. The initial problem was that the Port of Rotterdam is so large that there are six ports within the port (Botlek, Centrum, Delfshaven, Maasvlakte, Pernis and Waalhaven) if the United Nations Code for Trade and Transport Locations (UN/LOCODE) is used as the geographical tag. Dating back to 1981, UN/LOCODE originated within the Working Party on Trade Facilitation of the Economic Commission for Europe and is based on a code structure set up by the Economic Commission for Latin America and the Caribbean and a list of locations originating in the latter, developed in UNCTAD in cooperation with transport organizations and with active contributions from national Governments and commercial bodies. At the time of writing, the data for these subports were not available. However, in the bulk sectors, there was a close alignment between the port's official statistics, which indicated 1,177 dry bulk carriers, and the AIS category bulk carriers, which indicated 1,174 port calls (99.7 per cent).

Further analysis is needed to understand why North America does not feature more prominently in the dataset. This could relate to the greater use of combined ferries and freight traffic vessels, river traffic, a greater use of short sea shipping or simply the number of vessels fitted with AIS transponders. The data for the port of Seattle, Washington (United States) shows 12,674 dry cargo or passenger ships, which is twice the number of recorded calls for the next largest United States port in Galveston, Texas and just one sixth of that reported by the Northwest Seaport Alliance (Seattle and Tacoma ports combined) (The Northwest Seaport Alliance, 2016).

Table 4.1 shows a breakdown of the minimum number of port calls by category of ship per region. Asia and Europe represent the highest number of port calls. In Australia and the developed regions of Europe and North America, the category dry cargo/ passenger ships represents more than 50 per cent of the total.

Figure 4.2 shows the geographical distribution of the scale of 76,000 recorded port calls in Africa. Previously much research, albeit in the container sector, has identified Africa's corner points – Egypt, Morocco, and South Africa – as the busiest parts of the continent for maritime trade. This map of AIS data shows that there is considerable vessel traffic in the Gulf of Guinea. Luanda, Angola, is singled out as the second busiest port in the data sample, after Tangier, Morocco, with almost 4,000 port calls (2,105 dry cargo/passenger ships, 1,236 tankers, 507 container ships and 147 bulk carriers). Other leading ports in the data sample show significant levels of traffic in Durban, South Africa; Lagos, Nigeria; and Port Said, Alexandria and Suez, Egypt.

Figure 4.3 shows the number of AIS data recordings received for African countries. The AIS data represent 73 ports located in 37 countries (this figure includes the island of St. Helena, a British overseas territory). It does not include the 15 African landlocked countries, Cabo Verde or the Democratic Republic of the Congo, where data were not reported. The AIS data may not have systematically recorded every vessel's port call; therefore, these figures should be regarded as a minimum indication, and the accurate number of port calls will therefore be higher. Figure 4.4

Figure 4.2 Scale of vessel port calls in Africa, 2015

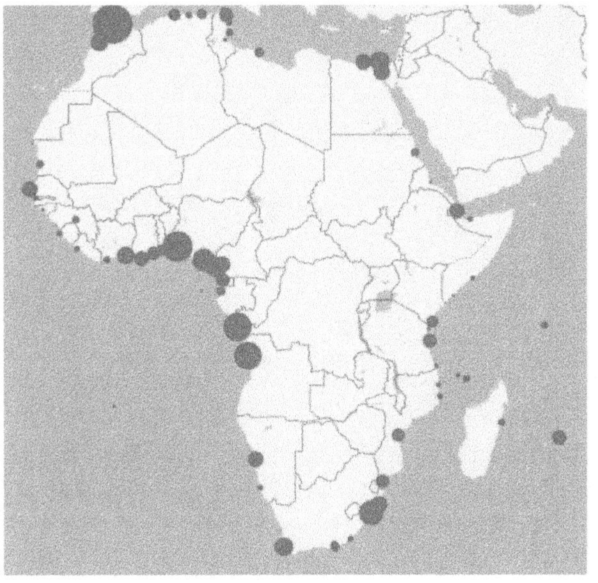

Source: UNCTAD secretariat calculations, based on raw observational data provided by MarineTraffic.

Figure 4.3 Vessel port calls in Africa, 2015

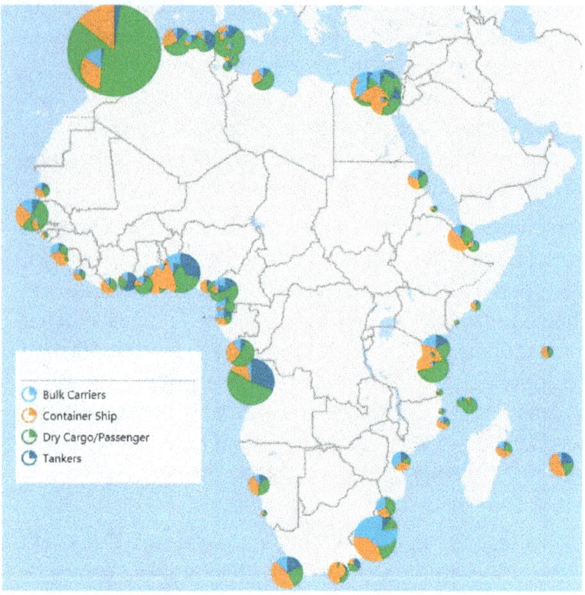

Source: UNCTAD secretariat calculations, based on raw observational data provided by MarineTraffic.

Figure 4.4 Vessel port calls in West Africa, 2015

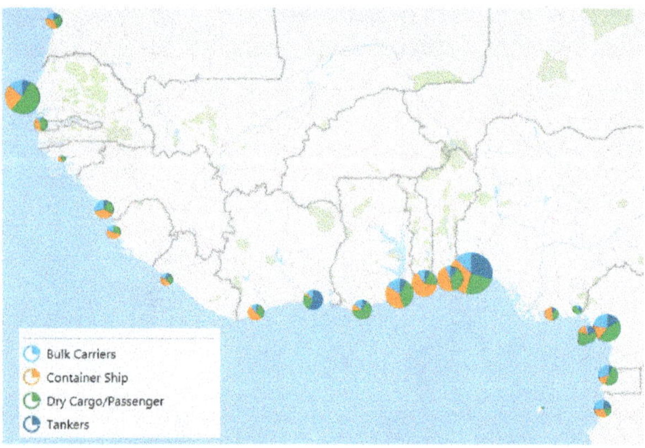

Source: UNCTAD secretariat calculations, based on raw observational data provided by MarineTraffic.

illustrates the specialty of the ports in West Africa. For instance, Abidjan (Côte d'Ivoire) has a large share of tankers, while Lomé (Togo) has a large share of container ships and Owendo (Gabon), a fairly even split of different vessel types. The uniqueness of the dataset concerning the type of vessels calling at ports relates back to UNCTAD work on the aforementioned balanced scorecard methodology. Using the AIS data to identify ports with similar vessel characteristics makes it possible to compare a sample of similar ports at the same time and counters the long-standing argument that ports cannot be compared because each is unique.

C. CONTAINER PORT DEVELOPMENTS

The dearth of available port statistics is less prevalent with regard to container ports because they are common user facilities, that is, they represent the trade of thousands of cargo owners. Table 4.2 shows throughput volumes for the world's 20 leading container ports from 2013 to 2015. The top 20 container ports, which account for 55 per cent of the throughput of the top 100 ports, showed a 95 per cent decline in growth, from 5.6 per cent in 2014 to 0.5 per cent in 2015. Although this does not appear to be true of other smaller ports, which experienced larger gains. The top 100 container ports are estimated to have handled a throughput of 539 million TEUs in 2015, up by about 6.8 per cent from the 505 million reported in 2014 (Informa PLC, 2016) . The list of top 20 container ports includes 15 ports from developing economies, and as in the previous year, are located in Asia; the remaining five ports are from developed countries, three of which are located in Europe (the Netherlands, Belgium and Germany) and two in North America (Los Angeles and Long Beach, California). The top 10 ports continue to be located in Asia. Nine of the top 20 container ports are located in China, and seven of these (excluding Dalian and Hong Kong, China) experienced positive growth. Overall, the top 20 container ports in China grew by 3.7 per cent in 2015, in spite of the economic slowdown (JOC.com, 2016a). Seven of the top 20 ports experienced a negative growth rate in container port throughput, compared with the previous year, while an additional two barely managed a positive growth rate at less than 1 per cent. The most significant declines occurred in Hong Kong (China), Hamburg (Germany) and Singapore at -9.5, -9.3 and -8.7 per cent, respectively. Conversely the ports of Port Klang (Malaysia), Antwerp (Belgium) and Tanjung Pelepas (Malaysia) experienced the most growth at 8.6 per cent, 7.5 per cent and 7.4 per cent, respectively. The port of Tanjung Pelepas made significant strides in 2014, with 11.4 per cent growth on the completion of infrastructure investments. Growth was expected to be reduced to around 4.4 per cent in 2015 but proved much better. Malaysian ports have consistently expanded their throughput during the last decade so that both Port Klang and Tanjung Pelepas are now handling twice the volume of 2005.

Operational performance of container ports

Table 4.3 shows improvements in container berth productivity in selected developing countries in 2015, compared with 2014. The highest growth is in the

Table 4.2	Top 20 container terminals and their throughput, 2013, 2014 and 2015 (Thousands of 20-foot equivalent units and percentage change)						
Rank	**Port Name**	**Country**	**2013**	**2014**	**2015**	**Percentage change 2014-2013**	**Percentage change 2015-2014**
1	Shanghai	China	33 617	35 290	36 540	4.98	3.54
2	Singapore	Singapore	32 579	33 869	30 922	3.96	-8.70
3	Shenzhen	China	23 279	24 040	24 200	3.27	0.67
4	Ningbo and Zhoushan	China	17 351	19 450	20 630	12.10	6.07
5	Hong Kong	China	22 352	22 200	20 100	-0.68	-9.46
6	Busan	Republic of Korea	17 686	18 683	19 467	5.64	4.20
7	Guangzhou	China	15 309	16 610	17 590	8.50	5.90
8	Qingdao	China	15 520	16 580	17 430	6.83	5.13
9	Dubai Ports	United Arab Emirates	13 641	15 200	15 590	11.43	2.57
10	Tianjin	China	13 000	14 060	14 110	8.15	0.36
11	Rotterdam	Netherlands	11 621	12 298	12 235	5.83	-0.51
12	Port Klang	Malaysia	10 350	10 946	11 887	5.76	8.60
13	Kaohsiung	Taiwan	9 938	10 593	10 260	6.59	-3.14
14	Antwerp	Belgium	8 578	8 978	9 654	4.66	7.53
15	Dalian	China	10 015	10 130	9 450	1.15	-6.71
16	Xiamen	China	8 008	8 572	9 180	7.04	7.09
17	Tanjung Pelepas	Malaysia	7 628	8 500	9 130	11.43	7.41
18	Hamburg	Germany	9 257	9 720	8 821	5.00	-9.25
19	Los Angeles	United States	7 868	8 340	8 160	6.00	-2.16
20	Long Beach	United States	6 648	6 818	7 190	2.56	5.46
	Total top 20		**294 245**	**310 877**	**312 546**	**5.65**	**0.54**

Source: Various sources, including Port of Rotterdam (2015).

port of Sohar, Oman, 160 km from Dubai, which experienced a doubling in the number of container-handling operations following improvements made by its operator, Hutchinson Port Holdings (Handy Shipping Guide, 2015). The figures show that double-digit growth in terminal efficiency is possible. These terminals often benefit from the experience of a global terminal operator who is part owner, part operator (see column 2 of the table for a list of the leading international terminal operators). It is not unusual for more than one competing international terminal operator to have a presence in the same port at different terminals, and in a limited number of cases, within the same terminal. For example, in 2013, the Antwerp Gateway common user terminal at Deurganck Dock was a joint-venture between DP World (42.5 per cent), ZIM ports (20 per cent), the former China Ocean Shipping Pacific (20 per cent), Terminal Link/CMA CGM (10 per cent) and Duisport (7.5 per cent), with DP World acting as the operator (DP World, 2013). As reported in previous editions of the *Review of Maritime Transport*, improvements in terminal operational performance are difficult to sustain year on year.

D. OVERALL PORT DEVELOPMENTS

Unlike container ports, bulk and liquid ports are not common user ports and tend to represent the interests of a few cargo owners. This makes it difficult to obtain statistics on these sectors. Table 4.4 shows the world's leading ports by volume. Fourteen of these top 20 ports are in China, a further three in Asia and one each in Australia, Europe and North America. These 20 ports experienced an 85 per cent decline in growth, from 6.3 per cent in 2014 to 0.9 per cent in 2015. Of the seven ports that experienced declines

Table 4.3 Container berth productivity, selected developing countries, 2015

Terminals	International terminal operators	Ports	Countries	Regions	Improvement (percentage)
Oman International Container Terminal	HPH	Sohar	Oman	Middle East	101
Luanda Container Terminal	APMT	Luanda	Angola	Africa	52
Tanzania International Container Terminal Services	HPH	Dar es Salaam	United Republic of Tanzania	Africa	37
Nam Hai Terminal		Haiphong	Viet Nam	Asia	22
DP World Maputo	DP World	Maputo	Mozambique	Africa	21
Tecon Suape Container Terminal	ICTSI	Suape	Brazil	South America	20
South Container Terminal	DP World	Jeddah	Saudi Arabia	Middle East	20
Shuaiba Area Container Terminal		Shuaiba	Kuwait	Middle East	18
Jawaharlal Nehru Container Terminal	DP World	Nehru	India	Asia	18
Evergreen Container Terminal – LCB2	Evergreen	Laem Chabang	Thailand	Asia	17
Manzanillo International Terminal	SSA Marine	Manzanillo	Panama	South America	16
Panama Ports Company	HPH	Cristobal	Panama	South America	16
First Container Terminal	Global Ports	St. Petersburg	Russian Federation	Europe	14
Société de manutention du terminal à conteneurs	Bolloré Group	Cotonou	Benin	Africa	13
Terminal Petikemas Surabaya	DP World	Surabaya	Indonesia	Asia	11
Korea Express Busan Container Terminal	China Shipping Group	Busan	Republic of Korea	Asia	9
South Harbor International Container Terminal (ATI)	ICTSI	Manila	Philippines	Asia	8
Aqaba Container Terminal	APMT	Aqaba	Jordan	Middle East	7
Walvis Bay Container Terminal		Walvis Bay	Namibia	Africa	6
PSA Singapore Terminals	PSA	Singapore	Singapore	Asia	6
Terminal 2 – Rio Multitermais Container Terminal		Rio de Janeiro	Brazil	South America	5
Dongbu Pusan Container Terminal	Evergreen	Busan	Republic of Korea	Asia	3
Port Akdeniz	Global Ports Holding	Antalya	Turkey	Asia	2
APM Terminals Pecem	APMT	Pecem	Brazil	South America	2

Source: UNCTAD secretariat calculations, based on the port productivity database of JOC.com (2016b) and other sources.

Note: For the purpose of this research, berth productivity is defined by JOC.com as "the average number of container moves per crane, per hour while a ship is at berth". The relative improvement has been measured and then weighted by call size to achieve actual improvement in year-on-year performance.

in throughput in 2015, Singapore was the only one not located in China. The Chinese port of Suzhou experienced the largest increase in throughput, 12.5 per cent. The next largest gain in port throughput was recorded by Rotterdam, the Netherlands, which experienced a growth of 4.9 per cent. Rotterdam's growth stemmed from increased trade in liquid bulks, in particular crude oil (up 8 per cent), mineral oil products (up 18 per cent) and liquefied natural gas (up 92 per cent) (Port of Rotterdam, 2016).

Despite the difficulty of obtaining dry bulk port statistics, UNCTAD has been successful in obtaining a unique dataset from a leading shipping agency, Wilhelmsen Ships Service. Table 4.5 shows data from bulk vessels calling at ports in several countries engaged in the iron ore and coal trades. The data are part of the company's internal record keeping and include port calls serviced by the company or observed to have taken place. The database recorded nearly 34,000 port calls in 2014 and 2015.

The database includes information on individual vessels, arrival times, berthing times and departure times that have been entered manually. The risk of manually entering data is the introduction of human error caused by creating shortcuts. That said, because there were numerous data fields, the data were filtered for obvious errors or questionable figures, for example where the load factor was greater than 100 per

Table 4.4 World's leading ports by total volume, 2013–2015 (Thousands of tons)

Rank	Port	Country	2013	2014	2015	Percentage change 2014–2013	Percentage change 2015–2014
1	Ningbo and Zhoushan	China	809 800	873 000	889 000	7.80	1.83
2	Shanghai	China	776 000	755 300	717 400	-2.67	-5.02
3	Singapore	Singapore	560 800	581 300	574 900	3.66	-1.10
4	Tianjin	China	500 600	540 000	541 000	7.87	0.19
5	Suzhou	China	454 000	480 000	540 000	5.73	12.50
6	Guangzhou	China	454 700	500 400	519 900	10.05	3.90
7	Qingdao	China	450 000	480 000	500 000	6.67	4.17
8	Tangshan	China	446 200	500 800	490 000	12.24	-2.16
9	Rotterdam	Netherlands	440 500	444 700	466 400	0.95	4.88
10	Port Hedland	Australia	326 000	421 800	452 900	29.39	7.37
11	Dalian	China	408 400	420 000	415 000	2.84	-1.19
12	Rizhao	China	309 200	353 000	361 000	14.17	2.27
13	Yingkou	China	330 000	330 700	338 500	0.21	2.36
14	Busan	Republic of Korea	292 400	312 000	323 700	6.70	3.75
15	South Louisiana	United States	241 500	264 700	265 600	9.61	0.34
16	Hong Kong	China	276 100	297 700	256 600	7.82	-13.81
17	Qinhuangdao	China	272 600	274 000	253 100	0.51	-7.63
18	Port Klang	Malaysia	200 200	217 200	219 800	8.49	1.20
19	Shenzen	China	234 000	223 300	217 100	-4.57	-2.78
20	Xiamen	China	191 000	205 000	210 000	7.33	2.44
	Total top 20		**7 974 000**	**8 474 900**	**8 551 900**	**6.28**	**0.91**

Source: Various sources, including Port of Rotterdam (2015).

Table 4.5 Average dwell times for bulk vessels, selected countries, 2015

	2014				2015			
Row labels	Sample size	Quantity (thousand tons)	Average waiting time (days)	Average working time (days)	Sample size	Quantity (thousand tons)	Average waiting time (days)	Average working time (days)
Australia	4 438	455 907	5.50	10.95	2 461	517 066	4.52	5.55
Brazil	1 533	252 707	6.44	12.08	1 537	258 899	5.17	2.04
Canada	151	17 779	5.08	2.58	36	3 327	2.33	2.69
China	599	76 347	3.73	2.74	1 470	183 976	1.81	2.42
Taiwan	..	..	..	..	107	8 858	0.68	3.40
Colombia	48	4 838	1.75	0.82	213	19 304	0.36	1.95
India	2 302	163 729	3.96	10.68	1 865	124 192	2.28	3.63
Indonesia	2 609	182 875	2.55	4.06	281	19 430	2.99	4.05
Netherlands	51	7 416	0.12	2.78	72	8 947	1.09	2.59
Republic of Korea	..	..	..	..	167	19 145	2.64	3.75
South Africa	..	..	..	..	994	89 376	2.32	2.33
United States	188	13 819	4.74	2.31	55	5 129	1.51	1.63
Grand total	**11 925**	**1 176 315**	**4.53**	**8.80**	**9 258**	**1 257 650**	**3.46**	**3.86**

Source: UNCTAD secretariat calculations, based on raw observational data provided by Wilhelmsen Ships Service.

cent or lower than 10 per cent or the IMO number corresponded to a different type of vessel incapable of carrying the specified cargo. In addition, in some instances, the time element showed dates, not hours; therefore, the time averages and fiscal calculations are estimated averages. The data entries were cross-checked with datasets of IMO for details concerning the ship type (IMO number) and of the Economic Commission for Europe concerning the location (UN/LOCODE). This process removed around 40 per cent of the data received to provide a database of 20,000 port calls for analysis.

The data, based on a sample size of almost 12,000 port calls in 2014, shows that the average waiting time for a berth was 4.5 days and the average time spent alongside a berth was 8.8 days, either loading or discharging a total of 1.176 billion tons of cargo, equivalent to approximately 12 per cent of the annual global seaborne trade. For 2015, the comparable figures are around 9,250 observations with an average of 3.5 days spent waiting for a berth and 3.9 days alongside a berth, handling 1.257 billion tons of cargo. The waiting time can be attributed to any number of reasons such as undertaking repairs, loading victualling, awaiting new instructions and cargo or port and sea-lane congestion. The most significant improvements in waiting times occurred in ports located in Brazil (83 per cent less waiting), India (66 per cent less waiting) and Australia (49 per cent less waiting).

Dwell time in Colombian ports increased by 137 per cent, as the recorded number of observations doubled. This may be attributable to the rebound effect of an export ban imposed on one of the largest exports of thermal coal in the first half of 2014. In 2015, Colombian thermal coal exports rose by 7.6 per cent, while coking coal exports declined by 1 per cent (S and P Global Platts, 2016). At 19.3 million tons, the Wilhelmsen Ships Service data sample covers about a quarter of Colombia's coal exports in 2015. For Indonesia, the data sample covers around 40 per cent of the country's coal exports in 2014 (Indonesia Investments, 2016). Yet for 2015, the Indonesian data sample size dropped by 90 per cent, while the average work time figures remained the same. This may relate to an internal change in the collection of data, and a longer time series would therefore be needed to highlight any trends.

The estimated cost of the sample wait is derived by taking the average daily charter rate over the year for the specific size of vessel carrying the cargo and multiplying this by the time. Both yearly figures involve different samples sizes and cannot be directly

Table 4.6 Estimated cost of dwell time, selected countries, 2014–2015

Country	2014			2015		
	Sample size	Average waiting time (days)	Estimated cost of sample wait (thousands of dollars)	Sample size	Average of waiting time (days)	Estimated cost of sample wait (thousands of dollars)
Australia	4 438	5.50	421 352	2 461	4.52	182 815
Brazil	1 533	6.44	188 822	1 537	5.17	73 630
Canada	151	5.08	13 594	36	2.33	702
China	599	3.73	43 636	1 470	1.81	26 087
Taiwan	..	..	..	107	0.68	703
Colombia	48	1.75	1 349	213	0.36	690
India	2 302	3.96	128 000	1 865	2.28	33 640
Indonesia	2 609	2.55	82 442	281	2.99	6 424
Netherlands	51	0.12	129	72	1.09	713
Republic of Korea	..	..	..	167	2.64	4 470
South Africa	..	..	..	994	2.32	19 067
United States	188	4.74	12 785	55	1.51	757
Grand total	**11 925**	**4.53**	**892 379**	**9 258**	**3.46**	**349 699**

Source: UNCTAD secretariat calculations, based on data supplied by Clarksons Research (2016) and raw observational data provided by Wilhelmsen Ships Service.

Note: ".." indicates data unavailable or sample too small.

compared. The cost is part of the price (that is, it excludes other factors such as crew wages, victualling and fuel oil) of an underutilized asset, which will ultimately be borne by consumers as a higher transport cost component of the value of the final good.

The estimated cost of dwell time in selected countries was calculated using average yearly charter rates for various sized vessels based on financial data from Clarksons Research (table 4.6). In 2014, this cost was estimated at $0.9 billion and in 2015, for a different sample, it was estimated at $350 million. The financial figures are approximate, since the charter rate would have fluctuated throughout the year. The figures pertain to coal and iron ore loading and discharging. The waiting costs for the two samples were significantly different because of a reduction in waiting time and the average daily charter hire rate that may have occurred as a result of the downturn in trade described in chapter 1. The total costs are estimates with regard to the economy as a whole, since this will either be a loss of revenue incurred by the shipowner or an extra cost incurred by a charterer having to pay hire for the use of the vessel. Regardless of which party directly pays for these costs, they will be passed onto the consumer through higher transport costs as a component of the final purchase price of the goods. In any business, the goal should always be to eliminate idle time of equipment within the source of production to improve efficiency. The data are useful to policymakers in exploring ways to increase a county's competitiveness and serve to highlight the need for more statistics on port operations.

E. CONCLUSION

This chapter has shown that the port industry experienced growth in 2015, but by a significantly lower rate than in 2014. Although this analysis was based on a limited sample, it is one that represents a significant market share. The largest ports recorded the sharpest declines in growth, which for the most part remained positive. Container ports suffered more of a downturn than the overall port sector, signifying that production capacity remains strong but demand for finished goods remains weak.

With the help of third parties, it is now possible to obtain an alternative view of official statistics and fill in certain gaps. Data derived from a seemingly unconnected need to provide ships with a collision avoidance system can be used to see how trade within a region, country or port is performing. As in most pioneering studies, the data initially ask more questions than they answer. Further analysis of the data is ongoing, with a view to reporting on information such as ship dwell time, vessel-carrying capacity and port productivity.

When companies encounter difficulties in reporting on growth metrics, such as market share, turnover or throughput, they focus on other factors, such as productivity or efficiency. A continued downward pressure in trade may therefore put pressure on ports to be seen as more operationally efficient. This means the release of statistics not previously considered newsworthy may become more common. Alternatively, the publication of third-party data that could be used to assess port performance may compel ports to issue their own data to prevent any negative interpretations.

Importantly, statistics should not be produced for the sake of statistics alone, but to explain how the world works and how it can be improved. Any increase in data on port metrics may influence shippers or carriers on which ports to use, and the resulting competition for business may drive improvements. If that data were freely available and centrally stored for analysis by researchers, greater insight into the workings of ports could be ensured. This could then lead to improvements in ports that would help lower transport costs and make international trade cheaper for all.

One of the factors influencing the growth of globalization has been the increased certainty in quotas and trade tariffs though membership of the World Trade Organization. A gradual reduction in trade tariffs, combined with improvements in industry practices, such as increased use of containerization, communications and banking, has also helped fuel this process. Improvements in port efficiency, facilitated by the availability of data, could add further to a reduction in transport costs and provide a much-needed boost to international trade.

In today's world of increased technology, people and businesses are more likely to be assessed by third parties. This thought should thus be a stimulus for port authorities to share more of their own data.

REFERENCES

Agence nationale des ports. Available at http://www.anp.org.ma/ (accessed 14 October 2016).

Clarksons Research (2016). *Shipping Review and Outlook*. Spring.

DP World (2013). Press release. 17 May. Available at http://www.npgenergy.be/assets/Uploads/Press-release-DPW-17052013.pdf (accessed 17 October 2016).

JOC.com (2016a). China port volume set for slowdown after 2015 growth. Available at http://www.joc.com/port-news/asian-ports/port-hong-kong/china-ports-data-shows-slowing-growth-2015_20160122.html (accessed 16 September 2016).

JOC.com (2016b). Port productivity. Available at http://www.joc.com/special-topics/port-productivity (accessed 13 October 2016).

Handy Shipping Guide (2015). Container handling facility plans for 6 million TEU following significant investment. 25 April. Available at http://www.handyshippingguide.com/shipping-news/container-handling-facility-plans-for-6-million-teu-following-significant-investment_6334 (accessed 7 June 2016).

Informa PLC (2016). Lloyd's List. Top 100 container ports 2015. 26 August. Available at https://www.lloydslist.com/ll/incoming/article504618.ece#country (accessed 6 October 2016).

Kozak M (2004). *Destination Benchmarking: Concepts, Practices and Operations*. CABI Publishing. Oxon, United Kingdom and Cambridge, United States.

Kowalski P (2005). Impact of changes in tariffs on developing countries' government revenue. Working Party of the Trade Committee. Organization for Economic Cooperation and Development Trade Policy Working Paper No. 18.

Indonesia Investments (2016). Production and export down, coal consumption in Indonesia up. 18 January. Available at http://www.indonesia-investments.com/news/todays-headlines/production-export-down-coal-consumption-in-indonesia-up/item6392 (accessed 6 October 2016).

MarineTraffic.com (2007–2016). Available at http://www.marinetraffic.com/en/ais/home/centerx:25/centery:37/zoom:7 (accessed 6 October 2016).

Progressive Economy (2013). Tariffs raised 30 per cent of government revenue in 1912, and now raise 1 per cent. April 10. Available at http://www.progressive-economy.org/trade_facts/tariffs-raised-30-percent-of-government-revenue-in-1912-and-now-raise-1-percent/ (accessed 16 September 2016).

Port of Rotterdam (2015). *Port Statistics. A Wealth of Information. Make it Happen*. Rotterdam Port Authority. Rotterdam.

Port of Rotterdam (2016). The Port of Rotterdam achieves a record throughput thanks to a growth of 4.9%. 15 January. Available at https://www.portofrotterdam.com/en/news-and-press-releases/the-port-of-rotterdam-achieves-a-record-throughput-thanks-to-a-growth-of-49 (accessed 6 October 2016).

S and P Global Platts (2016). Colombian 2015 thermal coal exports rise 7.6% on year to 80.64 million mt. 11 January. Available at http://www.platts.com/latest-news/shipping/london/colombian-2015-thermal-coal-exports-rise-76-on-26334265 (accessed 16 September 2016).

Standing Committee for Economic and Commercial Cooperation of the Organization of Islamic Cooperation (2015). *Evaluating the Ownership, Governance Structures and Performances of Ports in the OIC Member Countries* (Ankara). Available at http://www.comcec.org/wp-content/uploads/2015/12/5-Transport-Report.pdf (accessed 13 October 2016).

The Northwest Seaport Alliance (2016). Cargo stats. Available at https://www.nwseaportalliance.com/stats-stories/cargo-stats (accessed 16 September 2016).

UNCTAD (2007–2015). *Review of Maritime Transport*. United Nations publications. Sales Nos. E.07.II.D.14, E.08.II.D.26, E.09.II.D.11, E.10.II.D.4, E.11.II.D.4, E.12.II.D.17, E.13.II.D.9, E.14.II.D.5 and E. 15.II.D.6, respectively. New York and Geneva.

UNCTAD (1976). *Port Performance Indicators*. United Nations publication. Sales No. E.76.II.D.7. Geneva.

UNCTAD (1979). Manual on a Uniform System of Port Statistics and Performance Indicators. First edition. United Nations publication. Geneva.

UNCTAD (1983). Manual on a Uniform System of Port Statistics and Performance Indicators. Second edition. United Nations publication. Geneva.

UNCTAD (1987a) Manual on a Uniform System of Port Statistics and Performance Indicators. Third edition. United Nations publication. Geneva.

UNCTAD (1987b). *Measuring and Evaluating Port Performance and Productivity*. Monograph No. 6. UNCTAD/SHIP(494(6). United Nations publication. Geneva.

UNCTAD (2016). *Port Performance: Linking Performance Indicators to Strategic Objectives*. Port Management Series. Vol. 4. United Nations publication. New York and Geneva.

United Nations Department of Economic and Social Affairs (2002). *Improving Resource Mobilization in Developing Countries and Transition Economies*. ST/ESA/PAD/SER.E/30 (New York, United Nations publication).

United States Coast Guard (2016). Nationwide automatic identification system. Available at http://www.uscg.mil/acquisition/nais/(accessed 3 October 2016).

VT Explorer (2006–2013). Coverage. Vessel statistics. Available at http://www.vtexplorer.com/vessel-tracking-coverage.php (accessed 3 October 2016).

Xiao F, Han Ligteringen H, van Gulijk C and Ale B (2015). Comparison study on AIS data of ship traffic behaviour. *Ocean Engineering*. 95:84–93.

ENDNOTES

1 The Port Management Programme of the Human Resources Development Section of the Division on Technology and Logistics of UNCTAD is known as TrainForTrade in the Knowledge Development Branch. The Programme supports port communities from developing countries in their efforts to achieve higher efficiency and competitiveness.

5

LEGAL ISSUES AND REGULATORY DEVELOPMENTS

During the period under review, important developments included the adoption of the 2030 Agenda for Sustainable Development in September 2015 and the Paris Agreement under the United Nations Framework Convention on Climate Change in December 2015. Their implementation, along with that of the Addis Ababa Action Agenda, adopted in July 2015, which provides a global framework for financing development post-2015, is expected to bring increased opportunities for developing countries.

Among regulatory initiatives, it is worth noting the entry into force on 1 July 2016 of the SOLAS amendments related to the mandatory verification of the gross mass of containers, which will contribute to improving the stability and safety of ships and avoiding maritime accidents. At the International Maritime Organization (IMO), discussions continued on the reduction of greenhouse gas emissions from international shipping and on technical cooperation and transfer of technology particularly to developing countries. Also, progress was made in other areas clearly related to sustainable development. These included work on technical matters related to the imminent entry into force and implementation of the International Convention for the Control and Management of Ships' Ballast Water and Sediments, 2004 (known as the Ballast Water Management (BWM) Convention) and on developing an international legally binding instrument under the United Nations Convention on the Law of the Sea on the conservation and sustainable use of marine biological diversity of areas beyond national jurisdiction.

Continued enhancements were made to regulatory measures in the field of maritime and supply chain security and their implementation. Areas of progress included the implementation of authorized economic operator (AEO) programmes and an increasing number of bilateral mutual recognition agreements that will, in due course, form the basis for the recognition of AEOs at a multilateral level. As regards suppression of maritime piracy and armed robbery, in 2015, only a modest increase of 4.1 per cent was observed in the number of incidents reported to IMO, compared with 2014. The number of crew members taken hostage or kidnapped and those assaulted, and the number of ships hijacked, decreased significantly compared with 2014. In this respect, a circular on combating unsafe practices associated with mixed migration by sea and interim guidelines on maritime cyber risk management were approved at IMO. In the context of International Labour Organization (ILO) conventions, progress was also made on the issue of recognition of seafarers' identity documents and on improving their living and working conditions.

INTRODUCTION

In September 2015, the 2030 Agenda for Sustainable Development was adopted at the United Nations summit for the adoption of the post-2015 development agenda, representing consensus by the international community on a plan of action involving 17 Sustainable Development Goals, with 169 associated targets, which are "integrated and indivisible, global in nature and universally applicable" (see United Nations General Assembly resolution 70/1).[1] The Sustainable Development Goals are much more wide-ranging and comprehensive than the earlier Millennium Development Goals. They aim to eradicate, rather than reduce, global poverty, as well as harmonize the development and environment agendas and address inequality by leaving no one behind. Sustainable and resilient transport is among the cross-cutting issues, of relevance for achievement of progress on several of the Goals and targets, e.g. Sustainable Development Goal 9, to "build resilient infrastructure, promote inclusive and sustainable industrialization and foster innovation", and Sustainable Development Goal 13, to "take urgent action to combat climate change and its impacts".

Of particular relevance in the context of maritime transport, ship-source pollution and coastal zone management is also Sustainable Development Goal 14, to "conserve and sustainably use the oceans, seas and marine resources for sustainable development". Target 14.1 calls for significantly reducing all kinds of marine pollution by 2025, while target 14.2 calls for sustainably managing and protecting marine and coastal ecosystems by as early as 2020. Other targets are dedicated to minimizing and addressing the impacts of ocean acidification (target 14.3); by 2020, conserving at least 10 per cent of coastal and marine areas, consistent with national and international law and based on the best available scientific information (target 14.5); by 2020, effectively regulating harvesting and ending overfishing, illegal, unreported and unregulated fishing and destructive fishing practices (target 14.4); and by 2020, prohibiting certain forms of fisheries subsidies which contribute to these practices (target 14.6). Target 14.7 particularly calls for increasing the economic benefits to small island developing States and the least developed countries, from the sustainable use of marine resources, including through sustainable management of fisheries, aquaculture and tourism, by 2030. In addition, target 14.a calls for increasing scientific knowledge, developing research capacity and transferring marine technology, in order to improve ocean health and to enhance the contribution of marine biodiversity to the development of developing countries, in particular small island developing States and the least developed countries, while target 14.b calls for providing access for small-scale artisanal fishers to marine resources and markets.

Of particular importance in the context of legal and regulatory developments related to maritime transport is target 14.c: "Enhance the conservation and sustainable use of oceans and their resources by implementing international law as reflected in the United Nations Convention on the Law of the Sea, which provides the legal framework for the conservation and sustainable use of oceans and their resources, as recalled in paragraph 158 of "The future we want".[2] Worth noting is the broad and inclusive wording of this target, which directs the international community to implement international law as reflected in the Convention on the Law of the Sea. This would seem to cover, inter alia, a broad range of international legal instruments adopted under the auspices of IMO, for example, in the field of ship safety and marine environmental protection and pollution control.

UNCTAD contributes to the implementation of the 2030 Agenda, including Sustainable Development Goal 14, by working towards enhancing the regulatory governance of the oceans, including with respect to international shipping, marine pollution, security and safety, energy efficiency, fisheries and economic and environmental issues, particularly with a view to considerations arising for developing countries. UNCTAD research and analysis in the field of transport law, published as part of the *Review of Maritime Transport* and in individual studies and reports, as well as the relevant technical assistance and advice of UNCTAD aims to assist policymakers and other stakeholders in their understanding of the existing regulatory framework and in assessing the merits of accession to relevant international legal instruments and in their effective implementation and application at the national level.[3]

In December 2015, after nearly a decade of negotiations, a new and comprehensive global climate treaty, the Paris Agreement,[4] was agreed at the twenty-first Conference of the Parties to the United Nations Framework Convention on Climate Change by all 196 participating Parties. The Paris Agreement is applicable to all countries and includes long-term goals. It reflects a new type of deal without binding emission reduction targets but with national plans and a framework for transparency of effort and progression towards the purpose. The Paris Agreement expressly deals with domestic emissions, but emissions from international aviation and maritime transport are not explicitly covered within the framework of nationally determined contributions, which reflect national targets and actions. The Paris Agreement will enter into force when 55 Parties to the Convention, representing at least 55 per cent of global greenhouse gas emissions, ratify the agreement.

A. IMPORTANT DEVELOPMENTS IN MARITIME TRANSPORT LAW

Entry into force of the amendments to chapter VI/2 of the International Convention for the Safety of Life at Sea related to the mandatory verification of the gross mass of a container

An important regulatory development in 2016 is the entry into force of amendments to chapter VI/2 of SOLAS related to the mandatory verification of the gross mass of a container, which will have important implications for the whole transport supply chain. While the new requirements became mandatory as of 1 July 2016,[5] a number of problems related to implementation and compliance have been identified, and IMO advised on adopting a pragmatic approach to implementation, particularly for the first three months immediately after 1 July 2016, while stakeholders refine their procedures for documenting, communicating and sharing relevant electronic data (IMO, 2016a). An overview of the substantive rules, as well as of potential problems identified, and efforts made so far towards the effective implementation of the amendments, is provided below.

Background

It is critical for the safety of ships, their crew and cargo to ensure the stability of any ship during a sea voyage. As cargo is loaded on a ship, a responsible ship officer has to decide where each particular item is to be placed. This becomes more challenging with container ships, rather than with tankers or bulk carriers, as the weight of each packed container tends to vary depending on the type of cargo that it contains. Shippers have always been required to include the declared weight on the container manifest, but these were often only estimates or inaccurate. Despite the existence of a number of IMO instruments[6] regulating the stability and safe operation of ships, including safe packing, handling and transport of containers, there were no requirements to verify the actual weight of packed containers prior to vessel loading.

If weight is incorrectly declared, and ships are overloaded with overweight or misplaced containers, their structural integrity and stability risk being compromised, containers may fall overboard and be lost at sea, and serious incidents may occur, as illustrated by a number of high-profile casualties.[7] Although in many cases the difference between the declared and actual weight of containers was, in the event, not the named cause of the accidents, it was an aggravating factor. Thus, weighing containers may help avoid accidents, as well as any possible misdeclaration of exports.

Efforts to improve container security

Following the *MSC Napoli* incident in 2007, the World Shipping Council and the International Chamber of Shipping developed industry best practices for safe container handling.[8] However, these guidelines remained only voluntary.[9] After several years of study and discussion, IMO, in November 2014, approved the amendments to regulation 2 (Cargo information), part A of chapter VI, related to mandatory verification of gross mass of a container (SOLAS verified gross mass (VGM) amendments)[10] (IMO, 2014a, annex I), set to enter into force on 1 July 2016. The Maritime Safety Committee also adopted implementing guidelines regarding the verified gross mass of a container carrying cargo (VGM guidelines) (IMO, 2014b). Under the SOLAS VGM amendments, the shipper is responsible for the verification of the gross mass of a container carrying cargo, before it is loaded onto a vessel, by one of two methods. The shipper can either (a) weigh the packed container using calibrated and certified equipment (method 1); or (b) weigh all packages and cargo items, and then add the weight of the empty container, using a certified method approved by the competent authority of the State in which packing of the container was completed (method 2). In addition, the shipper of a container shall ensure that the VGM is stated in the shipping document (e.g. a bill of lading), signed by a person duly authorized by the shipper, and submitted to the master or his or her representative, sufficiently in advance to be used in preparing the ship's stowage plan. If the VGM of the container is not provided as described above, the container shall not be loaded onto the ship unless the master or his or her representative and the terminal representative have obtained the VGM through other means.

Potential problems in implementing the amendments

Concerns were expressed that not all shippers would be ready to comply with the amendments by 1 July 2016. Although aware of the VGM rules, many shippers complained that they lacked sufficient information by service providers (*Journal of Commerce*, 2016a; INTTRA, 2015). Problems identified included the following:

Lack of appropriate infrastructure and equipment

Accurate container weights need to be verified before vessel loading. Vessels themselves do not have the capability to weigh the containers, so verification has to be obtained on shore and provided to the port terminal operator prior to loading. That also depends on whether the terminal has the facilities to weigh the containers, and whether these facilities are calibrated and certified under national law.

Concerns have been expressed that the situation might be more challenging for smaller exporters, and for those shipping combinations of packaged products with various stowage equipment or loose products in containers, particularly as regards their lack of infrastructure, weighing machinery, information technology and other relevant processes (*Lloyd's List*, 2016a).

Form of communicating verified gross mass information

SOLAS does not mandate any particular form of communication between the parties exchanging the VGM information. It is important, however, to ensure that such information is correctly transmitted to and used by the carrier and the terminal when making the decision on whether to load a container on board a ship or not. Under both methods stipulated in the amendments, information required by the shipper is the same: the VGM of the packed container, identified as such and signed by the shipper or a person duly authorized by the shipper. The information and signature may be transmitted electronically. Normally, electronic data interchange messaging is used with respect to VGM. However, the form of exchange and precise content normally needs to be agreed between the commercial parties (*Lloyd's List*, 2016b).[11]

Difficulties in national implementation

Some concerns have been expressed regarding the effective national implementation of the SOLAS VGM amendments. While the amendments indicate what needs to be done and how, and while they became effective as of 1 July 2016, it is left to the competent authorities of member States and industry actors to provide clarifications about them, through issuing relevant policies that are expected to help achieve consistent implementation. Industry guidelines (European Association for Forwarding, Transport, Logistics and Customs Services, 2016), issued in January 2016 by a forwarders' group, suggest that such policies should, among other things, clarify the following points: how shipping lines will treat VGM from forwarders acting as carriers;[12] how VGM is to be transmitted to carriers; what tolerance level Governments will allow; and which certification programmes will be recognized as equivalent.

An IMO circular letter (IMO, 2016b), issued in February 2016, notes that information about the VGM amendments should be circulated to all relevant parties ahead of their implementation. It states that while the VGM guidelines provide the basis for consistent implementation, "there is still a need for SOLAS Contracting Governments to communicate, at a national level, with all parties involved in maritime containerized transport (e.g. shippers, port authorities, container terminals, shipping agents and carriers) on how methods 1 and 2 will be given effect, together with any measures that will be put in place to ensure compliance".

National implementation guidance by the competent authorities of a number of countries has been posted on the websites of the World Shipping Council[13] and the TT Club.[14] However, it has been reported that by 1 July 2016, around 80 per cent of SOLAS Contracting Parties had yet to publish such guidance (*Lloyd's List*, 2016d). Industry associations have also issued joint guidelines on aspects of the new mandatory requirements (European Chemical Industry Council and others 2016; TT Club, 2015). In any event, adjusting contractual arrangements in light of the new requirements, and communication between regulatory agencies, port authorities, shipping lines, terminals, shippers and exporting companies, still remain crucial for effective national implementation.

Distorted competition

Potentially, stakeholders, including ports, terminals and carriers, in countries where preparations for the implementation of the SOLAS VGM amendments were made earlier could be at a competitive advantage compared with those in other countries where such preparations were not made.

While expressing full support for the new rules, several European industry associations, representing various stakeholders, have called for uniform container weight rules in IMO member States, as variations in implementation may lead to distortion in competition. For countries in Europe for instance, uniform implementation would include the following: a common acceptance of weighing equipment; adopting similar standards on certification that do not have an adverse impact on the functioning of the logistics chain and are not overly restrictive; accepting a five per cent VGM weight variation that would reduce the risk of bottlenecks in ports due to the fact that more of the current equipment could be used; and communicating VGM at the earliest opportunity, and if possible before the packed container is delivered to a port facility, in order to avoid complications (European Association for Forwarding, Transport, Logistics and Customs Services and others, 2016). Similar implementation practices and procedures could also be applied in developing countries.

Consequences of not achieving full compliance by 1 July 2016

SOLAS VGM amendments impose an obligation on the shipper named on the ocean bill of lading,[15] as the party responsible for providing the carrier and the terminal operator with the VGM of the packed container. The shipper may be a manufacturer, ship agent or freight forwarder, for example, and due to the complex nature of the international transport transactions, the person identified as the "shipper" in the bill of lading may not have direct or physical control over the process by which the VGM is determined, or indeed may not be responsible as contractual shipper under the contract of carriage. Nevertheless, the named shipper still remains responsible and must ensure that arrangements are in place for accurately determining and declaring the VGM in compliance with the SOLAS requirements. Normally, the parties to the contract of sale will need to determine by which method the VGM will be obtained[16] and how this information is to be provided to the carrier by the shipper identified in the bill of lading (TT Club, 2015, sections A.1, C.1 and C.2).

On the other hand, SOLAS VGM amendments impose an obligation on the carrier and the terminal operator not to load the container on board a ship for which no VGM has been provided or obtained. Any costs associated with the non-loading, storage, demurrage or eventual return of the container to the shipper should be subject to contractual arrangements between the commercial parties. Also, section 13 of the VGM guidelines provides that in order to allow the continued onward movement of containers received without a declared VGM, the ship master or his or her representative and the terminal representative may obtain the VGM of the packed container on behalf of the shipper. This may be done by weighing the packed container in the terminal or elsewhere, but whether and how to do this, including the apportionment of the costs involved, should be agreed between the commercial parties. If containers are weighed at the terminal and are found to be over the declared VGM, they may also be rejected, and fines and penalties may be imposed on shippers, in accordance with national legislation of the port State. In addition, if ports do not have the facilities to weigh by the 1 July 2016 date, which is in fact not a requirement under SOLAS, containers could be turned away at the gate causing problems, including increased congestion for facilities.[17]

United States position

There has been some confusion regarding the United States position on the SOLAS VGM amendments. Shippers, particularly the Agriculture Transportation Coalition, whose members constitute the majority of United States agriculture and forest products exporters, issued a position paper (Agriculture Transportation Coalition, 2016) in February 2016, calling for a delay in enforcement of VGM until all parties could agree on industry best practices. Concerns were expressed in the paper, including on the competitive disadvantage that the SOLAS VGM amendments would potentially cause to United States exporters, and the fact that the shipper does not know the container weight, but only the weight of cargo, while the rule appears to impose on the shipper liability to certify equipment which is owned/leased/controlled by the carriers. Concerns were also raised that tare weights printed on the back of the container were not necessarily accurate, that the amendments did not account for container or weight variance and that the new rules imposed significant new implementation costs on all participants in the United States export supply chains.

Responding to this, the World Shipping Council, representing global container lines, supported the SOLAS VGM amendments, pointing out, among other things, that the tare weight of containers was painted on the door, and freely available, and that the shipper was not responsible for certifying that the tare weight painted on the container was accurate. This remained the responsibility of the container operator. The World Shipping Council also noted that providing an accurate weight of the packed container was an existing requirement under SOLAS and, therefore, it could not reasonably be argued that the VGM requirements introduced a new cost for weighing. It was actually a cost that should have already been built into the supply chain (World Shipping Council, 2016).

The United States Coast Guard determined that existing United States laws and regulations for providing VGM of containers were equivalent to the requirements in the SOLAS VGM amendments. In a letter to IMO, the United States Coast Guard explained that certain alternative approaches to determining VGM of containers could be equivalent to those outlined in the SOLAS amendments, stating that "shippers, carriers, terminals and maritime associations have outlined multiple acceptable methods for providing VGM, among which are that (a) 'the terminal weighs the container and when duly authorized, verifies the VGM on behalf of the shipper', and (b) 'the shipper and carrier reach agreement whereby the shipper verifies the weight of the cargo, dunnage and other securing material, and the container's tare weight is provided and verified by the carrier'" (United States Coast Guard, 2016). Close to the implementation date, the United States Federal Maritime Commission declared that steps taken by ocean carriers, in cooperation with terminal operators, were encouraging signs that the SOLAS VGM amendments were being implemented in a flexible, practical and pragmatic manner (United States, 2016a).

Outlook

In order to avoid delays and other adverse business consequences, stakeholders in IMO member States need to work together to develop clear procedures for the implementation of the SOLAS VGM amendments as soon as possible. So far, there appears to be no common resolution among shippers and carriers on how the verification of the container weight is to take place on the ground, and views regarding the full implications of the new requirements appear to differ. There also appears to be some frustration among shippers regarding potentially questionable and unspecified administration fees and other service charges imposed by some terminals and carriers (*Journal of Commerce*, 2016b). Additional costs are of particular concern from the perspective of developing countries, many of which already face disproportionately high transport costs. In the meantime, as already briefly noted above, IMO has recommended in a circular (IMO, 2016a) that port State control officers should be pragmatic for the first three months immediately after 1 July 2016, while the stakeholders refine their procedures for documenting, communicating and sharing electronic VGM data. A number of States have already adopted the IMO advice.[18] In this context, it is also worth noting that, according to the International Federation of Freight Forwarders' Associations, during the first two weeks of implementation of the SOLAS VGM amendments, no major disruptions were observed, although there was some lengthening of the transit times (*Lloyd's List,* 2016e).

B. REGULATORY DEVELOPMENTS RELATING TO THE REDUCTION OF GREENHOUSE GAS EMISSIONS FROM INTERNATIONAL SHIPPING AND OTHER ENVIRONMENTAL ISSUES

Reduction of greenhouse gas emissions from international shipping and energy efficiency

As outlined in previous issues of the *Review of Maritime Transport*, a new set of technical and operational measures to increase energy efficiency and reduce emissions of greenhouse gases from international shipping were adopted at IMO in 2011 (IMO, 2011, annex 19).[19] These introduced the Energy Efficiency Design Index for new ships and the Ship Energy Efficiency Management Plan for all ships, included by way of amendments to International Convention for the Prevention of Pollution from Ships (MARPOL 1973 and its Protocol of 1978) annex VI[20] through the introduction of a new chapter 4, entitled "Regulations on energy efficiency for ships", which entered into force on 1 January 2013. A number of guidelines and unified interpretations to assist in the implementation of this set of technical and operational measures were subsequently adopted at IMO in the following years (2012–2015). Furthermore, IMO is continuing its activities to support the 2013 resolution on the promotion of technical cooperation and transfer of technology relating to the improvement of energy efficiency of ships. The issue of possible market-based measures for the reduction of greenhouse gas emissions from international shipping was not addressed during the last four sessions of the IMO Marine Environment Protection Committee (MEPC), each of which postponed further discussion. Information about relevant deliberations and outcomes during the sixty-ninth session of the MEPC (18–22 April 2016) is presented below.

Reduction of greenhouse gas emissions from international shipping

United Nations Framework Convention on Climate Change matters

MEPC considered a document (IMO, 2016c) providing information on the outcomes of the United Nations Climate Change Conferences held in 2015. The Committee welcomed the adoption of the Paris Agreement[21] at the twenty-first session of the Conference of the Parties, under the United Nations Framework Convention on Climate Change, held in Paris, in December 2015, and recognized the continuing role of IMO in mitigating the impact of greenhouse gas emissions from international shipping.

The Paris Agreement

The Paris Agreement was opened for signature on 22 April 2016 at a high-level signature ceremony convened by the United Nations Secretary-General in New York, United States, and has since been ratified by 60 States.[22] In it, States commit to reducing emissions fast enough to achieve the goal of "holding the increase in the global average temperature to well below 2°C above pre-industrial levels and to pursue efforts to limit the temperature increase to 1.5°C" (article 2). States are required to commit to climate mitigation goals by submitting and implementing increasingly ambitious nationally determined contributions in five-year cycles. The review of implementation of individual nationally determined contributions shall be made under an "enhanced transparency framework", comprising a technical expert review and multilateral consideration (article 13). A global stocktake every five years is established "to assess the collective progress towards achieving the purpose of this Agreement and its long-term goals" (article 14), preceded by a mitigation-focused facilitative dialogue in 2018 that will "take stock of collective country actions in relation to progress towards the long-term goals" in the Agreement (paragraph 20 of the decision).[23] The Agreement also establishes a mechanism "to facilitate implementation of and promote compliance with the provisions of this Agreement" through "a committee that shall be expert-based and facilitative in nature and function in a manner that is transparent, non-adversarial and non-punitive" (article 15). However, further details regarding each of these processes are left to future decisions.

In addition, the Agreement recognizes the need for adaptation efforts, "enhancing adaptive capacity, strengthening resilience and reducing vulnerability to climate change, with a view to contributing to sustainable development" (article 7(1)).[24] It also contains a loss and damage provision, which is intended to help vulnerable countries establish early warning systems, risk insurance facilities and other means of coping with climate change impacts (article 8). The Agreement calls for developed countries to provide support, including financial resources for mitigation and adaptation in developing countries under the United Nations Framework Convention on Climate Change (article 9). In addition, developed country Parties commit to communicate "quantitative and qualitative information... including, as available, projected levels of public financial resources to be provided to developing country Parties. Other Parties providing resources are encouraged to communicate biannually such information on a voluntary basis" (article 9 (5)). Parties have also agreed that by 2025, the Conference of the Parties shall set a new "collective quantified goal from a floor of $100 billion per year, taking into account the needs and priorities of developing countries" (paragraph 54 of the decision).

Emission reduction targets for international shipping

Neither the Paris Agreement nor the related decision of the twenty-first Conference of the Parties included any reference to international shipping and aviation. Despite that, progress is expected to be made in each of these sectors with respect to emissions reduction. By way of background, according to the 1997 Kyoto Protocol[25] to the United Nations Framework Convention on Climate Change, the responsibility to limit and reduce international aviation and shipping emissions belongs to the International Civil Aviation Organization and IMO, as the two United Nations specialized agencies responsible for regulating these sectors.

Efforts have been made over the years by both agencies to adopt policies for reducing international emissions for which their respective sectors are responsible, albeit with somewhat slow progress. The Third IMO Greenhouse Gas Study 2014 (IMO, 2014c) estimated that international shipping emitted 796 million tons of CO_2 in 2012, compared with 885 million tons in 2007. This represented 2.2 per cent of the global emissions of CO_2 in 2012, compared with 2.8 per cent in 2007. The study also forecasted CO_2 emissions from shipping to increase by 50, to 250 per cent, by 2050. A similar scenario exists for aviation (International Civil Aviation Organization, 2013). Thus, both agencies, under current policies, may not be delivering sufficient measures to reduce emissions from these sectors, consistent with the 1.5°C/2°C objective of the Paris Agreement. Recently, the United Nations Secretary-General reminded both agencies of the urgent need to address the growth of emissions under their mandates (IMO, 2016d; International Civil Aviation Organization, 2016). The Assembly of the International Civil Aviation Organization, at its next meeting (September–October 2016), is expected to take a decision on the establishment of a global market-based measure for international aviation, to be fully implemented in 2020.[26]

At IMO, MEPC at its sixty-ninth session considered a number of documents related to a possible reduction target for international shipping, which, among other actions:

(a) Proposed that the Organization should develop an "Intended IMO Determined Contribution" on CO_2 reduction for the international shipping sector as a whole, taking account of the Paris Agreement of the twenty-first Conference of the Parties to the United Nations Framework Convention on Climate Change (IMO, 2016e);[27]

(b) Invited the Committee to develop a work plan to define international shipping's fair share of the international community's efforts to curb greenhouse gas emissions (IMO, 2016f);

(c) Proposed four key areas in which progress was needed at that session if IMO was to remain relevant and respond in an appropriate and timely manner to the Paris Agreement: agreement on a work plan to identify shipping's fair share of greenhouse gas emission reductions, continuation of work leading to revised phase 2 Energy Efficiency Design Index requirements, agreement to advance consideration of measures for existing ships, including market-based measures and adoption of a transparent global data collection system (IMO, 2016g);

(d) Commented on views expressed in document MEPC 69/7/2 (IMO, 2016f), concerning the role of international shipping in the reduction of global carbon emissions (IMO, 2016h).

In its submission proposing an "Intended IMO Determined Contribution", the International Chamber of Shipping, representing the global shipping community, noted that the UNCTAD *Review of Maritime Transport 2015* confirms that more than half of current international shipping activity now services developing economies, a proportion that is expected to increase in the future. The submission further argues that it would be inconsistent with the "spirit of Paris" and the principle of common but differentiated responsibilities set out in article 2 of the Paris Agreement to expect that international shipping should decarbonize at the same rate at which developed nations have committed to decarbonize their economies in their intended nationally determined contributions. The International Chamber of Shipping also suggested that, since the concept of reduction targets had not yet been applied to individual Parties under the Paris Agreement, or any other industrial sector, the term "Intended IMO Determined Contribution" was appropriate. This would avoid the implication that some kind of sanction might follow any reduction target not being reached, which was one of the key reasons for the success of the twenty-first Conference of the Parties and consensus being achieved among all nations (IMO, 2016e).

Following discussion,[28] MEPC:

1. Welcomed the Paris Agreement under the United Nations Framework Convention on Climate Change and acknowledged the major achievement of the international community in concluding the agreement;

2. Recognized and commended the current efforts and those already implemented by IMO to enhance the energy efficiency of ships;

3. Widely recognized and agreed that further appropriate improvements related to shipping emissions can and should be pursued;

4. Recognized the role of IMO in mitigating the impact of greenhouse gas emissions from international shipping;
5. Agreed to the common understanding that the approval at this session and subsequent adoption of the data collection system was the priority;
6. Reiterated its endorsement of the three-step approach consisting of data collection, analysis and decision-making;
7. Agreed to establish a working group under this item at MEPC 70, with a view to an in-depth discussion on how to progress the matter, taking into account all documents submitted to this session and comments made, and any further related proposals (IMO 2016i, p. 38).

Energy efficiency for ships

As mentioned above, the Energy Efficiency Design Index for new ships and associated operational energy-efficiency measures for existing ships became mandatory in 2013, with the entry into force of relevant amendments to MARPOL annex VI. The regulations require IMO to review the status of technological developments and, if proven necessary, amend the time periods and the Energy Efficiency Design Index reference line[29] parameters for relevant ship types and reduction rates.

MEPC at its sixty-ninth session considered an interim report of its Correspondence Group tasked with reviewing the status of technological developments relevant to implementing phase 2 of the Energy Efficiency Design Index regulations. It instructed the group to continue considering the status of technological developments for roll-on/roll-off cargo ships and roll-on/roll-off passenger ships and to make recommendations to MEPC 70 on whether the time periods, the Energy Efficiency Design Index reference line parameters for relevant ship types and the reduction rates (in regulation 21 of MARPOL annex VI) should be retained or, if proven necessary, amended (IMO, 2016i, p. 27).

Technical cooperation and transfer of technology

MEPC discussed the importance of implementing the resolution on the promotion of technical cooperation and transfer of technology relating to the improvement of energy efficiency of ships (IMO, 2013, annex 4). It considered a report (IMO, 2015a) which assessed the potential implications and impacts of the implementation of the "Regulations on energy efficiency for ships" in chapter 4 of MARPOL annex VI, in particular on developing countries, as a means of identifying their technology transfer and financial needs. For instance, the report identified that, as with any new regulation, relevant national maritime legislation might need to be updated and training of flag State and port State control officers could be needed. It also indicated that the level of awareness varied from region to region and, within regions, from country to country (IMO, 2015a, annex 1). In addition, the report identified barriers to transfer of technology, in particular to developing States, including associated costs and possible sources of funding to support transfer of technology relating to the improvement of energy efficiency of ships (IMO, 2015a, annex 3). It also noted that the scoping document on the establishment of an inventory of energy efficiency technologies for ships (IMO, 2015a, annex 2) had been forwarded to the Global Maritime Energy Efficiency Partnerships Project. An information portal for energy efficiency technologies for ships was also developed as part of the project.[30]

The Committee approved a model agreement on technological cooperation for the implementation of the regulations in chapter 4 of MARPOL annex VI (IMO, 2015a, annex 4), which would be issued by the IMO secretariat as a circular (MEPC.1/Circ. 861), to encourage its use by member States. It also endorsed a set of recommendations to guide and assist member States, industry and other entities within States in implementing the regulations in chapter 4 of MARPOL annex VI (IMO, 2015a, annex 5).

Further technical and operational measures for enhancing the energy efficiency of international shipping

MEPC approved draft amendments to chapter 4 of MARPOL annex VI (data collection system for fuel consumption of ships) (IMO, 2016i, annex 7), which will be used, among other things, to estimate CO_2 emissions, with a view to adoption at the seventieth session. The amendments contain mandatory requirements for ships of 5,000 gross tons and above to record and report data on their fuel consumption, along with additional data on proxies for the transport work undertaken by the ship.

MEPC reaffirmed its agreement that data collection was the first step in a three-step approach, the second step being data analysis and the third step being decision-making on what further measures, if any, are required (IMO, 2016i, pp. 27–34).

Ship-source pollution and protection of the environment

Air pollution from ships

MEPC continued its work on developing regulations to reduce emissions of other toxic substances from burning fuel oil, particularly NO_x and SO_x. Together with CO_2, these significantly contribute to air pollution from ships, and are covered by MARPOL annex VI, amended in 2008 to introduce more stringent emission controls.

Emissions of nitrogen oxides

As highlighted in previous issues of the *Review of Maritime Transport*, measures have been adopted at IMO that require ships to gradually produce NO_x emissions below certain levels. Requirements for the control of NO_x apply to installed marine diesel engines of over 130 kW output power, and different levels (tiers) of control apply based on a ship's construction date. Tier III limits that apply in emission control areas, for ships constructed from 1 January 2016 onwards, are almost 70 per cent lower than those of the previous tier II. Thus, applying these limits would require additional expensive technology to be installed, including catalytic reduction and exhaustive gas circulation systems. Outside emission control areas designated for NO_x control, tier II limits, required for marine diesel engines installed on ships constructed on or after 1 January 2011, apply.

MEPC continued its consideration of issues related to progressive reductions in NO_x emissions from ship engines, and in particular adopted amendments to MARPOL and the NO_x Technical Code 2008, which are expected to enter into force on 1 September 2017, namely:

- Amendments to regulation 13 of MARPOL annex VI (record requirements for operational compliance with NO_x tier III emission control areas) (IMO, 2016i, annex 2);
- Amendments to the NO_x Technical Code 2008 (testing of gas-fuelled and dual fuel engines) (IMO, 2016i, annex 3).

Emissions of sulphur oxides

With effect from 1 January 2012, MARPOL annex VI established reduced SO_x thresholds for marine bunker fuels, with the global sulphur cap reduced from 4.5 per cent (45,000 parts per million (ppm)) to 3.5 per cent (35,000 ppm), outside emission control areas. The global sulphur cap is expected to be reduced further to 0.5 per cent (5,000 ppm) from 2020. Depending on the outcome of an IMO fuel availability study, to be completed by 2018, this requirement could be deferred to 2025. Within emission control areas where more stringent controls on SO_x emissions apply, the sulphur content of fuel oil must be no more than 0.1 per cent (1,000 ppm) from 1 January 2015.[31] To meet these new requirements, shipowners and operators are adopting a variety of strategies, including installing scrubbers and switching to liquefied natural gas and other low-sulphur fuels.

Experts suggest that shipowners should prepare for a 2020 deadline. For instance, regardless of the IMO outcomes, European Union rules are already in place limiting sulphur in fuel to 0.5 per cent in European waters, as of 1 January 2020 (European Parliament and Council of the European Union, 2012). It has also been reported that as of 1 January 2016, in some of China's key ports, a voluntary sulphur reduction limit of 0.5 per cent applies, which will become mandatory in port waters from 1 January 2017, and then expand to emission control areas by 1 January 2019 (*Lloyd's List*, 2016f; *Fairplay*, 2016a).

The 2010 guidelines for monitoring the worldwide average sulphur content of fuel oils supplied for use on board ships (IMO, 2010, annex I) provide for the calculation of a rolling average of the sulphur content for a three-year period. The rolling average based on the average sulphur contents calculated for the years 2013–2015 is 2.45 per cent for residual fuel and 0.11 per cent for distillate fuel (IMO, 2014d, 2015b and 2016j). Following discussion, MEPC took the following steps:

- Adopted amendments to the 2010 guidelines for monitoring the worldwide average sulphur content of fuel oils supplied for use on board ships (IMO, 2016i, annex 6);
- Agreed to initiate the revision of the guidelines on the approval of systems for removing sulphur from exhaust gases (scrubbers) (IMO, 2016i, p. 59).

Fuel oil quality

MEPC considered a report of the Correspondence Group on fuel oil quality (IMO, 2016k and 2016l), established to consider possible quality-control measures prior to fuel oil being delivered to a ship. MEPC discussed three aspects of possible draft guidance on best practice for fuel oil providers, fuel oil purchasers/users and for member States/coastal States, and instructed the group to continue its work.

MEPC also discussed the ongoing review by the IMO secretariat of the availability of compliant fuel oil to meet the global requirement that the sulphur content of fuel oil used on board ships shall not exceed 0.5 per cent as from 1 January 2020. MEPC agreed in principle that a final decision on the date of implementation[32] of the global 0.5 per cent limit should be taken at MEPC 70, so that maritime administrations and industry can prepare accordingly.

Ballast water management

As seaborne trade continues to grow, with more than 50,000 merchant ships trading internationally, approximately 3–5 billion tons of ballast water per year are being transferred globally by ships (*The Maritime Executive*, 2015). Along with this growth, the risk of introduction and proliferation of non-native species following the discharge of untreated ships' ballast water – one of the four greatest threats to the world's oceans, and one of the major threats to biodiversity – increases as well.[33] Even though ballast water is essential to ensure safe operating conditions and stability for ships, it often carries with it a multitude of marine species, which may survive to establish a reproductive population in the host environment – becoming invasive, out-competing native species, multiplying into pest proportions and potentially bringing devastating consequences.

In February 2004, the BWM Convention was adopted under the auspices of IMO to prevent, minimize and ultimately eliminate the risks to the environment, human health, property and resources arising from the transfer of harmful aquatic organisms carried by ships' ballast water from one region to another. Several related resolutions were also adopted[34] and, since then, a number of guidelines and other instruments have been developed by IMO to encourage the uniform implementation of the Convention.[35] As explained in a recent article (UNCTAD, 2015a)[36] many countries have unilaterally developed or are developing national or local legislation, which remains generally consistent with these guidelines. Such action taken by States will assist in the consistent implementation of the BWM Convention after its entry into force, given also the fact that IMO does not have direct enforcement power. However, sometimes national rules can impose obligations that are different from or additional to the IMO standards.

Upon entry into force of the BWM Convention, shipowners will be obliged to install a ballast water management system to comply with its requirements. However, shipping companies have been concerned that the expensive new treatment equipment they are required to install, even if it has been type-approved in accordance with IMO guidelines, may not be regarded as fully compliant by some Governments. For instance, in the United States, the United States Coast Guard standard is consistent with the IMO Ballast Water Performance standard, but the respective implementing guidelines are not. It appears that the United States Coast Guard considers the IMO treatment technology type-approval guidelines, known as "G8", insufficient, and has adopted its own unilateral regulations. Under these circumstances, shipping companies trading with the United States that will also need to satisfy the United States Coast Guard standards are concerned that, if they decide to install a system approved in accordance with IMO guidelines, it could be accepted by the United States Coast Guard only for a limited time. After that, they would have to install a fully United States Coast Guard approved system, which may give rise to additional costs. However, currently, no treatment technology that has obtained full approval by the United States Coast Guard is commercially available. Nor is there any guarantee that a ballast water management system approved in accordance with IMO guidelines will be later granted full approval and/or found compliant by the United States Coast Guard. Until these issues are fully resolved, some States may continue to be reluctant to ratify the BWM Convention. However, it is also worth noting that, in the meantime, transitional arrangements have been in place for ships entering United States waters, which include (a) allowing them to install a United States Coast Guard accepted system approved in accordance with the current IMO guidelines (G8), as well as (b) granting extensions to dates for installing the required ballast water management systems. At the same time, IMO has agreed that while current IMO guidelines are being revised and might potentially change, ships that install ballast water management systems approved in accordance with the current guidelines (G8) should not be penalized.

The BWM Convention finally fulfilled its remaining entry into force criterion (tonnage), in September 2016, following ratification by Finland.[37] As at 20 September 2016, it had 52 Parties representing 35.14 per cent of the world's merchant gross tonnage, thus slightly exceeding the 35 per cent requirement. As a result of the latest ratification, the BWM Convention will enter into force on 8 September 2017.

At its sixty-ninth session, MEPC agreed to grant final approval to three[38] further ballast water management systems that make use of active substances, and noted that the total number of systems of a type approved by IMO is currently 65. It also re-established a Correspondence Group on the review of the guidelines for approval of ballast water management systems (G8).

MEPC approved two drafts that would be circulated and subsequently adopted upon entry into force of the BWM Convention, namely:

- Draft amendments to regulation B-3 of the BWM Convention (IMO, 2016i, annex 4), providing an appropriate timeline for ships to comply with the ballast water performance standard prescribed in regulation D-2 of the Convention;
- Draft resolution on determination of the date referred to in regulation B-3, as amended, of the BWM Convention (IMO, 2016i, annex 5).

Ballast water management is clearly linked with sustainable development as various international instruments indicate.[39] As part of the general IMO regulatory strategy regarding ship safety, cleaner seas and internationally agreed upon standards, the BWM Convention contributes to the implementation of Sustainable Development Goal 14.[40] In addition, the spread of invasive species has been recognized as one of the greatest threats to biodiversity and to the ecological and economic well-being of the planet.[41] Therefore, prevention, control or eradication of invasive alien species by 2020 is also specifically addressed under Sustainable Development Goal 15, target 15.8.[42]

Legally binding instrument under the United Nations Convention on the Law of the Sea

Worth noting is ongoing related work[43] towards the development of an internationally legally binding instrument under the United Nations Convention on the Law of the Sea on the conservation and sustainable use of marine biological diversity of areas beyond national jurisdiction. Negotiations shall address topics identified in a package agreed in 2011, including "the conservation and sustainable use of marine biological diversity of areas beyond national jurisdiction, in particular, together and as a whole, marine genetic resources, including questions on the sharing of benefits, measures such as area-based management tools, including marine protected areas, environmental impact assessments and capacity-building and the transfer of marine technology".[44] These are all matters of interest to developing countries. An important principle established in the United Nations Convention on the Law of the Sea, the global legal framework for all ocean-related activities, is freedom of the high seas (parts of the sea beyond national jurisdiction), for both coastal and landlocked States. However, such freedom is subject to a number of conditions, as specified by the relevant rules of international law, including the United Nations Convention on the Law of the Sea. For instance, when engaging in various activities in the high seas, States have to consider, among other issues, the positions of other interested States and other interests, including the sustainable use of living resources and the protection of the environment.[45] Also according to the United Nations Convention on the Law of the Sea, the regime of common heritage of humanity applies to the seabed beyond the limits of national jurisdiction. This implies that the resources found there are to be used for the benefit of humanity as a whole with particular consideration for the interests and needs of developing countries.[46] Genetic resources are commercially valuable and their exploitation may in the near future become a promising activity taking place beyond the limits of national jurisdiction. However, neither the United Nations Convention on the Law of the Sea nor the United Nations Convention on Biological Diversity (1992) provide any specific legal framework regarding the international regime applying to genetic resources in areas beyond national jurisdiction. Therefore, a new instrument needs to be negotiated. In addition, as regards benefit sharing and capacity-building, it is critical that the special challenges and needs of developing countries, in particular small island developing States and the least developed countries, are taken into account when drafting the instrument.[47]

Developments regarding the International Convention on Liability and Compensation for Damage in Connection with the Carriage of Hazardous and Noxious Substances by Sea, 1996, as amended by its 2010 Protocol

With more than 200 million tons of chemicals traded annually by tankers, the number of ships carrying hazardous noxious substance cargoes is growing steadily, and so is the risk of related accidents. While it is clearly important to ensure that those who have suffered damage caused by hazardous noxious substance cargoes have access to a comprehensive international liability and compensation regime (IMO, 2016n), no relevant international convention is yet in force. The International Convention on Liability and Compensation for Damage in Connection with the Carriage of Hazardous and Noxious Substances by Sea (HNS Convention), originally adopted in 1996, was amended in 2010 in an effort to overcome a number of perceived obstacles to its ratification. However, despite the recognized importance of an international liability and compensation regime for hazardous noxious substances carried by sea, to date no State has ratified the HNS Convention, as amended in 2010, and it is not clear if and when it will enter into force.[48] This leaves an important gap in the global liability and compensation framework, while a comprehensive and robust international liability and compensation regime is in place in respect of oil pollution from tankers (International Oil Pollution Compensation Fund regime),[49] as well as in respect of bunker oil pollution from ships other than tankers (International Convention on Civil Liability for Bunker Oil Pollution Damage, 2001).

The IMO Legal Committee at its 103rd session (8–10 June 2016) encouraged all States to consider acceding to the 2010 HNS Convention as soon as possible, in order to bring it into force (IMO, 2016m).

Liability and compensation for transboundary pollution damage resulting from offshore oil exploration and exploitation

As also highlighted in the *Review of Maritime Transport 2015*, offshore oil exploration is characterized by particular technical, safety and operational challenges, which are increased in areas prone to earthquakes. Potentially devastating consequences may result from associated oil pollution incidents, both in terms of economic loss and in terms of effects on marine biodiversity and ecosystem health, in particular in sensitive marine environments such as the Arctic. However, no international legal instrument to provide for liability and compensation in cases of accidental or operational oil spills exists at present.

Recent incidents at offshore platforms, such as that in August 2009 on the *Montara* situated in the Australian exclusive economic zone, causing an oil spill reaching the shores of Australia and Indonesia, as well as that of the Deepwater Horizon drilling platform in the Gulf of Mexico, in April 2010, which exploded and killed 11 members of the crew and injured others, and caused a leak of 4 million barrels of oil into the waters of the Gulf, have highlighted the important need for effective regulation of related liability issues. Given that no relevant international legal instrument exists, the need for such an instrument has been considered at the IMO Legal Committee since 2011 and was again raised at the Committee's 103rd session.

The Committee recalled its recommendation that member States should send examples of existing bilateral and regional agreements to the IMO secretariat. In this context, it noted a document (IMO, 2016o) presenting two examples of regional agreements which had been provided by one member State, as well as a revised draft guidance for bilateral/regional arrangements or agreements on liability and compensation issues connected with transboundary oil pollution damage resulting from offshore exploration and exploitation activities (IMO 2016p, annex), which contained an introduction and examples of elements that may be included and/or considered when negotiating bilateral/regional arrangements or agreements; or when developing or revising national law.

Following discussion, the Legal Committee restated its view that there was no compelling need to develop an international instrument to provide for liability and compensation for transboundary pollution damage resulting from offshore exploration and exploitation activities. However, guidance on bilateral or regional agreements should continue to be developed (IMO, 2016m, pp. 19–20).

While according to the United Nations Convention on the Law of the Sea, the global framework convention, it is normally the responsibility of coastal States to adopt adequate legislation with respect to pollution from seabed activities,[50] the extensive risks associated with offshore oil exploration and the considerable potential for extensive transboundary pollution underline the need for an international liability and compensation regime. While the reluctance of IMO to deal with the issue appears to be related to its mandate, which focuses on ship-source pollution (IMO, 2014e), the continued absence of an international liability regime leaves an important gap in the international legal framework and is a matter of concern, in particular for potentially affected developing countries.

Key developments in summary

During the period under review, important developments included, notably, the adoption of the 2030 Agenda for Sustainable Development and the Paris Agreement under the United Nations Framework

Convention on Climate Change, the implementation of which is expected to bring increased opportunities for developing countries. Among regulatory initiatives, worth noting is the entry into force on, 1 July 2016, of the SOLAS VGM amendments, which will contribute to improving the stability and safety of ships and avoiding maritime accidents. Discussions continued at IMO on the reduction of greenhouse gas emissions from international shipping, and on technical cooperation and transfer of technology, particularly to developing countries. Also, progress was made in other areas clearly related to sustainable development. These included work on technical matters related to the imminent entry into force and implementation of the 2004 BWM Convention and on developing an international legally binding instrument under the United Nations Convention on the Law of the Sea on the conservation and sustainable use of marine biological diversity of areas beyond national jurisdiction.

C. OTHER LEGAL AND REGULATORY DEVELOPMENTS AFFECTING TRANSPORTATION

This section highlights key issues in the field of maritime security and safety that may be of particular interest to parties engaged in international trade and transport. These include developments relating to maritime and supply chain security, maritime piracy, unsafe migration by sea, maritime cybersecurity and seafarers' issues.

Maritime and supply chain security

Framework of Standards to Secure and Facilitate Global Trade of the World Customs Organization

As highlighted in previous editions of the *Review of Maritime Transport*, the Framework of Standards to Secure and Facilitate Global Trade (also known as the "SAFE Framework") adopted in 2005 has become a widely accepted instrument as an important reference point for customs and economic operators alike, and has evolved over the years.[51] A number of mutual recognition agreements of respective AEOs continue to be adopted, mostly on a bilateral basis, whereby two customs administrations agree to recognize the AEO authorization issued under the other programme and provide reciprocal benefits to AEOs. It is however hoped that these bilateral agreements will, in due course, form the basis for multilateral agreements at the subregional and regional levels. During the period under review, the number of mutual recognition agreements signed and those under negotiation increased, indicating greater engagement by all relevant stakeholders. As at May 2016, 40 bilateral mutual recognition agreements had been concluded, and a further 30 were being negotiated. In addition, 69 AEO programmes had been established in 79 countries,[52] with an additional 16 programmes planned to be launched in the near future.[53]

Developments in the European Union and in the United States

A summary of relevant developments in the field of maritime and supply chain security in the European Union and in the United States, both important trade partners for many developing countries, is provided here.

The Union Customs Code adopted on 9 October 2013 aims to streamline, simplify and modernize customs legislation, rules and procedures, as well as offer greater legal certainty, uniformity and clarity for businesses and customs officials throughout the European Union (European Parliament and Council of the European Union, 2013). It also aims to help complete the shift by customs to a paperless and fully electronic and interoperable environment, and reinforce swifter customs procedures for compliant and trustworthy AEOs.[54]

While most of the substantive provisions of the Union Customs Code entered into force on 1 May 2016, a transition period before full implementation, expected to last until 31 December 2020 at the latest, has been envisaged, mainly to develop and/or upgrade information technology systems needed to fully implement the legal requirements.[55] Detailed rules aiming to ensure a smooth and gradual transition from the existing regime to the new Union Customs Code are contained in the Transitional Delegated Act (European Commission, 2016a) and the Union Customs Code work programme (European Commission, 2016b). Their practical application is addressed in guidance documents,[56] including the AEO guidelines (European Commission, 2016c) that aim to provide common understanding, and a tool to facilitate the correct and harmonized application of the legal provisions on AEOs.

The AEO guidelines provide general information about the European Union AEO programme, including the benefits of the status and mutual recognition (part 1); describe the AEO criteria and the different aspects of the security requirements and supply chain security (part 2); deal with the overall decision-making process concerning both customs authorities and economic operators (part 3); describe different aspects of the exchange of information between customs authorities including consultation (part 4); cover all aspects related to the management of the already granted status, including monitoring, re-assessment, amendment, suspension and revocation (part 5); and deal with mutual recognition of AEO programmes (part 6).

According to information provided by the European Commission's Taxation and Customs Union Directorate General, as at 10 June 2016, 19,512 applications for AEO authorizations had been submitted and 16,791 authorizations issued. The number of applications rejected up to 10 June 2016 was 2,031, and the number of authorizations revoked was 1,775.[57] The European Union has so far concluded six AEO mutual recognition agreements with third countries, including major trading partners, and further negotiations are currently taking place or will be launched in the near future with others of the most important trading partners.[58]

As regards developments in the United States, it is worth noting that legislative requirements to scan 100 per cent of all United States-bound containers – part of the Safe Port Acts of 2006, highlighted in previous issues of the *Review of Maritime Transport* – were supposed to enter into force in 2012. However, a three-year pilot project found that such a requirement could not be accomplished without causing disruption to the supply chain and at great expense. Therefore, the United States Department of Homeland Security issued successive two-year extensions to the entry into force deadline, in 2012 and 2014.[59] A third deadline extension request was sent to Congress on 2 May 2016, which postponed implementation another time, until May 2018 (*Fairplay*, 2016b).

In May 2016, the Department of Homeland Security issued a request for information (United States, 2016b), seeking input on new programmes, capabilities, models, strategies or approaches that could be used to make progress towards 100 per cent scanning of both containerized and non-containerized maritime cargo bound for the United States. Of particular interest were solutions that built on existing programmes, such as the Customs–Trade Partnership against Terrorism, and leveraged private sector resources and expertise. The desired outcomes were to increase the amount of United States-bound maritime cargo scanned, improve global radiological/nuclear detection capability and capacity, and reduce nuclear and other radioactive materials out of regulatory control in the global maritime shipping environment. Inputs that were to be submitted in June 2016 are intended to be reviewed in the following months (additional information may be requested during this time) with a view to further discussing a limited number of well-qualified submissions in late 2016.

In addition, in a joint letter[60] addressed to the Secretary of Homeland Security, a number of organizations representing United States manufacturers, farmers, wholesalers, retailers, importers, agribusiness, distributors and transportation and logistics providers reiterated their position against the 100 per cent scanning requirement as impractical, ineffective and a danger to global commerce, as illustrated by a series of pilot tests. The letter also expressed concern about some of the issues raised in the request of the United States Department of Homeland Security for information, particularly a potential expansion of the mandate to non-containerized cargo and the search for "quick wins". While fully supporting the two-year waiver of the 100 per cent scanning, the letter urged that the Administration, instead of going through a waiver exercise every two years, should recommend to the Congress a comprehensive re-evaluation of the 100 per cent scanning requirement and focus on finding practical supply chain security solutions.

Programmes such as the Container Security Initiative and the Customs–Trade Partnership against Terrorism, in which representatives of the trade community participate, continue to be implemented with the aim of increasing supply chain security.[61] The Container Security Initiative is now operational at 58 ports in North America, Europe, Asia, Africa, the Middle East, and Latin and Central America, pre-screening over 80 per cent of all maritime containerized cargo imported into the United States,[62] while the Customs–Trade Partnership against Terrorism currently includes more than 10,000 certified partners from the trade community. As with AEOs, members of the Customs–Trade Partnership against Terrorism are considered low risk and are therefore less likely to be examined. The Customs–Trade Partnership against Terrorism signed its first mutual recognition agreement in June 2007 and, since then, has signed similar arrangements with nine countries or territories and the European Union.[63]

In addition, through the voluntary Importer Self-Assessment programme, in place since June 2002, interested importers who are participating members of the Customs–Trade Partnership against Terrorism may assume responsibility for monitoring their own compliance in exchange for benefits,[64] while the Trusted Trader programme, already in the test phase, aims to join the existing Customs–Trade Partnership against Terrorism and Importer Self-Assessment programmes, integrating and streamlining the processes of supply chain security and trade compliance within one partnership programme.[65] Worth noting in this context is the Proliferation Security Initiative, which aims to stop trafficking of weapons of mass destruction, and related materials, and is currently endorsed by over 100 countries around the world.[66]

International Organization for Standardization

Previous issues of the *Review of Maritime Transport* reported on developments related to the International Organization for Standardization (ISO) 28000 series of standards entitled "Security management systems for the supply chain," which are designed to help the industry successfully plan for, and recover from, any ongoing disruptive event. The core standard in this series is ISO 28000:2007, "Specification for security management systems for the supply chain", which serves as an umbrella management system that enhances all aspects of security – risk assessment, emergency preparedness, business continuity, sustainability, recovery and resilience and/or disaster management – whether relating to terrorism, piracy, cargo theft, fraud or many of the other security disruptions. The standard also serves as a basis for AEO and Customs–Trade Partnership against Terrorism certifications. Various organizations adopting such standards may tailor an approach compatible with their existing operating systems.

There have been no new developments to report during the period under review. However, for ease of reference, the current status of the ISO 28000 series is detailed in box 5.1.

Box 5.1 Current status of the International Organization for Standardization 28000 series of standards

Standards published

- **ISO 28000:2007**, "Specification for security management systems for the supply chain".

This standard provides the overall "umbrella" standard. It is a generic, risk-based, certifiable standard for all organizations, all disruptions and all sectors. It is widely in use and constitutes a stepping stone to the AEO and Customs–Trade Partnership against Terrorism certifications.

- **ISO 28001:2007**, "Security management systems for the supply chain – Best practices for implementing supply chain security, assessments and plans".

This standard is designed to assist the industry to meet the requirements for AEO status.

- **ISO 28002:2011**, "Security management systems for the supply chain – Development of resilience in the supply chain – Requirements with guidance for use".

This standard provides additional focus on resilience, and emphasizes the need for an ongoing, interactive process to prevent, respond to and assure continuation of an organization's core operations after a major disruptive event.

- **ISO 28003:2007**, "Security management systems for the supply chain – Requirements for bodies providing audit and certification of supply chain security management systems".

This standard provides guidance for accreditation and certification bodies.

- **ISO 28004-1:2007**, "Security management systems for the supply chain – Guidelines for the implementation of ISO 28000 – Part 1: General principles".

This standard provides generic advice on the application of ISO 28000:2007. It explains the underlying principles of ISO 28000 and describes the intent, typical inputs, processes and typical outputs for each requirement of ISO 28000. The objective is to aid the understanding and implementation of ISO 28000. ISO 28004-1:2007 does not create additional requirements to those specified in ISO 28000, nor does it prescribe mandatory approaches to the implementation of ISO 28000.

- **ISO/PAS 28004-2:2014**, "Security management systems for the supply chain – Guidelines for the implementation of ISO 28000 – Part 2: Guidelines for adopting ISO 28000 for use in medium and small seaport operations".

This standard provides guidance to medium-sized and small ports that wish to adopt ISO 28000. It identifies supply chain risk and threat scenarios, procedures for conducting risk/threat assessments and evaluation criteria for measuring conformance and effectiveness of the documented security plans in accordance with ISO 28000 and ISO 28004 implementation guidelines.

- **ISO/PAS 28004-3:2014**, "Security management systems for the supply chain – Guidelines for the implementation of ISO 28000 – Part 3: Additional specific guidance for adopting ISO 28000 for use by medium and small businesses (other than marine ports)".

This standard was developed to supplement ISO 28004-1 by providing additional guidance to small and medium-sized businesses (other than marine ports) that wish to adopt ISO 28000. The additional guidance in ISO/PAS 28004-3:2012, while amplifying the general guidance provided in the main body of ISO 28004-1, does not conflict with the general guidance nor does it amend ISO 28000.

- **ISO/PAS 28004-4:2014**, "Security management systems for the supply chain – Guidelines for the implementation of ISO 28000 – Part 4: Additional specific guidance on implementing ISO 28000 if compliance with ISO 28001 is a management objective".

This standard provides additional guidance for organizations adopting ISO 28000 that also wish to incorporate the best practices identified in ISO 28001 as a management objective in their international supply chains.

- **ISO 28005-1:2013**, "Security management systems for the supply chain – Electronic port clearance (EPC) – Part 1: Message structures".

This standard deals with computer-to-computer data transmission.

- **ISO 28005-2:2011**, "Security management systems for the supply chain – Electronic port clearance (EPC) – Part 2: Core data elements".

This standard contains technical specifications that facilitate efficient exchange of electronic information between ship and shore for coastal transit or port calls, as well as definitions of core data elements that cover all requirements for ship-to-shore and shore-to-ship reporting as defined in the International Ship and Port Facilities Security Code, the IMO Convention on Facilitation of International Maritime Traffic, 1965, and relevant IMO resolutions.

- **ISO/PAS 28007-1:2015**, "Ships and marine technology – Guidelines for private maritime security companies (PMSC) providing privately contracted armed security personnel on board ships (and pro forma contract) – Part 1: General".

This standard provides guidelines containing additional sector-specific recommendations, which companies (organizations) that comply with ISO 28000 can implement to demonstrate that they provide privately contracted armed security personnel on board ships.

- **ISO 20858:2007**, "Ships and marine technology – Maritime port facility security assessments and security plan development".

This standard establishes a framework to assist marine port facilities in specifying the competence of personnel to conduct a marine port facility security assessment and to develop a security plan as required by the International Ship and Port Facilities Security Code. In addition, it establishes certain documentation requirements designed to ensure that the process used in performing the duties described above is recorded in a manner that permits independent verification by a qualified and authorized agency.

Combating maritime piracy and armed robbery

As the issues covered in a recent two-part report on maritime piracy prepared by UNCTAD (UNCTAD 2014b and 2014c) show, maritime piracy has evolved from a localized maritime transport concern into a cross-sectoral global challenge, with a range of important repercussions for the development prospects of affected regional economies, as well as for global trade. Just as the ships targeted by pirates, maritime piracy remains a "moving target". Given the issues at stake and the broad range of costs and trade-related implications of maritime piracy at both the regional and the global levels, sustained long-term efforts to combat and repress piracy clearly remain a matter of strategic importance. Addressing the challenge of piracy in an effective manner requires strong cooperation at the political, economic, legal, diplomatic and military levels, as well as collaboration between diverse public and private sector stakeholders across regions.

The Maritime Safety Committee at its ninety-sixth session (11–20 May 2016) noted that the number of acts of piracy and armed robbery against ships reported to IMO, which occurred or were attempted in 2015, was 303, a modest increase by 12 incidents (4.1 per cent) over the 291 reported in 2014. The areas most affected were the Straits of Malacca and Singapore (134), the South China Sea (81) and the western Indian Ocean with 38 in total, followed by West Africa (35), South America and the Caribbean (5), the North Atlantic and Pacific Ocean (4), the Yellow Sea (4) and the Mediterranean Sea (2). The number of incidents caused by Somalia-based pirates (Arabian Sea) increased to 15, from 12 in 2014, still significantly lower than the 78 incidents reported in 2007 when Somalia-based piracy was prevalent. No ship was reported hijacked by Somali pirates in 2015.

In addition, approximately 46.5 per cent of attacks worldwide were reported to have occurred or to have been attempted in territorial waters, largely due to an increase in armed robbery activity in the Strait of

Malacca. Furthermore, in 141 (46.5 per cent) of the 303 reports received, the crews were violently attacked by groups of one to four people, who also reportedly carried knives or guns in 109 (77.3 per cent) out of those 141 incidents. The data also reveal that during the period under review, one crew member was reported killed in West Africa. This number remains the same as in 2014. About 71 crew members were reportedly taken hostage or kidnapped. This was a significant decrease from 137 incidents reported in 2014. In 2015, the crew were assaulted in 25 cases, almost half the number of cases reported in 2014 (49 cases). Worldwide, 5 ships were reportedly hijacked, as compared with 21 in 2014. The total number of incidents of piracy and armed robbery against ships reported to have occurred or to have been attempted from 1984 to the end of December 2015 has risen to 7,346 (IMO, 2016q).

The Maritime Safety Committee also noted the release of a new regional guide to counter piracy and armed robbery against ships in Asia by the Information Sharing Centre of the Regional Cooperation Agreement on Combating Piracy and Armed Robbery against Ships in Asia, as well as the formal opening of the Djibouti Regional Training Centre building, intended to support regional maritime security and counter-piracy training in the region. In addition, expanding the use of a Long-Range Identification and Tracking Distribution Facility for the automatic provision of long-range identification and tracking information on flag States to the Maritime Trade Information Sharing Centre – Gulf of Guinea was supported, because of an increasing number of piracy attacks there, and the positive results from its use in the Gulf of Aden and the western Indian Ocean (IMO, 2016r).

Unsafe mixed migration by sea

The Maritime Safety Committee approved a circular (IMO, 2016s) aiming to promote awareness and cooperation among IMO member States so that they may address more effectively unsafe practices associated with the trafficking, smuggling or transport of migrants by sea, which have an international dimension. Recommended actions by States include compliance with international obligations, including ensuring compliance with SOLAS,[67] and taking appropriate action against masters, officers and crew members engaged in unsafe practices; cooperation to the fullest extent possible to prevent and suppress unsafe practices associated with the trafficking, smuggling or transport of migrants by sea, in conformity with the international law of the sea and all generally accepted relevant international instruments; and measures and procedures that can be followed when States have reasonable grounds to suspect that a ship is engaged in unsafe practices associated with the trafficking, smuggling or transport of migrants by sea.

Measures towards enhancing maritime cybersecurity

With the ever-increasing use of software, the Internet and technologies, the importance of cybersecurity continues to increase. In recognition of this fact, the Maritime Safety Committee at its ninety-sixth session approved interim guidelines on maritime cyber risk management (IMO, 2016t). The guidelines provide recommendations aiming to safeguard shipping from current and emerging cyberthreats and vulnerabilities, due to the ever increasing use of software, the Internet and technologies on board ships and potential cyberattacks against them. Therefore, appropriate technical and procedural controls need to be in place to protect the company, ship operations, and information and data pertaining to a ship and its crew, passengers and cargo. The guidelines also include functional elements that support effective cyber risk management. For detailed guidance, users of the guidelines shall also refer to IMO member Governments' and flag administrations' requirements, as well as to relevant international and industry standards and best practices.[68]

Seafarers' issues

Over 1.2 million seafarers operate ships around the world,[69] and the vast majority of them come from developing countries. Establishing internationally agreed standards on the working conditions of seafarers, providing them with necessary training and protecting their welfare are important, not only for them, but also for sustainable development, as these help to improve the ability of the global shipping industry to operate ships safely and in an environmentally responsible manner.

Amendments to the Maritime Labour Convention, 2006

The Maritime Labour Convention, 2006, which consolidates and updates more than 68 international labour standards relating to seafarers, and sets out their responsibilities and rights with regard to labour and social matters in the maritime sector, entered into force on 20 August 2013. As at 23 September 2016, it had 79 Parties, representing over 91 per cent of the world's gross tonnage,[70] and is considered the fourth pillar of the global maritime regulatory regime.

At times, certain shipowners who do not take their responsibilities seriously and find themselves in financial difficulty abandon seafarers in ports far from home without fuel, food, water or medical care and without pay for months. The IMO Legal Committee noted that, as at March 2016, the ILO Abandonment of Seafarers Database listed 192 abandoned merchant ships, some dating back to 2006, with abandonment cases still unresolved. Therefore, it agreed that it should keep the issue under consideration.[71]

In order to better protect abandoned seafarers and to provide financial security for compensation to seafarers and their families in cases of seafarers' death or long-term disability,[72] amendments to the Maritime Labour Convention were approved by the International Labour Conference in June 2014, and are set to enter into force on 18 January 2017.

Fair treatment of seafarers in the event of a maritime accident

The International Transport Workers' Federation provided further information (IMO, 2016u) to the IMO Legal Committee on the analysis of the laws of IMO member States implementing the 2006 guidelines on fair treatment of seafarers in the event of a maritime accident (IMO, 2015c). Such analysis had revealed that member States had adopted different approaches with regard to the implementation of the guidelines, including their scope of application; the extent to which the legal principles contained in the guidelines were adopted; and the types of legal instruments employed. The reasons for those different approaches appear to include different interpretations by member States; different gap analyses revealing that the legal principles contained in the guidelines already exist to greater or lesser degrees in the national laws of member States; different legal systems and legislative drafting traditions between member States; and different government ministries and/or independent legal entities within member States that implement, administer and/or enforce the guidelines (IMO, 2016u).

As the Legal Committee concluded, different approaches in the implementation of the guidelines could be streamlined through the development of guidance.

International Labour Organization Convention on Seafarers' Identity Documents (Revised), 2003 (No. 185)

As highlighted in the *Review of Maritime Transport 2015*, the Convention on Seafarers' Identity Documents, 2003 (No. 185), relates to the issuance and recognition of the seafarers' identity document, which facilitates the temporary admission of seafarers to foreign territory, for the purposes of their well-being while in port, accessing onshore welfare facilities or taking shore leave, and for transit through a country related to the operation of ships. These are all vital elements for the realization of decent working conditions for seafarers, as part of the core mandate of the ILO.

Promoting the issuance of seafarers' identity documents by member States was the aim of amendments introduced to Convention No. 185. Discussions on those amendments were held during an ILO meeting of the Ad Hoc Tripartite Maritime Committee (10–12 February 2016). The amendments aim to identify cost-effective technical and administrative solutions to overcome problems that have arisen in the implementation of the Convention and to encourage further ratifications, particularly by ILO member States with maritime interests. It is worth noting that, although Convention No. 185 was adopted in 2003, only 32 out of 187 ILO member States had ratified it or were provisionally applying it as of 30 June 2016,[73] and that number includes only a few port States. Consequently, countries that had made considerable investment to properly implement Convention No. 185 could count on only a few other countries to recognize the seafarers' identity documents issued under it. In addition, only a few countries that had ratified Convention No. 185 were in a position to actually issue seafarers' identity documents conforming to it. These were also hampered by the fact that the fingerprint technology and biometric products required in annex I of the Convention were already considered out of date and were not used by the border authorities of many countries concerned. Many of these countries are using the International Civil Aviation Organization standards for travel documents instead, which are exclusively based on the facial image in a contactless chip as the biometric, rather than a fingerprint template in a two-dimensional barcode.

After discussion, the Committee adopted the proposed amendments to annexes I, II and III of Convention No. 158. Amendments established that the seafarers' identity document shall conform to the mandatory requirements contained in International Civil Aviation Organization document 9303 on machine-readable travel documents, which are now universally followed for travel, and similar documents. In the meantime, member States that were already implementing

Convention No. 185 were given sufficient time to make any necessary revisions to their national seafarers' identity documents and procedures for implementing the proposed amendments.[74]

Key developments in summary

During the period under review, enhancements were made to regulatory measures in the field of maritime and supply chain security and their implementation. Areas of progress included the implementation of AEO programmes and an increasing number of bilateral mutual recognition agreements that will, in due course, form the basis for the recognition of AEOs at a multilateral level. As regards piracy and armed robbery against ships, the number of incidents reported to IMO to have occurred or to have been attempted in 2015, was 303, a modest increase of 4.1 per cent, compared with 2014. The number of crew members taken hostage or kidnapped, those assaulted and the number of ships hijacked decreased significantly compared with 2014. In addition, a circular on combating unsafe practices associated with mixed migration by sea and interim guidelines on maritime cyber risk management were approved. In the context of ILO conventions, progress was also made on the issue of recognition of seafarers' identity documents for seafarers and improving their living and working conditions.

D. STATUS OF CONVENTIONS

A number of international conventions in the field of maritime transport were prepared or adopted under the auspices of UNCTAD. Table 5.1 provides information on the status of ratification of each of those conventions as at 30 June 2016.

Table 5.1 Contracting States Parties to selected international conventions on maritime transport, as at 30 June 2016

Title of convention	Date of entry into force or conditions for entry into force	Contracting States
United Nations Convention on a Code of Conduct for Liner Conferences, 1974	6 October 1983	Algeria, Bangladesh, Barbados, Belgium, Benin, Burkina Faso, Burundi, Cameroon, Cabo Verde, Central African Republic, Chile, China, Congo, Costa Rica, Côte d'Ivoire, Cuba, Czechia, Democratic Republic of the Congo, Egypt, Ethiopia, Finland, France, Gabon, Gambia, Ghana, Guatemala, Guinea, Guyana, Honduras, India, Indonesia, Iraq, Italy, Jamaica, Jordan, Kenya, Kuwait, Lebanon, Liberia, Madagascar, Malaysia, Mali, Mauritania, Mauritius, Mexico, Montenegro, Morocco, Mozambique, Niger, Nigeria, Norway, Pakistan, Peru, Philippines, Portugal, Qatar, Republic of Korea, Romania, Russian Federation, Saudi Arabia, Senegal, Serbia, Sierra Leone, Slovakia, Somalia, Spain, Sri Lanka, Sudan, Sweden, Togo, Trinidad and Tobago, Tunisia, United Republic of Tanzania, Uruguay, Venezuela (Bolivarian Republic of), Zambia **(76)**
United Nations Convention on the Carriage of Goods by Sea, 1978 (Hamburg Rules)	1 November 1992	Albania, Austria, Barbados, Botswana, Burkina Faso, Burundi, Cameroon, Chile, Czechia, Dominican Republic, Egypt, Gambia, Georgia, Guinea, Hungary, Jordan, Kazakhstan, Kenya, Lebanon, Lesotho, Liberia, Malawi, Morocco, Nigeria, Paraguay, Romania, Saint Vincent and the Grenadines, Senegal, Sierra Leone, Syrian Arab Republic, Tunisia, Uganda, United Republic of Tanzania, Zambia **(34)**
International Convention on Maritime Liens and Mortgages, 1993	5 September 2004	Albania, Benin, Congo, Ecuador, Estonia, Lithuania, Monaco, Nigeria, Peru, Russian Federation, Spain, Saint Kitts and Nevis, Saint Vincent and the Grenadines, Serbia, the Syrian Arab Republic, Tunisia, Ukraine, Vanuatu **(18)**
United Nations Convention on International Multimodal Transport of Goods, 1980	Not yet in force – requires 30 Contracting Parties	Burundi, Chile, Georgia, Lebanon, Liberia, Malawi, Mexico, Morocco, Rwanda, Senegal, Zambia **(11)**
United Nations Convention on Conditions for Registration of Ships, 1986	Not yet in force – requires 40 Contracting Parties with at least 25 per cent of the world's tonnage as per annex III to the Convention	Albania, Bulgaria, Côte d'Ivoire, Egypt, Georgia, Ghana, Haiti, Hungary, Iraq, Liberia, Libya, Mexico, Morocco, Oman, Syrian Arab Republic **(15)**
International Convention on Arrest of Ships, 1999	14 September 2011	Albania, Algeria, Benin, Bulgaria, Congo, Ecuador, Estonia, Latvia, Liberia, Spain, Syrian Arab Republic **(11)**

Note: For official status information, see the United Nations Treaty Collection (https://treaties.un.org).

REFERENCES

Agriculture Transportation Coalition (2016). Agriculture Transportation Coalition Position Paper: Safety of Life at Sea (SOLAS) Container Weight Documentation. Available at http://agtrans.org/wp-content/uploads/2016/02/AgTC-SOLAS-position-paper.pdf (accessed 29 July 2016).

European Association for Forwarding, Transport, Logistics and Customs Services (CLECAT) (2016). CLECAT guidelines on the implementation of the SOLAS amendments on container weighing. January. Available at http://www.clecat.org/media/CLECAT_guidelines_on_container_weighing.pdf (accessed 29 September 2016).

European Association for Forwarding, Transport, Logistics and Customs Services, European Shippers' Council, European Seaports Organization, Federation of European Private Port Operators and Terminals (2016). SOLAS requirements for weighing of containers: European organizations representing shippers, freight forwarders, terminal operators and port authorities call on national authorities to take action in coordination to preserve level playing field. 20 April. Available at https://www.espo.be/media/espoviews/2016.04.20_Joint_Statement_-_Weighing_of_Containers_-_CLECAT_ESC_ESPO_FEPORT.pdf (accessed 29 September 2016).

European Chemical Industry Council, European Association for Forwarding, Transport, Logistics and Customs Services, European Shippers' Council and Global Shippers' Forum (2016). Industry guidance for the implementation of SOLAS chapter VI, regulation 2 and the associated IMO guidelines regarding the verified gross mass of a container carrying cargo. Available at http://www.otmbe.org/infotheek/downloads/informatie/658-joint-industry-guidance-mandatory-weighing-of-containers-cefic-esc-clecat-gsf/file (accessed 29 July 2016).

European Commission (2016a). Commission Delegated Regulation (EU) 2016/341 of 17 December 2015 supplementing Regulation (EU) No. 952/2013 of the European Parliament and of the Council as regards transitional rules for certain provisions of the Union Customs Code where the relevant electronic systems are not yet operational and amending Delegated Regulation (EU) 2015/2446. Available at http://eur-lex.europa.eu/legal-content/EN/TXT/PDF/?uri=OJ:L:2016:069:FULL&from=NL (accessed 29 July 2016).

European Commission (2016b). Commission Implementing Decision (EU) 2016/578 of 11 April 2016 establishing the work programme relating to the development and deployment of the electronic systems provided for in the Union Customs Code. Available at http://eur-lex.europa.eu/legal-content/EN/TXT/PDF/?uri=CELEX:32016D0578&from=EN (accessed 29 July 2016).

European Commission (2016c). Authorized Economic Operators Guidelines. 11 March. TAXUD/B2/047/2011, Rev. 6. Available at http://ec.europa.eu/taxation_customs/sites/taxation/files/resources/documents/customs/policy_issues/customs_security/aeo_guidelines_en.pdf (accessed 14 October 2016).

European Parliament and Council of the European Union (2012). Directive 2012/33/EU of the European Parliament and of the Council of 21 November 2012, amending Council Directive 1999/32/EC as regards the sulphur content of marine fuels. Available at http://eur-lex.europa.eu/legal-content/EN/TXT/?uri=CELEX:32012L0033 (accessed 29 July 2016).

European Parliament and Council of the European Union (2013). Regulation (EU) No. 952/2013 of the European Parliament and of the Council of 9 October 2013 laying down the Union Customs Code. Available at http://eur-lex.europa.eu/legal-content/EN/TXT/PDF/?uri=CELEX:32013R0952&rid=1 (accessed 29 July 2016).

Fairplay (2016a). China investigates shore power to reduce emissions in port area. 14 July. Available at http://fairplay.ihs.com/ports/article/4271701/china-investigates-shore-power-to-reduce-emissions-in-port-areas (accessed 12 October 2016).

Fairplay (2016b). United States seeks "quick wins" towards 100 per cent container scanning. 12 May. Available at http://fairplay.ihs.com/safety-regulation/article/4268041/us-seeks-%E2%80%9Cquick-wins%E2%80%9D-towards-100-container-scanning (accessed 12 October 2016).

International Civil Aviation Organization (2013). *International Civil Aviation Organization Environmental Report 2013*. Available at http://cfapp.icao.int/Environmental-Report-2013/ (accessed 29 July 2016).

International Civil Aviation Organization (2016). United Nations Secretary-General underscores aviation's vital role in sustainable development and climate change. 12 February. Available at http://www.icao.int/Newsroom/Pages/United-Nations-Secretary-General-Underscores-Aviation%E2%80%99s-Vital-Role-in-Sustainable-Development-and-Climate-Change.aspx (accessed 29 July 2016).

IMO (2010). Report of the Marine Environment Protection Committee at its sixty-first session. MEPC 61/24. London.

IMO (2011). Report of the Marine Environment Protection Committee at its sixty-second session. MEPC 62/24. London.

IMO (2013). Report of the Marine Environment Protection Committee at its sixty-fifth session. MEPC 65/222. London.

IMO (2014a). Report of the Maritime Safety Committee on its ninety-fourth session. MSC/94/21. London.

IMO (2014b). Guidelines regarding the verified gross mass of a container carrying cargo.

MSC.1/Circ.1475. London.

IMO (2014c). Third IMO Greenhouse Gas Study 2014. Final report. MEPC 67/INF.3. London. Available at http://www.imo.org/en/OurWork/Environment/PollutionPrevention/AirPollution/Documents/Third%20Greenhouse%20Gas%20Study/GHG3%20Executive%20Summary%20and%20Report.pdf (accessed 13 October 2016).

IMO (2014d). Sulphur monitoring for 2013. MEPC 67/4. London.

IMO (2014e). Implications of the United Nations Convention on the Law of the Sea for the International Maritime Organization. Study by the secretariat of the International Maritime Organization. LEG/MISC.8. London.

IMO (2015a). Final report of the Ad Hoc Expert Working Group on Facilitation of Transfer of Technology for Ships. Note by the Chair of the Ad Hoc Expert Working Group. MEPC 69/5. London.

IMO (2015b). Air pollution and energy efficiency. Sulphur monitoring for 2014. MEPC 68/3/2. London.

IMO (2015c). Fair treatment of seafarers in the event of a maritime accident. Analysis of the questionnaire on the implementation of the 2006 Guidelines on fair treatment of seafarers in the event of a maritime accident. Submitted by the International Transport Workers' Federation, the International Federation of Shipmasters' Associations, Comité Maritime International and InterManager. LEG 102/4. London.

IMO (2016a). Advice to administrations, port State control authorities, companies, port terminals and masters regarding the SOLAS requirements for verified gross mass of packed containers. MSC.1/Circ.1548. London.

IMO (2016b). IMO Circular Letter No. 3624. 10 February. London.

IMO (2016c). Outcomes of the United Nations Climate Change Conferences held in Bonn in June, August and October 2015 and Paris in December 2015. Note by the Secretariat. MEPC 69/7. London.

IMO (2016d). United Nations Secretary-General visits IMO. 3 February. Available at http://www.imo.org/en/MediaCentre/PressBriefings/Pages/04-UNSG-visit-.aspx (accessed 29 July 2016).

IMO (2016e). Proposal to develop an Intended IMO Determined Contribution on CO_2 reduction for international shipping. Submitted by the International Chamber of Shipping. MEPC 69/7/1. London.

IMO (2016f). International shipping's share in international efforts to limit the rise of global average temperature. Submitted by Belgium, France, Germany, the Marshall Islands, Morocco and Solomon Islands. MEPC 69/7/2. London.

IMO (2016g). An appropriate IMO response to the Paris Agreement. Submitted by the Clean Shipping Coalition. MEPC 69/7/3. London.

IMO (2016h). Establishing a process for considering shipping's appropriate contribution to reducing CO_2 emissions. Submitted by World Shipping Council, Cruise Lines International Association, Intertanko and International Parcel Tankers Association. MEPC 69/7/4. London.

IMO (2016i). Report of the Marine Environment Protection Committee on its sixty-ninth session. MEPC 69/21. London.

IMO (2016j). Sulphur monitoring for 2015. MEPC 69/5/7. London.

IMO (2016k). Report of the Correspondence Group on fuel oil quality. Submitted by the United States. MEPC 69/5/3. London.

IMO (2016l). Report of the Correspondence Group on fuel oil quality – Collation of comments. Submitted by the United States. MEPC 69/INF.7. London.

IMO (2016m). Report of the Legal Committee on the work of its 103rd session. LEG 103/14. London.

IMO (2016n). Address of the Secretary-General at the opening of the 103rd session of the Legal Committee. 8 June. Available at http://www.imo.org/en/MediaCentre/SecretaryGeneral/Secretary-GeneralsSpeechesToMeetings/Pages/LEG-103-opening.aspx (accessed 29 July 2016).

IMO (2016o). Liability and compensation issues connected with transboundary pollution damage from offshore exploration and exploitation activities. Note by the secretariat. LEG 103/INF.2. London.

IMO (2016p). Liability and compensation issues connected with transboundary pollution damage from offshore exploration and exploitation activities. Guidance for bilateral/regional arrangements or agreements on liability and compensation issues connected with transboundary oil pollution damage resulting from offshore exploration and exploitation activities. Submitted by Indonesia and Denmark. LEG 103/13/1. London.

IMO (2016q). Reports on acts of piracy and armed robbery against ships. Annual Report – 2015. MSC.4/Circ.232. London.

IMO (2016r). Report of the Marine Safety Committee on its ninety-sixth session. MSC/96/25. London.

IMO (2016s). Interim measures for combating unsafe practices associated with the trafficking, smuggling or transport of migrants by sea. MSC.1/Circ.896/Rev.2. London.

IMO (2016t). Interim guidelines on maritime cyber risk management. MSC.1/Circ.1526. London.

IMO (2016u). Fair treatment of seafarers in the event of a maritime accident. Submitted by the International Transport Workers' Federation. LEG 103/5. London.

IMO (2016v). Guidelines on the Facilitation Aspects of Protecting the Maritime Transport Network from Cyberthreats. The Guidelines on Cybersecurity On Board Ships. Submitted by the International Chamber of Shipping, International Union of Marine Insurance, Baltic and International Maritime Council, International Association of Independent Tanker Owners, Cruise Lines International Association and International Association of Dry Cargo Shipowners. MSC 96/4/1. London.

INTTRA (2015). INTTRA survey finds widespread fears of disruption and lack of preparedness for new SOLAS container weight requirements. 2 December. Available at http://www.inttra.com/pr/article/inttra-survey-finds-widespread-fears-of-disruption-and-lack-of-preparedness-for-new-solas-container-weight-requirements (accessed 29 July 2016).

Journal of Commerce (2016a). Shippers, forwarders still confused over container weight rule. 23 May. Available at http://www.joc.com/regulation-policy/transportation-regulations/international-transportation-regulations/survey-finds-shippers-forwarders-fazed-over-container-weight-rule_20160523.html (accessed 29 July 2016).

Journal of Commerce (2016b). Shipper frustration with VGM fees intensifies. 1 July. Available at http://www.joc.com/regulation-policy/transportation-regulations/international-transportation-regulations/global-solas-disruption-minimal-shipper-frustration-over-fees-intensifies_20160701.html (accessed 29 July 2016).

Lloyd's List (2016a). Supply chain at risk as box weight rules approach. 29 January. Available at https://www.lloydslist.com/ll/sector/containers/article512218.ece (accessed 29 July 2016).

Lloyd's List (2016b). Containers – A weight on their minds. 9 February.

Lloyd's List (2016c). International Federation of Freight Forwarders' Associations calls for clarity on new box weight data requirements. 23 February.

Lloyd's List (2016d). The weight is over. 30 June.

Lloyd's List (2016e). VGM disruption limited in first two weeks, say forwarders. 19 July.

Lloyd's List (2016f). Outlook 2016: Environmental wrangling kicks a political football into play. 7 January.

Paris Memorandum of Understanding on Port State Control (2016). Paris Memorandum of Understanding agrees on a concentrated inspection campaign on MARPOL annex VI in 2018. 30 May. Available at https://www.parismou.org/paris-mou-agrees-concentrated-inspection-campaign-marpol-annex-vi-2018 (accessed 29 July 2016).

Rajamani L (2016). Ambition and differentiation in the 2015 Paris Agreement: Interpretative possibilities and underlying politics. *International and Comparative Law Quarterly*. 65(2):493–514.

The Maritime Executive (2015). Ballast Water Management Convention So Close... 24 November. Available at http://maritime-executive.com/article/ballast-water-management-convention-so-close (accessed 12 October 2016).

TT Club (2015). Verified gross mass. Industry FAQs. Available at http://www.ttclub.com/fileadmin/uploads/tt-club/Publications___Resources/New_Document_Store_2015/1SOLAS_VGM___Industry_FAQs_Dec_2015_A4_WEB.pdf (accessed 29 July 2016).

UNCTAD (2004). Container security: Major initiatives and related international developments. UNCTAD/SDTE/TLB/2004/1. Available at http://unctad.org/en/Docs/sdtetlb20041_en.pdf (accessed 29 July 2016).

UNCTAD (2007). Maritime security: International Ship and Port Facilities Security ISPS code implementation, costs and related financing. UNCTAD/SDTE/TLB/2007. Available at http://unctad.org/en/Docs/sdtetlb20071_en.pdf (accessed 29 July 2016).

UNCTAD (2011a). *Review of Maritime Transport 2011*. United Nations publication. Sales No. E.11.II.D.4. New York and Geneva.

UNCTAD (2011b). The 2004 Ballast Water Management Convention – with international acceptance growing, the Convention may soon enter into force. Transport Newsletter No. 50, Second Quarter. Available at http://unctad.org/en/Docs/webdtltlb20113_en.pdf (accessed 4 July 2016).

UNCTAD (2012a). *Review of Maritime Transport 2012*. United Nations publication. Sales No. E.12.II.D.17. New York and Geneva.

UNCTAD (2012b). *Liability and Compensation for Ship-source Oil Pollution: An Overview of the International Legal Framework for Oil Pollution Damage from Tankers.* Studies in Transport Law and Policy 2012 No. 1. United Nations publication. New York and Geneva.

UNCTAD (2013). *Review of Maritime Transport 2013*. United Nations publication. Sales No. E.13.II.D.9. New York and Geneva.

UNCTAD (2014a). *Review of Maritime Transport 2014*. United Nations publication. Sales No. E.14.II.D.5. New York and Geneva.

UNCTAD (2014b). *Maritime Piracy. Part I: An Overview of Trends, Costs and Trade-related Implications.* United Nations publication. New York and Geneva. Available at http://unctad.org/en/PublicationsLibrary/dtltlb2013d1_en.pdf (accessed 29 July 2016).

UNCTAD (2014c). *Maritime Piracy. Part II: An Overview of the International Legal Framework and of Multilateral Cooperation to Combat Piracy.* United Nations publication. New York and Geneva. Available at http://unctad.org/en/PublicationsLibrary/dtltlb2013d3_en.pdf (accessed 29 July 2016).

UNCTAD (2015a). The International Ballast Water Management Convention 2004 is set to enter into force in 2016. Transport and Trade Facilitation Newsletter No. 68. Available at http://unctad.org/en/PublicationsLibrary/webdtltlb2015d4_en.pdf (accessed 29 July 2016).

UNCTAD (2015b). *Review of Maritime Transport 2015*. United Nations publication. Sales No. E.15.II.D.6. New York and Geneva.

United States, Federal Maritime Commission (2016a). Announcements about gate weights are encouraging sign for smooth VGM implementation. 29 June. Available at http://www.fmc.gov/announcements_about_gate_weights_are_encouraging_sign_for_smooth_vgm_implementation/ (accessed 29 July 2016).

United States, Department of Homeland Security (2016b). Request for Information. Strategies to Improve Maritime Supply Chain Security and Achieve 100% Overseas Scanning. 2 May. Available at http://www.usfashionindustry.com/pdf_files/DHS-Request-for-Information-100-Percent-Overseas-Container-Scanning.pdf (accessed 14 October 2016).

United States Coast Guard (2016). United States declares an equivalency to regulation VI/2 of SOLAS. Marine Safety Information Bulletin. No. 009/16. Available at https://www.uscg.mil/msib/docs/009_16_4-28-2016.pdf (accessed 29 July 2016).

World Customs Organization (2011). The customs supply chain security paradigm and 9/11: Ten years on and beyond September 2011. World Customs Organization Research Paper No. 18. Available at http://www.wcoomd.org/~/media/WCO/Public/Global/PDF/Topics/Research/Research%20Paper%20Series/18_CSCSP_911.ashx?db=web (accessed 4 July 2016).

World Customs Organization (2015). *SAFE Framework of Standards to Secure and Facilitate Global Trade*. June. Available at http://www.wcoomd.org/en/topics/facilitation/instrument-and-tools/tools/~/media/2B9F7D49331 4432BA42BC8498D3B73CB.ashx (accessed 29 July 2016).

World Customs Organization (2016). *Compendium of Authorized Economic Operator Programmes*. Available at http://www.wcoomd.org/en/topics/facilitation/~/media/WCO/Public/Global/PDF/Topics/Facilitation/Instruments%20and%20Tools/Tools/Safe%20Package/AEO%20Compendium%20EN%20%202016.ashx (accessed 29 July 2016).

World Shipping Council (2014). History of the IMO effort to improve container security. Available at http://www.worldshipping.org/History_of_IMO_Effort_to_Improve_Container_Safety_May_2014.pdf (accessed 29 July 2016).

World Shipping Council (2016). Comments on Agriculture Transportation Coalition Position Paper: Safety of Life at Sea (SOLAS) Container Weight Documentation. 11 February. Available at http://www.worldshipping.org/public-statements/Comments_on_AgTC_Position_Paper_for_Release.pdf (accessed 29 July 2016).

ENDNOTES

1 Entitled "Transforming our world: the 2030 Agenda for Sustainable Development". For more information on the Goals and targets, see http://www.un.org/sustainabledevelopment/sustainable-development-goals/ (accessed 29 July 2016).

2 See General Assembly resolution 66/288, the outcome of the United Nations Conference on Sustainable Development, paragraph 158: We recognize that oceans, seas and coastal areas form an integrated and essential component of the Earth's ecosystem and are critical to sustaining it, and that international law, as reflected in the United Nations Convention on the Law of the Sea, provides the legal framework for the conservation and sustainable use of the oceans and their resources. We stress the importance of the conservation and sustainable use of the oceans and seas and of their resources for sustainable development, including through their contributions to poverty eradication, sustained economic growth, food security and creation of sustainable livelihoods and decent work, while at the same time protecting biodiversity and the marine environment and addressing the impacts of climate change. We therefore commit to protect, and restore, the health, productivity and resilience of oceans and marine ecosystems, to maintain their biodiversity, enabling their conservation and sustainable use for present and future generations, and to effectively apply an ecosystem approach and the precautionary approach in the management, in accordance with international law, of activities having an impact on the marine environment, to deliver on all three dimensions of sustainable development.

3 For more information and documentation, see the UNCTAD webpage on transport policy and legislation, available at http://unctad.org/en/Pages/DTL/TTL/Legal.aspx (accessed 29 July 2016).

4 For more information, see Rajamani (2016).

5 For States Parties to SOLAS, 1974. The first version of SOLAS, adopted in 1914, was a response to the *Titanic* disaster. The second version was adopted in 1929, the third in 1948 and the fourth in 1960. The convention in force today, SOLAS, 1974, updated and amended on numerous occasions, is a widely adopted instrument. It entered into force in 1980 and, as at 31 July 2016, it had 162 States Parties representing 98.53 per cent of world gross tonnage. For amendments to SOLAS, 1974, the "tacit acceptance" procedure is used, according to which an amendment shall enter into force at a particular date, unless before that date a specified number of Parties objects to it. For more information, see http://www.imo.org/en/About/Conventions/ListOfConventions/Pages/International-Convention-for-the-Safety-of-Life-at-Sea-(SOLAS),-1974.aspx (accessed 19 August 2016).

6 Including SOLAS regulations VI/2.1, VI/2.2 and VI/2.3.

7 Including *MSC Napoli* (2007), *Annabella* (2007), *MOL Comfort* (2013) and *Svenborg Maersk* (2014).

8 Presented to the IMO Maritime Safety Committee in December 2008. For more information on the 2009 *Safe Transport of Containers by Sea: Guidelines on Industry Best Practices* publication, see the World Shipping Council webpage at http://www.worldshipping.org/industry-issues/safety/cargo-weight (accessed 29 July 2016).

9 For a history of the IMO effort to improve container security, see World Shipping Council (2014).

10 The full text of the amendments is available at http://www.worldshipping.org/industry-issues/safety/SOLAS_CHAPTER_VI_Regulation_2_Paragraphs_4-6.pdf (accessed 29 July 2016).

11 See also TT Club (2015). For more information, see the Shipplanning Message Development Group website at http://www.smdg.org (accessed 4 July 2016).

12 For concerns expressed on this issue by the International Federation of Freight Forwarders' Associations, and related response by one container line, see *Lloyd's List* (2016c).

13 See http://www.worldshipping.org/industry-issues/safety/global-container-weight-verification-rule-effective-july-1-2016 (accessed 29 July 2016).

14 See http://www.ttclub.com/loss-prevention/container-weighing/stakeholder-digests/ (accessed 4 July 2016).

15 VGM guidelines define the "shipper" as "a legal entity or person named on the bill of lading or sea waybill or equivalent multimodal transport document as shipper and/or who (or in whose name or on whose behalf) a contract of carriage has been concluded with a shipping company".

16 As permitted by the State in which the packing of the container is completed.

17 For more information, see http://www.imo.org/en/MediaCentre/HotTopics/container/Pages/default.aspx (accessed 29 July 2016).

18 See, for instance, notices by the competent authorities of India, available at http://dgshipping.gov.in/WriteReadData/News/201606240423183653668m_s_notice_no_07_of_2016.pdf (accessed 4 July 2016), and Hong Kong, China, available at http://www.mardep.gov.hk/en/notices/pdf/mdn16087.pdf(accessed 4 July 2016), stating that they will enforce the requirements in a practical and pragmatic manner from 1 July 2016 to 30 September 2016.

19 For a summary of the content of the regulations, see UNCTAD (2012a), pp. 97–98; for an overview of the discussions on the different types of measures, see UNCTAD (2011a), pp. 114–116.

20 MARPOL annex VI came into force on 19 May 2005 and, as at 20 September 2016, had 87 States Parties representing 96.14 per cent of world tonnage.

21 See FCCC/CP/2015/L.9/Rev.1, annex, available at http://www.un.org/ga/search/view_doc.asp?symbol=FCCC/CP/2015/L.9/Rev.1 (accessed 3 October 2016).

22 At that ceremony, 174 States and the European Union signed the Paris Agreement, and 15 States also deposited their instruments of ratification. In accordance with article 21(1), the Agreement requires at least 55 Parties, accounting in total for at least 55 per cent of the total greenhouse gas emissions, for its entry into force. As at 23 September 2016, there were 191 signatories, of which 60, accounting for 47.76 per cent of total global greenhouse gas emissions, had become Parties. For more information on the status of the Paris Agreement, see http://unfccc.int/paris_agreement/items/9485.php(accessed 23 September 2016).

23 See FCCC/CP/2015/L.9/Rev.1, available at http://www.un.org/ga/search/view_doc.asp?symbol=FCCC/CP/2015/L.9/Rev.1 (accessed 3 October 2016).

24 It is worth noting, in this context, the role of UNCTAD within its mandate as recently reiterated by member States at the fourteenth session of the United Nations Conference on Trade and Development (Nairobi, 17–22 July 2016), to "continue to assist developing countries in enhancing the sustainability and climate resilience of their transport systems and infrastructure, including coastal transport infrastructure and services and transport corridors" (see the Nairobi Maafikiano, TD/519/Add.2, paragraph 55 (k)); as well as "contribute to policy dialogue and cooperation mechanisms in support of sustainable transport, climate change adaptation and disaster risk reduction for transport infrastructure, services and operations, including collaborative efforts to support and strengthen the conservation and sustainable use of oceans and their resources" (TD/519/Add.2, paragraph 55 (l)).

25 See article 2(2). The Protocol was adopted in 1997 and entered into force on 16 February 2005. It currently has 192 Parties. The text is available at http://unfccc.int/resource/docs/convkp/kpeng.pdf (accessed 29 July 2016).

26 For more information, see http://www.icao.int/environmental-protection/Pages/market-based-measures.aspx (accessed 29 July 2016).

27 This suggestion by the International Chamber of Shipping supports in principle a request by the Marshall Islands at MEPC 68, that MEPC should discuss the establishment of IMO commitments for CO_2 emissions reduction on behalf of the entire international shipping sector. This would mirror the commitments or intended nationally determined contributions made by nations under the Paris Agreement, from which international shipping is currently excluded.

28 For a summary of shared comments made during discussions, see IMO (2016i), pp. 35–38.

29 A reference line is defined as a curve representing an average index value fitted on a set of individual index values for a defined group of ships. The reference line value is formulated as: Reference line value = a (100 per cent dead-weight) – c where "a" and "c" are parameters determined from the regression curve fit. For more information, see IMO (2013), annex 14.

30 See http://glomeep.imo.org/ (accessed 17 August 2016).

31 MARPOL annex VI, regulation 14 "Sulphur oxides (SO_x) and particulate matter". The first two SO_x emission control areas, the Baltic Sea and the North Sea areas, were established in Europe and took effect in 2006

and 2007, respectively. The third established was the North American emission control area, taking effect on 1 August 2012. In July 2011, a fourth emission control area, the United States Caribbean Sea, was established. This latter area covers certain waters adjacent to the coasts of Puerto Rico (United States) and the United States Virgin Islands, and took effect on 1 January 2014.

32 1 January 2020 or 1 January 2025.

33 See http://globallast.imo.org (accessed 29 July 2016).

34 Conference resolution 1: Future work by the Organization pertaining to the International Convention for the Control and Management of Ships' Ballast Water and Sediments; Conference resolution 2: The use of decision making tools when reviewing the standards pursuant to Regulation D5; Conference resolution 3: Promotion of technical cooperation and assistance; Conference resolution 4: Review of the Annex to the International Convention for the Control and Management of Ships' Ballast Water and Sediments.

35 For a list of these instruments as at October 2015, see http://www.imo.org/en/OurWork/Environment/BallastWaterManagement/Documents/Compilation%20of%20relevant%20Guidelines%20and%20guidance%20documents%20-%20October%202015.pdf(accessed 29 July 2016).

36 See also UNCTAD (2011b), pp. 8–13.

37 The Convention is set to enter into force 12 months after the date on which no fewer than 30 States, the combined merchant fleets of which constitute not less than 35 per cent of the gross tonnage of world merchant shipping, have become Parties to it. Since the last session of MEPC, Belgium, Fiji, Ghana, Indonesia, Morocco, Peru, Saint Lucia and Finland have become Parties to the Convention. More countries have announced their intention to ratify the Convention, notably, Australia (IMO, 2016m).

38 Two proposed by the Republic of Korea and one by Japan.

39 Note, for instance that the Convention, in its preamble, refers to the 1992 United Nations Conference on Environment and Development and its request that IMO develop rules on ballast water discharge; the need for a precautionary approach in accordance with principle 15 of the Rio Declaration on Environment and Development; States' obligations under the United Nations Convention on the Law of the Sea to prevent the spread of alien species; the conservation and sustainable use of marine biodiversity and marine and coastal ecosystems under the Convention on Biological Diversity and related instruments; and the 2002 World Summit on Sustainable Development.

40 Particularly targets 14.1, 14.2, 14.3, 14.5, 14.a, 14.b and 14.c. For more details, see the first section of chapter 5.

41 See http://www.imo.org/en/OurWork/Environment/BallastWaterManagement/Pages/Default.aspx. Also see http://globallast.imo.org (accessed 29 July 2016).

42 Target 15.8 relates to both land and water ecosystems and reads: "By 2020, introduce measures to prevent the introduction and significantly reduce the impact of invasive alien species on land and water ecosystems and control or eradicate the priority species."

43 In accordance with United Nations General Assembly resolution 69/292 of 19 June 2015.

44 Ibid.

45 United Nations Convention on the Law of the Sea, article 87.

46 United Nations Convention on the Law of the Sea, article 150.

47 For more information, see http://www.un.org/Depts/los/biodiversity/prepcom.htm (accessed 29 July 2016).

48 Also highlighted in UNCTAD (2013), pp. 110–111.

49 The 1992 Civil Liability Convention and 1992 International Oil Pollution Compensation Fund Convention. For an analytical overview of the international legal framework, see UNCTAD (2012b).

50 United Nations Convention on the Law of the Sea, article 208.

51 As at October 2015, 169 out of 180 World Customs Organization member States had signed the letter of intent to implement the Framework of Standards to Secure and Facilitate Global Trade. Its latest revised version (World Customs Organization, 2015) was issued in June 2015. The latest package of the Framework, bringing together all World Customs Organization instruments and guidelines that support its implementation, is available at http://www.wcoomd.org/en/topics/facilitation/instrument-and-tools/tools/

safe_package.aspx (accessed 29 July 2016). For more information on the content of the latest revisions, as well as on the concept of AEOs, see UNCTAD (2015b).

52 Due also to the fact that 28 European Union countries have one common, uniform AEO programme.

53 For more information, see World Customs Organization (2016).

54 For more information, see http://ec.europa.eu/taxation_customs/customs/customs_code/union_customs_code/ucc/introduction_en.htm (accessed 29 July 2016).

55 Ibid.

56 Available at http://ec.europa.eu/taxation_customs/customs/customs_code/union_customs_code/ucc/guidance_en.htm (accessed 29 July 2016).

57 The breakdown reported per authorization type issued was: AEO/customs simplifications 7,726; AEO/security and safety 661; and AEO/customs simplifications–AEO/security and safety 9,916.

58 The European Union has already concluded mutual recognition agreements with Andorra, China, Japan, Norway, Switzerland and the United States. Negotiations are ongoing with Canada. For more information on AEOs, see http://ec.europa.eu/taxation_customs/customs/policy_issues/customs_security/aeo/index_en.htm (accessed 29 July 2016).

59 For more detailed information and analysis, see UNCTAD (2014a), pp. 86–87.

60 The letter is available at https://www.sfia.org/img/files/Final%20Multi%20Association%20DHS%20Letter%20on%20100%20Percent%20Maritime%20Cargo%20Scannin%20%20%20.pdf (accessed 29 July 2016).

61 For more information on the various security initiatives, see UNCTAD (2004).

62 For more information about the Container Security Initiative, see http://www.cbp.gov/border-security/ports-entry/cargo-security/csi/csi-brief (accessed 29 July 2016).

63 The nine countries/territories are Canada, Taiwan Province of China, Israel, Japan, Jordan, Mexico, New Zealand, the Republic of Korea and Singapore.

64 For more information, see http://www.cbp.gov/trade/isa/importer-self-assessment (accessed 29 July 2016). For information on the benefits for participants, see http://www.gpo.gov/fdsys/pkg/FR-2002-06-17/pdf/02-15308.pdf (accessed 29 July 2016).

65 For more information, see http://www.gpo.gov/fdsys/pkg/FR-2014-06-16/pdf/2014-13992.pdf (accessed 29 July 2016).

66 For more information, see http://www.state.gov/t/isn/c10390.htm (accessed 29 July 2016).

67 Available at http://www.mar.ist.utl.pt/mventura/Projecto-Navios-I/IMO-Conventions%20(copies)/SOLAS.pdf. For a brief history of SOLAS and a list of amendments to date and where to find them, see http://www.imo.org/en/KnowledgeCentre/ReferencesAndArchives/HistoryofSOLAS/Documents/SOLAS%201974%20-%20Brief%20History%20-%20List%20of%20amendments%20to%20date%20and%20how%20to%20find%20them.html (accessed 20 September 2016).

68 Including IMO (2016v).

69 See http://www.ilo.org/global/standards/subjects-covered-by-international-labour-standards/seafarers/lang--en/index.htm (accessed 18 August 2016).

70 For updated status information, see http://www.ilo.org/global/standards/maritime-labour-convention/lang--en/index.htm (accessed 16 October 2016).

71 Living and working conditions for seafarers were also a priority during the forty-ninth Committee meeting of the Paris Memorandum of Understanding on Port State Control, in May 2016, where great importance was given to a Concentrated Inspection Campaign on the Maritime Labour Convention, 2006, scheduled to be held from September to November 2016 (Paris Memorandum of Understanding on Port State Control, 2016).

72 For more information on the amendments, see UNCTAD (2014a), pp. 89–90.

73 For updated status information, see http://www.ilo.org/dyn/normlex/en/f?p=1000:11300:0::NO:11300:P11300_INSTRUMENT_ID:312330 (accessed 16 October 2016).

74 For more information, see http://www.ilo.org/global/standards/maritime-labour-convention/events/WCMS_411197/lang--en/index.htm (accessed 29 July 2016).

www.ingramcontent.com/pod-product-compliance
Lightning Source LLC
Chambersburg PA
CBHW082347230926
51846CB00004B/941

* 9 7 8 9 2 1 1 1 2 9 0 4 5 *